'"How did it get like this?" In this th[...] book, Geoff Raby draws on his pers[...] background to produce the answers many have been looking for, and to propose some ways forward. In essence, he argues that Australia should deepen its engagement with China and develop an independent foreign policy suited to our regional location. In these days of crisis, his rational argument is sorely needed.'

Jocelyn Chey AM has held diplomatic posts in
China and Hong Kong

'Raby is right. Australia–China relations are in a deep hole. "If you find yourself in a hole, stop digging", says a wise adage. This book offers a wise and thoughtful strategy for reversing course. Future generations of Australians, and indeed Asians, will be grateful to Raby for providing timely advice on how to manage a rising China.'

Kishore Mahbubani, Distinguished Fellow at the Asia Research
Institute, NUS, author of *Has China Won?*

'The most hard-headed, informed and useful extended discussion of ascendant China in our world since the freeze in Australia–China relations began. Raby's unsentimental look at how the world seems from Beijing, why the Chinese government behaves as it does, its weaknesses and vulnerabilities including the paucity of its soft power, and its emergence at the head of a new "bounded" order in a new multilateral globe, is a virtuoso masterclass in what is happening to our world and guide to how Australian diplomacy and statecraft can be marshalled to meet it.'

Stephen FitzGerald, former Australian Ambassador to China

CHINA'S GRAND STRATEGY AND AUSTRALIA'S FUTURE IN THE NEW GLOBAL ORDER

CHINA'S GRAND STRATEGY AND AUSTRALIA'S FUTURE IN THE NEW GLOBAL ORDER

GEOFF RABY

MELBOURNE
UNIVERSITY
PRESS

MELBOURNE UNIVERSITY PRESS
An imprint of Melbourne University Publishing Limited
Level 1, 715 Swanston Street, Carlton, Victoria 3053, Australia
mup-contact@unimelb.edu.au
www.mup.com.au

First published 2020
Reprinted twice 2020
Text © Geoff Raby, 2020
Design and typography © Melbourne University Publishing Limited, 2020

Cover design by Philip Campbell Design
Typeset in 12/15pt Bembo by Cannon Typesetting
Printed in Australia by McPherson's Printing Group

A catalogue record for this book is available from the National Library of Australia

9780522874945 (paperback)
9780522874952 (ebook)

This book is dedicated to COVID-19, without which it would not have been finished; to Grace, who endured it all; to Helena, who survived to see it; to my mother, who passed 100 waiting for it and is still going; and to little Alana, who is the light.

CONTENTS

AUTHOR'S NOTE

This book had its origins in Monash University's Richard Larkins Oration, which I delivered in August 2012. It was exactly one year after I concluded my four-and-a-half-year term as Australian ambassador to China, and after I resigned from government service following twenty-seven years working mainly on Australian foreign and trade policy, much of which was on China.

At the time of the oration, the subjects of China's rise, its security threats to Australia and its challenge to the US' pre-eminence in East Asia were just emerging as hot topics of public discussion. During president Barack Obama's visit to Australia in November 2011, while standing next to a gushing prime minister Julia Gillard, he'd announced the establishment of a US Marine base near Darwin. The previous day, breaching normal protocols and good manners, he'd used his speech to the joint houses of the Australian Parliament to attack China and reveal for the first time his new foreign policy doctrine: the Asian 'Pivot'.

Hugh White in 2010 published what has turned out to be a prescient and hence seminal book on the strategic challenges of China's rise. In *The China Choice*, he argued that soon the US would need to decide between accommodating China's rise and, in order to avoid war, ceding strategic space to China and ultimately hegemony in East Asia; or choosing to push back and seek to contain China.

The implications of this for Australia were massive, not least as China had by then become Australia's biggest trading partner, and this dependence would only grow. As a realist in foreign and strategic policy, White argued for the US to begin sharing power with China.

The torrent of invective, bile and ludicrous charges of 'appeasement' directed at White by some of Australia's conservative commentators took the country's public policy discussion to a new low.

It was against this background that the Larkins Oration was written, and it is probably why the turnout on a cold and damp Melbourne winter evening was unusually large. In the front row was former prime minister Malcolm Fraser. I had not met him before, but I remembered him as minister for the army in the Liberal government during the Vietnam War, a loathed figure among the anti-war student movement. And as leader of the Opposition, he engineered the ouster of prime minister Gough Whitlam by conniving with governor-general John Kerr. One of Whitlam's first acts on being elected prime minister in December 1972 was to end Australia's involvement in the Vietnam War and recognise the People's Republic of China (PRC). These were defining moments in Australia's relationship with the US, marking a return to an independent Australian foreign policy.

Over the many years since his time as minister for the army, Fraser had arrived at a view of the US as a country destined for war, driven by its military–industrial complex's insatiable appetite for conflict and the corruption of US politics which that involved. Fraser's views by the end of his life may have been even more anti-war and more anti-US than those of the student demonstrators during the Vietnam War. His journey had brought him to the Larkins Oration as a stooped, frail figure—he would pass away two-and-a-half years later—and he spoke at length with me afterwards, welcoming what I had said.

Now free after my government service, I tried to make the case for Australia to develop once again an independent foreign policy with respect to China's rise, one based on our interests and, equally importantly, on a well-grounded understanding of China.

This would involve not only China's potential as a security threat as its economy continued to grow, but also a realistic understanding of the constraints China was under and the real limits to its ability to project power and become a global hegemon. The rise of China would not, because it could not, be a re-run of the rise of the US. When viewed from Beijing, my point of reference, the world and the security challenges China faced looked very different than when viewed from Washington or Canberra.

This book has been a work in progress for many years. Over this time, China's rise has continued unabated despite its many internal and external challenges. Since 2012, China has found ways to shape the world order other than exercising military power—though it has been busily accumulating a formidable arsenal—to ensure its security and regime survival. In pursuing its grand strategy, it has cumulatively, and by its great weight in the world, changed the world order in its favour. As a consequence, Australia faces difficult foreign policy and security challenges. So far, unfortunately, it has been found wanting. This book addresses these issues.

The enforced stillness of the COVID-19 lockdown enabled me to finish the writing. However, it also denied me access to many books and materials that had been accumulating in Beijing over the years, as well as to libraries and bookshops, rendering it challenging to follow up sources and identify authorities. Google, Wikipedia and courageous e-commerce couriers helped.

This book is a summation of over thirty years working in and on China, including the past thirteen years spent first as Australia's ambassador to the People's Republic of China, and then, since late 2011, working in and with business. In all of these many and different roles, the hardest task has been explaining to policymakers in government and business the contemporary reality of China. Sometimes this has involved leaning against periods of enthusiasm, when Beijing is given the benefit of the doubt and government and business are dazzled by the prospect of endless opportunities.

At other times, it has involved leaning against periods of pessimism, as insecure optimism is disappointed by the realities on the ground and China has not done as was hoped, or worse, expected. Fortunately, Australia, until recent times, has largely been free of the ideological baggage that the US and many of the European states have carried with them into the China relationship.

I have also had wonderful opportunities to travel all over China, something that was much harder in the times before mine. I was the first Australian ambassador to visit officially all thirty-one provinces of China, and have had the good fortune since 1987 to visit Tibet on five occasions and Xinjiang on at least six. I have also travelled to Yunnan, Gansu and Inner Mongolia multiple times, and to the far north-east in both breezy summers and freezing winters. These travels have been drawn on here to enliven and inform the narrative.

Such is the vastness and complexity of China that I have often found anecdotes much more effective in helping decision-makers understand the realities of the country than any amount of sophisticated analyses and data. Accordingly, I have used personal stories throughout this study to add a sense of feel and texture to the narrative. Most importantly, they help provide context to perhaps the most remarkable story of our times: how China over the past forty years has gone from being a boutique foreign policy interest to transforming the world order, and in the West, viewed in most capitals as the major threat to global security. China's rise need not, and I believe will not, end in war, but this moment of managing a power shift of untold historical significance is replete with uncertainties and risks. Understanding China's grand strategy, the order it has created and the constraints on its exercise of power, may help statesmen avoid catastrophic miscalculations.

INTRODUCTION

How did it get like this? The Australia–China relationship is at its lowest point since diplomatic relations between the two countries began in 1972.

This is something the Australian Government doesn't wish to discuss. Its diplomats are paid to put a positive spin on things. Elements of the conservative populist media almost rejoice in this state of affairs.[1] Just when it seemed the situation could not get any worse, China took umbrage at Australian Prime Minister Scott Morrison's initial unilateral proposal for an international inquiry into the Chinese origins of, and responses to, the COVID-19 pandemic of 2020.[2] China invoked trade measures against Australian exports of barley and beef without senior government-to-government contact occurring.

Chinese students and tourists have been warned by the Chinese Government to avoid travelling to Australia because it is said to be unsafe—they may face racist attacks. The Australian Government, meanwhile, warned companies and government organisations that they were under unprecedented cyber-attack, with China clearly the unnamed culprit.[3] Some commentators now argue that Australia–China relations will never recover.

Ever since prime minister Bob Hawke embraced China's vision of reform and opening itself up to the outside world, imagining what it could mean for Australia's future prosperity and security,

China and Australia have endeavoured to maintain annual high-level exchanges. But three years ago, Australia was denied access to the highest levels of the Chinese political system, and official, national-level contact remains frozen by China.[4]

It was in March 2017 that the last senior bilateral visit occurred, when Premier Li Keqiang came to Canberra. At the state reception held in his honour in the Great Hall of the Australian Parliament, he made light-hearted, off-the-cuff jokes in English about how he thought he'd come to Australia to be sold beef, only to be served rubbery chicken at lunch. He did, however, have a pointed message to deliver. Using the analogy of flying through turbulence on his way to Australia, he said the Australia–China relationship had been going through some bumpy patches, but skilful pilots found ways to navigate into smoother air. Then it was all smiles again. The nosedive was still ahead.

From Cooperation to Strategic Competition

Within the small, tight Canberra policy circle, in the years since the Abbott government had been elected, the security–intelligence–military establishment had come to lead on China policy. The emerging dominant view of China was that it was seeking to overturn the US-led order in the region. As China's power grew, maintaining constructive positive relations came to be seen as less important than resisting what is believed to be China's ambition to build a Sino-centric order. The bilateral relationship was a second-order concern, and if it was in trouble, this might even be a badge of honour. Australia need do nothing to restore normal, constructive relations with China. Australia was getting tough with China.[5]

As the leaders were meeting in Canberra in that autumn of 2017, in the Department of Foreign Affairs and Trade (DFAT), drafting of the Malcolm Turnbull government's white paper on foreign affairs and trade was well advanced. Looking to the future, but with their eyes firmly fixed on the past, those preparing *Opportunity, Security, Strength: the 2017 Foreign Policy White Paper* saw the US as continuing to lead a liberal, rules-based order. Donald Trump's election and America-first policies, with their implication of the US turning away from global leadership and engagement, shook the easy assumptions of the foreign and strategic policy establishment. The US withdrawal from the Trans-Pacific Partnership (TPP) a few days after Trump began his presidency confirmed many of their worst fears. Nevertheless, as reflected in the white paper, the hope was that the US would return to its customary role of global leadership with which Australia felt secure—and for which it readily paid its dues, with participation in US military engagements in Iraq, Afghanistan and elsewhere.

The white paper acknowledged China's continuing economic importance to Australia and foreshadowed the sustainment of cooperative, mutually beneficial relations. It could hardly say anything else about Australia's biggest trading partner. At the same time, together with the US, Canberra was developing policies to push back against China's rise, even though no-one would say so publicly.[6] Australian officials would have been well briefed in private on the content of the forthcoming US National Security Strategy (NSS) and in turn would have been prepping the National Security Committee of Cabinet on the change in US doctrine. This paper replaced the Obama doctrine of the Pivot to Asia with one of 'geopolitical competition' with China.[7]

From this time, the weight of Australia's foreign and strategic policy began shifting from cooperation with China to pushing back against it. This was done by encouraging greater US engagement in the region, reinvigorating the Quadrilateral Security Dialogue with gradually expanded military dimensions, and embracing the Indo-Pacific strategic concept to draw an ambivalent India more directly into balancing against China. Predictably, however much Australia sought to present these initiatives as benign, almost innocent, natural evolutions of existing activities, the sorts of things most countries would do, the ultra-suspicious leaders in Beijing and their strategic think-tank advisers would only assume the worst, and with every reason to do so.

Australia was heading into uncharted policy waters, unaccompanied by our regional neighbours in the Association of Southeast Asian Nations (ASEAN) or New Zealand. Australia was travelling in company with China's strategic competitors, especially the US and Japan. It was replacing decades of cooperative relations, of building regional integration and common purpose, with strategic competition and division within the Asia-Pacific region.

In retrospect, the white paper now appears to have been a diversion from the Australian Government's real policy intention, which was to align itself even more closely with China's strategic competitors to contain China. Since then, Australia has had a fundamental contradiction at the heart of its foreign policy. It talks the talk of engagement in the white paper but walks the walk of competition and containment as stated so baldly in the NSS.

The NSS framed the new approach in stark ideological terms, stating that 'a geopolitical competition between free and repressive visions of world order is taking place in the Indo-Pacific'.[8] Commenting on this for the Brookings Institute, Ryan Hass observed that:

> No other country in the Indo-Pacific region creates such a dichotomy to distinguish between the US and China … By seeking to paint the region in such black-and-white terms, the United States sets itself apart from the rest of the region.[9]

Except for Australia, Hass could have noted. In the NSS, Australia received what might be seen as disproportionate praise as a US ally. Special mention was made of Australia for having fought alongside the US in every conflict since World War I, reinforcing economic and security arrangements in the region, and safeguarding 'democratic values'. Japan was mentioned only in passing as a 'critical ally', with India seen as an 'emerging strategic and defence partner'.[10]

It can now be seen that, well before the NSS proposed that China be classified as a 'strategic competitor', and before Vice President Mike Pence endorsed this as official policy with his Hudson Institute speech in 2018, Australian officials had quietly shifted Australia's doctrine from strategic cooperation with China to strategic competition. In view of the overwhelming importance of China to Australia's foreign policy and future economic wellbeing, this was a profound policy change, one made without public discussion.

Over this period, Australia's position on China's investment in 'strategic' assets progressively hardened. When the mainland Chinese private firm Landbridge was being awarded a 99-year lease for the Port of Darwin, it was not thought to be of sufficient strategic importance for either the Defence Department or the Foreign Investment Review Board (FIRB) to take an interest. But when the US raised concerns, it became a major controversy. In response to a complaint by president Obama that the US had not been advised of the sale, prime minister Turnbull replied that he could have read about it on the front page of Darwin's *NT Times*.[11]

The continuing controversy over the Port of Darwin led to greater attention being paid by Australian officials to Chinese foreign direct investment (FDI) in general and infrastructure in particular. Surprisingly, in view of the furore, the major Chinese state-owned power company, State Grid, through its Hong Kong subsidiary, nearly acquired a majority share in a 99-year lease for the NSW-based electricity provider Ausgrid. It was only in the final stages of the approvals process that it was blocked by the FIRB. Once again, a major public controversy ensued over Chinese investment.[12]

Critical infrastructure became a lightning rod for attempts to resist Chinese foreign investment more broadly. In January 2017, the Australian Government established the Critical Infrastructure Centre to 'safeguard' Australia's most important infrastructure from 'the increasingly complex national security risks of sabotage, espionage and coercion'.[13] It also appointed a former Australian ambassador to China and intelligence chief, David Irvine, to head the FIRB; previously, the FIRB had been led by former Treasury officials or people with commercial experience.[14]

China interpreted these actions, and the anti-foreign interference laws enacted in June 2018, as directed squarely at it, which they were, and as part of a broader coordinated geopolitical strategy. The semi-official *Global Times*, quoting officials and leading think-tank contributors, declared that 'Australia closely follows US steps, which is spearheading the Indo-Pacific strategy aimed at containing China'.[15]

The announcement in August 2018 to ban Huawei from all aspects of Australia's 5G telecommunications network brought relations with China to their lowest ever point. It was made by the acting minister for home affairs in the Australian Parliament, to ensure it would be well covered in the media. It was not just that the Australian Government had decided to make the announcement in such a high-profile way that angered China, but also that Australia was the first to do so. Its handling was gratuitously provocative. Turnbull recalls that when he told Trump in a phone call what he had done, the US President was 'both impressed and a little surprised that we'd taken this position'[16]—though it is not clear why he was surprised, as Turnbull had been discussing 5G with the President and Vice President Pence for 'some time'.[17]

Australia was joined by the US, New Zealand and Japan in the 5G ban. Although the UK is a member of the Five Eyes intelligence-sharing group—the other participants being Australia, Canada, New Zealand and the US—it found ways of permitting Huawei to participate in restricted elements of the 5G network, as Germany and France have done. However, under immense US pressure the UK Government has now decided to ban Huawei from the 5G networks from 2027.[18] Canada, meanwhile, has taken an inordinately long time to reach a decision. Huawei is being adopted in most other parts of the world as an efficient supplier. It is playing an increasingly important role in China's Belt and Road Initiative (BRI) in driving digital connectedness.[19] It is the digital backbone of Eurasia, the subcontinent and much of Africa.

China's Bad Behaviour

China also overreached through its United Front Work Department's attempts to influence domestic politics and interfere on university campuses in Australia, and it did so internationally too, especially with its unilateral assertion of sovereignty over disputed islets, reefs and rocky atolls in the South China Sea, culminating in a backlash.[20] China's bad behaviour invited pushback.

Trump's abandonment of the Pivot was part of burying Obama's legacy policies—as was done with the TPP, for instance. Although envisaging a greater US commitment in Asia across all aspects of its statecraft, the Pivot was still premised on engagement with China.[21]

The abandonment of the Pivot was the culmination of years of rising concern over China's challenge to the US-led order, beginning the shift from engagement to containment.[22]

It was now time for the intelligence and strategic policy community in Australia to prevail over foreign policy and diplomacy. Following the US, the terms of the relationship with China were to be redefined. Businesspeople who urged the government to do more to improve relations were casually dismissed as self-serving, as if concerns about the economic impact of a dysfunctional relationship were somehow illegitimate.

The external and internal elements of the China threat were drawn together into a powerful narrative. Domestically, China's political interference and growing influence over campuses, cyber-warfare, investment in critical infrastructure, and intellectual property theft have been highlighted. These are all tools of modern statecraft that those with the means to do so deploy. Externally, the South China Sea and China's grand strategy for global influence based on the BRI raise the spectre of a China-dominated order. The domestic dimension feeds the narrative that China must be resisted in foreign policy, while bad behaviour by China internationally is used to support the need for greater vigilance by other nations.[23]

Fears about China's challenge to the existing order derive largely from an historical view that its rise will trace a similar trajectory to that of the US. Just as the US established hegemony over the Western Hemisphere before challenging Great Britain as the leading global power, it is argued that China will establish hegemony in the Asia-Pacific region before eclipsing the US as the sole dominant global power. Hence, so much discussion about a shifting power balance is also couched in terms of values and norms: do you really want to live in a world dominated by the values of the Communist Party of China?[24]

Based on the expected economic trajectories pre-COVID-19, one could be excused for thinking that certain historical parallels may exist between the rise of China and the earlier rise of the US from the end of that country's civil war. Yet the reality is that China's geopolitical circumstances, and its strategic strengths and weaknesses, are far removed from those of the US during its ascendency. The external and internal conditions China faces are vastly different to those faced historically by the US. The differences are so great that studying the US ascendency has little relevance to understanding the effect of China's own rise on the world order.

Strategy and Constraints

China's grand strategy derives from a position of weakness, not strength. China is constrained by its geography, its history, and most of all by its resource endowments. The third-largest country in area globally, it must defend over 22 000 kilometres of land borders that it shares with fourteen countries; it has been in conflict with most of its neighbours and has ongoing hot disputes with India in several places along their border, most recently in Ladakh involving the first fatalities of troops in over fifty years. China is also still an empire with significant unresolved internal territorial issues—Xinjiang, Tibet, Taiwan and, more recently, Hong Kong. Most importantly of all, China, unlike the US, is utterly dependent on international markets and foreign suppliers for all the energy and resources it needs for its continued prosperity.

All of these vital inputs travel via strategic chokepoints, especially the Straits of Malacca and the South China Sea. In return, China's exports, so essential to its economy, mainly travel through those same chokepoints, as well as the Suez and Panama canals. In a conflict, the US could readily control any of these and disrupt the flow of China's trade in both directions.[25]

While China already has become the dominant power in East Asia, it is far from becoming the local hegemon; in fact, it faces formidable obstacles in doing so. The US presence in the region will continue, as it has massive interests, both economic and geopolitical, to defend. These interests require the US to continue to underpin regional stability. Alongside the Middle East, East Asia is the most dangerous place in the world.

Japan is the third-biggest economy in the world and likely to remain so, with a formidable military capacity. India commands the Indian Ocean due to its economic and geographical size and location.[26] Historical analogies with the US establishing hegemony over the Western Hemisphere, or a Chinese version of the Monroe Doctrine, are largely fantasies of Beijing's or Washington's strategic analysts. Certainly, Great Britain ceded strategic space to the US over the Western Hemisphere, but Britain had neither comparable interests to defend nor key powerful allied states to support it, and by the time of the US' ascendency, imperial overreach had set in.

Significantly, China is also constrained by an absence of soft power. As Henry Kissinger writes in *On Order*, states need both power and legitimacy. China has increasing, almost unchallenged economic power. Post-COVID-19, it is possible that, with China's early recovery from the pandemic, it will restart its commercial motors before others do and the economic gap between it and other nations will widen further. But China struggles for legitimacy, which is supported and reinforced by soft power. China is structurally constrained in the exercise of soft power because of its party-state system of government. Its soft power must ultimately conform to the Communist Party of China's (CPC) ideological narrative, which is intended to legitimise, at every turn, the Party's hold on power. As can be seen from the COVID-19 crisis, while the Party's narrative may resonate loudly within China, it usually does not work outside of the country. China's standing in global polling on measures of favourable attitudes towards it have been falling steeply since Xi Jinping assumed power in 2012 and took China in a more authoritarian direction, accompanied by a more muscular foreign policy.

China is decades away from matching the US militarily, and even when it does, armed conflict is most unlikely as neither side would risk nuclear conflict. As in the Cold War, the doctrine of mutually assured destruction (MAD) will deter direct conflict between the superpowers. Meanwhile, China has developed substantial force-denial capabilities that will dissuade US adventures closer to China's shores. Without either hard power (coercion) or soft power (persuasion without force) as an advantage, China has sought a strategic edge through various forms of sharp power using its economic strength. This has ranged through political interference; overseas investments; the acquisition of technology, whether legitimately or illegitimately;

cyberwarfare, in which it is only one of many participants; and its grand strategy of the BRI.

China's statecraft depends on geo-economics—pursuing national interests through economic instruments, such as the BRI, trade and aid—and institutional entrepreneurship, as represented by the Shanghai Cooperation Organisation (SCO), Asia Infrastructure Investment Bank, Silk Road Fund, the New Development Bank (formerly the BRICS Development Bank) and others. It now has the world's greatest number of diplomatic missions and, assisted by the Trump administration stepping back from multilateral institutions, it has strengthened its influence in and over these forums.[27] The debates over the role and behaviour of the World Health Organization (WHO) and its director general in the early days of COVID-19, in particular the WHO's tardiness in declaring a global pandemic, reflect a growing unease over the success of China's statecraft multilaterally.[28]

A Changed Order

The old order shaped and led by the US is over. The historic moment in the post–Cold War era, of a unipolar order in which the US pursued a liberal internationalist agenda, is already a fading memory. Whether or not the new order is settled is debatable, of course, but as argued in a book by Shashi Tharoor and Samir Saran, both commentators on strategic affairs, the old order has been replaced by a *new world disorder.* Stability, then, itself has been replaced by disorder.[29]

However, the notion of a single stable order of the past thirty years has itself been challenged. Oliver Stuenkel argues that the old order was neither stable nor peaceful, nor was it authentically international. To many developing countries, it was a Western order, not theirs. Moreover, it consisted of many orders of different rules that some states belonged to and others did not.[30]

The exact shape of the new international order is rapidly coming into sharper focus, and China's rise has been the principal catalyst in its remaking. This has been accelerated by the 'black swan' event of the election of Donald Trump with his 'Make America Great Again' policies, under which the US has withdrawn from its accustomed role of providing global leadership of a unipolar international order. It was inevitable that, if China developed into a major global economy, which it has, it would change the world order, in view of its absolute size, it being largely homogenous (95 per cent of its population is Han), and the sheer scale of its economy. As a 'civilisation state' with a continuous language and culture of some 3000 years, it has a strong sense of cultural identity, purpose and destiny.[31]

China's economy has been the world's great over-achiever under the reform and open-door policies first introduced in 1979. The world has benefited enormously from China's growth, not least Australia. For many years now, China's economy has been the biggest when measured using the economists' favoured metric, purchasing power parity, which tries to adjust for relative price differences between economies. Since 2009, it has been the second biggest on the more popular measure that uses current prices. Even on the latter measure, China will overtake the US to be the biggest economy in the world within a decade. This is an 'uncomfortable truth'.

No-one should be surprised that we are where we are. The biggest or second-biggest economy in the world will want the global order to reflect its interests and needs for security. It will define these in its own way based on its historical experiences, anxieties—real or imagined—and its cultural norms and assumptions.

Engagement and Disillusion—Buyer's Remorse

Engagement with China served the West's interests as well as China's. The West wanted to integrate a poor, backward, inward-looking, fearful China into the international system. China's massive population meant that this offered big economic benefits for the West, which have been realised on a scale vastly greater than could have been imagined when engagement began.

It was believed that a more prosperous, politically stable, confident and internationally oriented China would also be less of a threat to regional stability, a notion which has generally been correct. The economic collapse and political disintegration of a country with a vast population and a strategic geographic location could have seen waves of politically destabilising immigration across East Asia, and armed conflict that would have overwhelmed neighbouring states.

The decade-long Cambodia–Vietnam war ended in 1991, the last major conflict in this historically war-torn region. The US military presence in East Asia plus China's drive for economic development have largely secured peace in the region for over thirty years, despite the tremendous potential for conflict. On all metrics, engagement with China can be judged an overwhelming success.

China has also shown that it can be a responsible actor during regional and global economic crises. During the 1997 Asian financial crisis that badly shocked East Asian economies, China resisted the temptation to engage in tit-for-tat competitive devaluations of its currency, which would have been the logical but irresponsible response to protect its export industries.[32] In those days, China was far more dependent on its export sector than it is today. During the global financial crisis (GFC) in 2008, China implemented a massive stimulus package which supercharged its economy and contributed to global economic recovery. It also contributed significantly to Australia avoiding a recession.

The West also largely assumed that China, as a major beneficiary of an increasingly open, rules-based, multilateral trading system, would support the US-led global order in all its dimensions. This was articulated most explicitly by the US deputy secretary of state in the George W Bush administration, Bob Zoellick, in an important speech to the National Committee on US–China Relations in September 2005. Zoellick envisaged China signing up to support the existing order as a 'responsible stakeholder'.[33] The speech was influential, shaping policy thinking in Western capitals at the time. When he became prime minister in 2007, Kevin Rudd was still using Zoellick's notion of a 'responsible stakeholder' to frame Australian foreign and security policies towards China.[34]

For Beijing, signing up to the rules-based multilateral trading system, with its accession to the World Trade Organization (WTO) in 2001, was a significant step towards becoming a responsible stakeholder. To be sure, China was clearly a major beneficiary of accession, but as the WTO is based on an exchange of reciprocal concessions among its members, so were China's trading partners. While China's accession was taken as affirmation that it was now a fully subscribed member of the international rules-based system, China itself, like other great powers, notably the US, saw the system as à la carte in nature. The US, for example, has never ratified the Law of the Sea Convention and so is not a party to it, while China did not choose to recognise the International Court of Arbitration's jurisdiction over the South China Sea case.

Zoellick and others were not really paying attention to what China was doing at the time, taking little notice of its primary security concerns, mainly in Eurasia. The world looks very different from Beijing than it does from inside the beltway in Washington. By the time Zoellick made his speech, China had begun the process of gradually constructing a 'parallel order'. As early as 2003, it had initiated the SCO, with its Eurasia-focused military and security dimensions.[35] By 2007, Beijing had resumed more assertive policies in the South China Sea, well before Rudd embraced the 'responsible stakeholder' concept. All the indications were that China would engage with the international system on its own terms.

Many in the West, particularly in the US, believed that the introduction of market reforms and foreign trade and investment in a state run by a Leninist communist party would inevitably see the political transformation of China from an authoritarian dictatorship to a competitive political system, or 'democracy'. For those who held this view, it was to be another great civilising project in China, akin to the sending of Christian missionaries in big numbers in the nineteenth century—even though that was, in fact, one of the most unsuccessful of such foreign ventures.[36] South Korea and Taiwan's remarkable democratic transitions in the 1990s and, earlier, Japan's adoption of a democratic postwar constitution, created a sense of inevitability in Western policy circles: markets and private property would beget political liberalism. This optimistic assumption unhelpfully overlooked the preponderant role of the US within, and influence over, these states. Authoritarian Singapore even had enough of an approximation of the rule of law and a market economy for it to be seen as another win for 'democracy'.

Indeed, China has grown rapidly to create the biggest middle-class society in the shortest time in world history. It has all the attributes of the global middle class—never-satisfied material expectations; high-quality suburban housing; healthy, well-functioning families; kids in private schools, or subject to aspirations for them to be there; great value placed on university education, with an eye to the best colleges within China and, even better, in the US; expensive household pets like dogs that are exercised twice a day; digital connectedness, albeit with politically determined restrictions; and holidays in far-flung places within China and overseas.

This is how the great civilising project was supposed to end, except that by now, at these levels of material living standards, the CPC should have long ago disappeared into the dustbin of history, and China should be a democracy. It didn't and now across the political spectrum in Washington and some capitals in Europe, a sense of buyer's remorse has set in.

The CPC very nearly did disappear at the time of the country-wide demonstrations in 1989 that ended with the military's violent crackdown. It might have gone the same way as the old Soviet-dominated Eastern Bloc which fell to pieces in that year. As we know, it survived. Not only that, it has prospered.

An implicit social compact between the Party and the people promised rising living standards and greater personal space, with the Party withdrawing from managing the details of ordinary people's lives, while in return its rule would be unchallenged. Economic growth surged on the back of renewed reforms following Deng Xiaoping's 'Southern Tour' in 1992, and substantial personal freedoms were quickly accumulated. Complex and difficult to sustain as it has been over three decades—with external economic shocks such as the Asian financial crisis, the GFC and its sustained aftermath, the SARS epidemic of 2003 and the COVID-19 pandemic; the digital revolution of smartphones together with social media; and rising incomes, expectations and travel abroad by ordinary folk—the social compact has held fast and given China the political stability and internal cohesion for it to grow to the point where it has now changed the global order, as some, like Martin Jacques over a decade ago, predicted it would do.[37]

Parallel Orders

From the late 1990s, then president Jiang Zemin fought hard inside the Party to allow 'red capitalists' to join it, a struggle he eventually won. This was a significant achievement because it allowed the Party to modernise along with the rest of society as the economy grew and as the private sector, the agency of growth and social change, expanded. Red capitalists were wealthy individuals who had made their fortunes virtually overnight in the burgeoning private sector, but who sought Party membership less for ideological fidelity and more for the favours that membership could bestow to aid their businesses.

With over 92 million members, the CPC is by far the largest political party ever to have existed. Putting to one side the anachronistic nineteenth-century European labels and slogans inherited from the Soviet Union, with its clunky propaganda, it has continued to grow and adapt as China's economy and society have changed.[38]

All of this underpinned an extraordinary economic take-off during the 2000s. The decade was transformative for China. The country rapidly progressed through a series of tipping points to shift from being largely self-sufficient in all the energy and resources it needed to sustain high rates of growth, to becoming at first an importer, then a substantial net importer, and then, regarding some critical commodities such as crude oil and iron ore, the world's single biggest importer.

This changed Beijing's thinking about its security, highlighting its massive and unanticipated dependence on foreign sources of supply and on congested and contested shipping lanes. Suddenly, China's leaders had to respond to these new vulnerabilities. Under Hu Jintao, the 'going out' policy was launched, encouraging Chinese enterprises to invest overseas and put a foot on commodities to ensure resources security. Subsequently, this was supplanted by Xi Jinping's BRI. In addition to resource security, it also sought, among other things, to reduce strategic transport vulnerabilities via routes that avoided maritime chokepoints.

A decade or so ago, the idea of a Group of Two was ventilated within think tanks both in the West and China. This was naively conceived of as having the US and China providing leadership of the existing order by cooperating across a range of common issues, from trade and investment liberalisation to the tackling of asymmetrical security threats such as terrorism, crime, environment and pandemics, thereby ensuring stability in world affairs. It did not gain much traction in part because China itself ten years ago was not ready to put up its hand and take on a leadership role with all the responsibilities and limits on its own behaviour that would entail. More importantly, the old order was not of China's making and, by the beginning of the second decade of the twenty-first century, China was clearly signalling that things had changed. Of course, the US then, as now, was not ready to share global leadership. Such is the way of the dominant power, until the ground has given way under its feet or, as with Thucydides' Trap, where Sparta attacks Athens, the ascendant power, to prevent its rise.

A reformulation of the G2 suggests a multipolar order, with China and the US being by far the two most powerful states, but neither being capable of providing, nor willing to provide, leadership and costly global public goods. This will weaken multilateral institutions, as the two major states will prefer to deal with each other bilaterally, as can be seen with the US–China trade deal agreed in December 2019. It marks a return to managed trade, thereby undermining the WTO's founding principle of non-discrimination which was intended to prevent such arrangements. Lesser states will seek coalitions among themselves, such as the TPP, to which neither the US nor China belong.[39] The parallel orders will intersect at many places, but they also have their own institutions and arrangements between states to support cooperation within each bounded order, led by one of the two superpowers.

Australia's Dystopian Future

From a liberal perspective, the new world order will be dystopian. It will not, however, be Hobbesian, as the powers will generally regard the pursuit of stability and balance as being in their own interests, so as to continue to raise living standards and thus ensure domestic political steadiness. Lesser powers like Australia will need to learn to work with states on specific issues of national interest, even where they are not like-minded in terms of adherence to liberal values, including respect for human rights. The Philippines under President Rodrigo Duterte is a case in point.

Australian foreign policy in the new order must be based on realism. As its starting point, Australia should take the world as it finds it, not how it may wish it to be. The most immediate and complex foreign policy challenge is China.

Central to understanding the emerging world order is to comprehend China's strategic intentions and potential. The question of whether China is an expansionary power or not becomes crucial in understanding how the new order will unfold.

This book argues that China will not be an expansionary power that seeks to establish global hegemony. This is not because of lack of intent or ambition, nor is it because historically China has not been an expansionary power—as it was when ruled by the Manchus—but rather because China is a constrained superpower. This book tries to understand how China sees the world, its security and threats, and, most importantly, the constraints on its actions and how it seeks to overcome these. It also tries to understand how Chinese leaders want to shape the global order so as to advance their country's interests as defined by the party-state.

A more pluralistic and competitive domestic political system in China most likely would define some aspects of these differently, but it might only be at the margins. Geography, history, population, resources and culture bear on Beijing's understanding and definition of interests and security however China is governed.

It is noteworthy that democratic Taiwan makes the same claims as communist China over the South China Sea, as well as Tibet and Xinjiang. Democratic Taiwan, however, is far more expansionist than communist China when it comes to Mongolia, the Russian Far East and much of eastern Kazakhstan—the old Manchu empire. Much Western strategic discussion ignores this, seeing only a caricatured party-state geopolitical agenda, without reference to China's geographic and historical experiences.[40]

China is invariably seen as thrusting outwards, its imperial ambitions now stretching far and wide. Like any state, China seeks security, influence, and recognition of the legitimacy of its interests. More peculiar to China is the perceived need—rightly or wrongly—to defend the party-state from external attack. Few other countries' political systems are subject to sustained attack and criticism from other governments, such as when Australian foreign minister Julie Bishop said China's political system made it unfit for leadership in the Asia-Pacific, or when Vice President Pence effectively called for regime change.[41] As the old saying goes: 'Just because you're paranoid doesn't mean you're not being followed'.

Australia will need to demonstrate that it wishes to pursue an independent foreign policy towards China. It is a long road back to how things stood at the start of the decade, when relations were in a constructive phase. There was no frothiness but rather a clear understanding of the mutual benefits to be had from a cooperative relationship. Australia–China relations had been through some difficult periods, but there was enough of a ballast of goodwill and mutual interest in the relationship to get through the difficult patches. Australia then still spoke the language of strategic cooperation and engagement, and, importantly, acted on that basis. Foreign policy towards the region was still directed at promoting greater integration, not division. The pursuit of a free trade agreement (FTA) with China was not just about selling more beef and wine. It was also about higher levels of economic integration around services, investment and intellectual property.

It will be argued that China was different then, and that things changed appreciably after Xi Jinping took over as leader in 2012. That is true up to a point, as Xi adopted a more muscular foreign policy and began to change course on economic policy in a less market, more statist direction.[42] A more assertive foreign policy from China should have been anticipated as its economy and power grew commensurately. In fact, Beijing has not given up on economic reform and still continues its policy of opening up, but as it has become richer, it has become less needy of foreigners. Nevertheless, reforms in the financial sector, such as permitting majority ownership by foreigners of domestic securities companies continue.[43] China post-COVID-19 may attempt a partial decoupling from the international economy, pursuing domestic consumption-led growth and seeking higher levels of self-reliance, especially in technology.[44]

Had China's threat to the old order been understood more widely, would the correct policy response have been to thwart China's economic rise? Certainly not, just as policies to try to contain China today are not appropriate. Australia and the US, and the West more generally, have no option but to accept China as it is—for better or for worse—and work out how to respond in ways that avoid war and maximise benefits.

The Asia-Pacific region is more stable and prosperous than at any time in the past 200 years. This is not only because of the US military presence but also because of China's economic development and its internal political stability, despite the odds being against it. Alternative histories can be imagined, but we only have the one we have.

As distasteful as it may be for neo-cons on the right and liberals on the left, it is necessary to recognise both the legitimacy of the party-state and China's interests, namely territorial integrity and security in all of its dimensions—military, energy, resources, food, environment, water. It is also necessary to recognise that, no matter how overweening a leader's ambitions may be, China is a constrained power and all its grand schemes, from the BRI to a global soft power effort at great expense, will always over-promise and under-deliver. It is important not to jump at shadows but to assess Beijing's initiatives and actions on their merits.

When Beijing's actions challenge the interests of states, it will of course be necessary and legitimate to push back against it both individually and collectively. Beijing needs to understand that its bad behaviour has a cost for itself. Ultimately, an inclusive framework of norms, rules and habits of consultation which include China and of which it is an author, will be the best means of constraining bad behaviour.

Understanding China's actual constraints and capacities should help reduce strategic mistrust, the purpose of which is to build the conditions for 'competitive coexistence'.[45] This in turn is required to create the conditions whereby Australia can work cooperatively on issues of common concern in order to advance its own interests.

The new world order is here. While uncongenial to the West, it is not obviously threatening to Australia's security. To hedge against a dominant China, Australia needs to work within constantly changing coalitions of states, forming around specific issues and then dissolving when no longer required. Australian diplomacy must be creative, flexible, resolute and consistent. It must also be well resourced and led.

In 2013, David Shambaugh wrote of China as a 'partial power', at a time when its rise was just beginning to be felt globally. Shambaugh thought in terms of China's 'spread' globally rather than its depth and capacity to challenge the old order. He was concerned that China's insecurities, vulnerabilities, brittleness, and unwillingness to accept responsibility for leadership, would prevent it from being a complete power and taking a global leadership role.[46] It is suggested in this book that these things cannot be expected to go away as China grows more powerful; rather, they are structural and existential but have not prevented China constructing its parallel, bounded order.

China the 'constrained power' is the China that Australia must learn to work with in its own interests. Having as our major economic partner a wilful, difficult, abrasive but nonetheless brittle and still weak power, one that is more comfortable with tyranny than democracy, but on which Australia's economic wellbeing and security in the region rest, is the dystopian future that Australian policymakers will need to learn to navigate. If nothing else, it is hoped that this book demystifies China, thereby enabling Australia's foreign and strategic policy discussions to be based on a contemporary understanding of that society as it is, not as some fear it might become.

PART I

STRATEGY AND ORDER

CHAPTER 1

CHINA'S GRAND STRATEGY AND THE NEW WORLD ORDER

On a cold, cloud-wrapped morning in late September 2006, I crossed from China into Pakistan at the Khunjerab Pass. At 4700 metres, it is the highest sealed border crossing in the world. Getting to the pass on the Chinese side involved a 420-kilometre drive from the ancient Silk Road trading centre of Kashgar, flanked by the barren Pamir Mountains to the south and, for much of the journey, the Taklamakan Desert to the north—the 'sea of sand', as it was known to late-nineteenth-century European explorers.[1] We'd cleared customs 130 kilometres short of the border, at the Xinjiang transport-hub town of Tashkurgan.

At the highest point of the pass, marking the international border, was a large stone cairn, honouring the 'heroic' Chinese workers who in 1982 gave their lives to build this narrow strip of paved road in tough conditions. On the Pakistani side, the Karakoram Highway looked as if it had not been maintained since, turning into a steeply descending, twisting, single-lane passage, rutted and with its asphalt regularly shattered by rockfalls.

To be fair, it would be an impossible job to keep this road in good repair. Pakistan's Hunza Valley, into which the road from the pass disappears, forms the intersection of some of the world's highest mountains—the Himalayas, Kunlun, Karakoram, Pamir and

Hindu Kush. This is young geology and it's in constant motion. The only benefit to be had from the long delays caused by treacherous rockslides and bottlenecks of heavy trucks was that there was ample time to gaze in awe at the rivers kilometres below on the valley floor and at the peaks soaring kilometres above.

The Karakoram Highway is part of the main artery connecting Central Asia with the Arabian Sea. Such are the constraints of topography and geography which have shaped the economic and political development of Central Asia, and which China is now shaping through its geo-economic stratagem, the Belt and Road Initiative. When I visited the Khunjerab Pass, teams of Chinese surveyors were preparing to assist the Pakistani Government in upgrading this vital route. This was long before the BRI was presented publicly as the key organising principle for China's foreign engagements by President Xi in a speech in Astana, Kazakhstan in 2013. In time, as a major BRI undertaking, the Karakoram Highway would become the China–Pakistan Economic Corridor (CPEC), opening a modern link between far western China, Central Asia and the Port of Gwadar on the Indian Ocean, and the markets of Europe beyond.

Alone, Insecure and Weak—China's Grand Strategy

Kissinger has argued that only the US had the resources and will to construct the post–World War II order.[2] US idealism and exceptionalism were essential for this, as was its capacity. For China, its will to refashion the order comes from necessity, and a deep sense of vulnerability and abiding insecurity. Like the US, it also now has the economic weight to achieve this.[3]

Leading strategic thinkers in China have long discussed what its grand strategy should be without any settlement of the issue in the way the US, for example, did at the end of the Cold War: as the leader of a unipolar, liberal internationalist order.[4] From the founding of the People's Republic, China's leaders based their strategies on fear. Mao Zedong took control of a country that had disintegrated and was beset by enemies on its borders and abroad. Sulman Wasif Khan describes a 'surrounding world alive with danger, [China's] integrity and its stability forever uncertain'.[5] Mao did not win 'the state', but rather inherited a China shattered into many pieces. The CPC had to make a state out of the rubble it had acquired. It had to ensure control of its creation, to be recognised as the rightful governing party.[6] When viewed from the outside today, China looks secure, but when viewed from the central leadership compound in Zhongnanhai, in Beijing, the same anxieties and insecurities still shape China's grand strategy.

Though never explicitly articulated as such, China's grand strategy has consistently had as its goals the defence of territorial integrity and protection of the CPC as China's legitimate ruling party. In the 1960s, Mao's 'three worlds theory' linked the external threats of the Soviet Union and the US with domestic threats. Pro-Soviet 'revisionists' and pro-American 'class enemies' at different times were held to be seeking to overthrow Communist Party rule.[7]

Deng Xiaoping saw that China could co-exist with both the US and Russia, and that foreign policy should serve the paramount task of domestic economic reconstruction. Nevertheless, the CPC was always on high alert against foreign forces—namely the US and its allies—promoting 'peaceful evolution'.[8] Western sanctions in response to the Tiananmen Square violent intervention by the People's Liberation Army (PLA) in June 1989 reminded the leadership how closely linked were domestic and international security. The sanctions at the time reinforced conservative elements' will to reject political reform and reaffirm the option of using force should Taiwan formally declare independence.[9]

The next twenty years saw a fairly benign international environ-ment. Western condemnation of China over riots in Tibet in 2008 and Urumqi (the capital of Xinjiang) in 2009, and the awarding of the Nobel Peace Prize to dissident Liu Xiaobo in 2010, were each viewed by the leadership as further evidence of 'Westerners' ill-intentions'.[10] Foreign policy under Hu Jintao, albeit without a formal doctrine, continued to be defined as territorial integrity, support for CPC rule, and social and economic development providing the underpinnings of domestic stability.

In many respects, Xi Jinping has been successful in realising the original goals of the strategy. He has responded to insecurities by strengthening internal Party control, shoring up support internationally, and ensuring that China has the military strength to protect itself. But as Khan observes, this strategy still derives from weakness and vulnerability, both external and internal. The paradox facing China's leaders is that continuing to pursue these goals when China is now so powerful 'inspires fear, and fear resistance'.[11]

China scares its neighbours. The US has declared it a strategic competitor and now also in Europe China's strategic intentions and potential threat are under review. The Chinese leadership's suspicion that the world is out to get it leads to behaviour that begets suspicion, and the way the world responds feeds that suspicion, in the end 'creating the very insecurity that Xi has been trying to avoid'.[12] In this way, successful defence of China's core strategic interests has taken the country back to where it was in the early 1960s, beset with enemies—real or imagined—within and without.[13]

If anything, China's strategic vulnerabilities have increased with its successful economic growth and rising military power. It needs to commit ever more resources to defending its borders as both inland and other neighbours become more uneasy with its rise; unsettled internal territorial issues have still not been resolved; and, most importantly, China has become utterly dependent on world markets for significant shares of its resource and energy needs. Meanwhile, its soft power does not correspond to its economic and military weight.

Following Xi's Astana speech in 2013, the BRI evolved as a key element of China's grand strategy. It is intended to increase China's security by addressing strategic vulnerabilities in peripheral borders and maritime chokepoints, and to project soft power through the agency of economic and social development in the countries involved. It has also been suggested that it was in part a response to president Obama's speech in Darwin in 2011 announcing the Pivot to Asia as his new strategic doctrine,[14] with its accompanying promise to direct greater military and diplomatic attention towards Asia.

A grand strategy should also reflect the vision a state has of itself, and how it intends to shape the international environment to meet the state's strategic objectives. Xi Jinping sought to give BRI a moral dimension in his speech to the World Economic Forum in Davos in 2017 when he spoke of a 'Community of Common Destiny'. It has been suggested that this was China's first attempt to define (at least publicly) a vision for the strategy.[15] Nonetheless, debate and uncertainty continue about the extent of China's ambitions and whether it will attempt to remake the world in its own authoritarian image. The notion of a Community of Common Destiny has been likened to the ancient Confucian governing philosophy of 'All under Heaven', with the emperor at the centre of a world order, ruling with a mandate from heaven.[16]

Considering all of the intended ambiguity typical of speeches by politicians addressing multiple audiences, a Community of Common Destiny may be interpreted in various ways. It may be a vision of an order that converges on an illiberal capitalist system similar to China's, a Pax Sinica. Or it may involve the replacement of rivalry with cooperation between states of different forms of political and social organisation. On either interpretation, it is an order in which China feels secure, and one in which China aims to replace the US as the 'dominant commercial player and influencer in the world'.[17]

Some would argue that China is well on the way to achieving the latter and therefore needs to be resisted at every turn by the upholders of the old liberal order: the US and its allies.[18] As usually happens, however, a big gap exists between conception and the creation. Grand objectives have a way of falling short of intentions. Already, China's conception of an order is meeting resistance on numerous fronts, especially over the indebtedness arising from BRI projects, China's overweening ambitions regarding its own incarnations of Russia's 'near abroad', and the abundance of exuberance demonstrated by the CPC's United Front Work Department in interfering in other countries' domestic politics.[19]

The BRI has become the central organising principle of China's foreign trade and investment relations, and indeed its foreign policy more generally. Highlighting the power and authority of Xi Jinping, it was written into the CPC's constitution in 2017. It provides a hierarchy of priorities for decision-making within China. Demonstrating remarkably little understanding of current Chinese policy, Malcolm Turnbull said to Premier Li Keqiang during the last bilateral meeting between leaders that 'Australia would not sign up to a slogan when we had no control over its content or substance'.[20]

The geo-economic dimension under the BRI of China's grand strategy has captured much international attention, but China's institutional entrepreneurship has also been significant. It has sought to influence, and shape, existing multilateral institutions created for the liberal universalist order, especially the United Nations (UN) and the WTO. It has done this by paying diplomatic attention to its bilateral relations with all states, big and small. China has also displayed an expansive capacity to create new institutions, including the SCO, the New Development Bank, and the Asia Infrastructure Investment Bank (AIIB). Some are international and open to all states to join; others are not and, as such, form a China-led order.[21]

Destined for Peace

Exercising military power to create the new order is not part of China's grand strategy. Military strength is for China's own security, not regional or global hegemony. This is entirely a practical matter, not one of philosophy, national disposition or history.[22] China's vulnerabilities and weaknesses all but rule out the projection of power by military means beyond its near abroad.

China's doctrine has been force-denial in and around its littoral waters, Taiwan, and extending to the first island chain, and supporting its claims—or at least raising the costs of denial by others—in the South China Sea. Also, Japan is a major potential military threat, with its substantial and sophisticated forces, and its geographic location. China has rapidly built formidable capabilities in a number of areas, notably in its submarine fleet and missiles, especially those designed to destroy aircraft carriers, one of the US' singular advantages.

China's rapid accumulation of ground-launched intermediate-range missiles has led to a strong US response. In August 2019, the US unilaterally withdrew from its bilateral Intermediate-Range Nuclear Forces Treaty, asserting persistent Russian violations. The treaty banned fielding ballistic missiles, cruise missiles and launchers that could carry either conventional or nuclear warheads.

China had not been a party to the treaty and the US' withdrawal from it has opened the way for the US to rebuild these capabilities in East Asia.[23]

China's expanding blue-water navy, including its aircraft carrier program, suggests a bigger and more expansive military ambition. China intends to expand its naval presence in the Indian Ocean, including the Arabian Sea. This is consistent with Beijing's existential anxiety about having the capacity to protect its extended vital supply lines. As it opens more pipelines and direct land transport routes across Eurasia, and as it seeks energy and resource security along the Belt, so it will seek to secure its supplies and access to markets along the maritime Road.

Since Graham Allison's 2015 *Atlantic* article, international strategic analysts' attention has focused again on Thucydides' Trap, with a rising China challenging the US' dominant role at the top of the international order being analogous to Athens and Sparta and, accordingly, suggesting the inevitability of conflict. Others have written about a rising Wilhelmine Germany and Britain using a similar focus.[24] Allison modified his thesis in a subsequent book, arguing that conflict was not inevitable. While his researchers found that over the past 500 years, a major rising power had led to war on twelve occasions and not on four of them, Alison argued that, 'As far as the eye can see, the defining question about global order is whether China and the US can escape the Thucydides Trap'.[25]

The threat of nuclear conflict, or mutually assured destruction (MAD), means that the US and China are not destined for war. Beijing has long subscribed to a 'no first use' policy, though of course that could change. Reviewing *Destined for War*, Arthur Waldron argues that China has brought upon itself an arms race among Japan, India and other American allies, in response to its bullying behaviour in the South China Sea. Rather than just copping China's rise, as Foreign Minister Yang Jiechi brazenly admonished ASEAN states to do in 2010, long before Xi's ascendency to power, 'all of China's neighbours are now building up strong military capabilities'.[26]

Allison discusses 'power shift' or 'power transition' theories as the causes of war, potentially between China and the US. Conflicts can arise because of uncertainty about what the rising power might do in the future. The dominant power may therefore strike to prevent what it fears is a transition that will jeopardise its position. Hawks in the US are drawing attention to this and the possibility of nuclear conflict.[27]

Oliver Stuenkel argues instead that, rather than a power shift making war the common destiny for China and the US, it more usefully could be compared not with Wilhelmine Germany but with how the US went on to have a cooperative relationship with Great Britain after it displaced the latter as the dominant power.[28] Historically, rising powers have pursued a variety of strategies when dealing with a declining power, from support to predation, depending on the perceived value along the spectrum from accommodation to conflict.[29]

On this analysis, it is difficult to see that China would not want to prop up the US in view of the US' experience in managing and leading the old international order, its leadership of the many international institutions that China will still value, its preparedness to provide global public goods on which China can free-ride, and its underpinning of the international economy which provides the stability on which China's leaders depend domestically.

A major difference between the power shift involving the US and Great Britain, and that involving China and the US, however, is that China's leaders believe that the US has never accepted the legitimacy of the Chinese political system, and so it will never willingly concede its status as the pre-eminent regional and global power. As Kevin Rudd has argued, the Chinese leadership views the US approach to it as the 'five tos': 'to contain China; to isolate China; to diminish China; to internally divide China; and to sabotage China's leadership'.[30]

These capture all the anxieties and insecurities shaping China's foreign and strategic policies, and the challenges, albeit not insurmountable, of constructing a cooperative relationship between the US and China. Insecurity begets insecurity, with suspicion and mistrust on both sides. This has profound implications for how Australia positions itself in this dynamic, unfolding power shift.

Super-connectivity—Many Belts and Roads

As discussed further in Part II of this book, China is 'Prometheus bound': constrained by history, geography, an utter dependency on foreign suppliers of resources and energy, and—from the perspective of world leadership—a debilitating soft power deficit. It understands that it needs to find other ways to establish and then build and exercise power and influence.[31]

From a Washington or Canberra perspective, the BRI is seen as mainly about the 'Road', China's maritime reach into the Indian Ocean, South-East Asia and the Pacific.[32] This is understandable, as China's development of maritime power is relatively recent and directly challenges areas that had previously been the exclusive security realm of the US, whose activities there had been uncontested. In East Asia and the Pacific, China will continue to encounter strong US competition. In the Indian Ocean, India will continue to dominate militarily and China will have no choice but to work out various accommodations with it. It is in Eurasia that China will encounter the least resistance and where the BRI will be most effective in advancing its goals.[33]

The Eurasian 'heartland' was defined over a century ago by the geostrategic realist Halford John Mackinder as the world's geopolitical pivot.[34] Since the end of the Cold War, it has been an area contested between the US, Russia and China. The US has had only tenuous influence in the region, one where Russia historically has long been the unchallenged dominant power but, for now at least, is resigned to China's growing influence. China has been assiduous in building relations with other Eurasian regional powers, including Turkey and Iran, as well as the states of Central Asia. This Eurasian heartland is where China has the greatest chance of achieving strategic primacy over the US.[35]

In terms of transport connectivity as a means of executing a grand geopolitical strategy, we have been there before. Unlike President Trump, past US presidents did not build walls in the Western Hemisphere but sought to bind the vast dispersed geostrategic area together by means of highways. The Pan-American Highway runs for 30 000 kilometres from Alaska to Tierra del Fuego.

The convention to build it was signed in 1937, and in 1952 Mexico was the first state to complete its section of the road. Typically, it was justified on both political grounds (fortifying anti-fascist defences in the 1930s and 1940s) and economic grounds (selling more US automobiles). It was also said to promote broader social and economic development. Like all such projects, it attracted its share of resistance from countries that suspected the motives of those building it. Argentina, for one, saw it as a Trojan Horse for US imperialism.[36] Similarly, some today see the Hambantota Port, which a Chinese firm acquired in a debt-for-equity swap because the Sri Lankan Government could not service the loan, as Chinese imperialism under the BRI.[37]

The sheer scale of the BRI demands attention (see Figure 1). It involves some trillion dollars of initial investment, and seventy-one countries along the Belt and Road corridors, accounting for 50 per cent of the world's population, 40 per cent of global GDP,

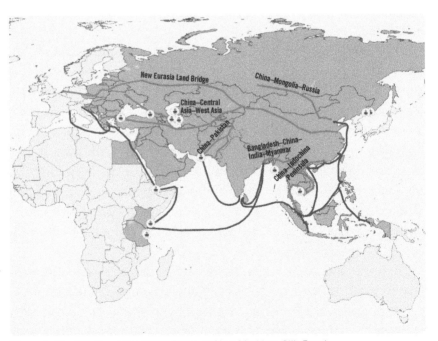

Figure 1. The Silk Road Economic Belt and New Maritime Silk Road
Source: World Bank Group, 'Belt and Road Economies: Opportunities and Risks of Transport Corridors', Washington, DC, June 2019, p. 3

and 75 per cent of the world's energy resources.[38] Such numbers attest to the scale of China's ambitions and are why participation for many governments is compelling.[39]

The core areas remain Eurasia and the Indian Ocean, across to the central east coast of Africa, with extensions through South-East Asia and more recently the Pacific. Countries as far away as Italy, Brazil, Chile and New Zealand have also sought formally to be associated with it. Beyond the corridor countries, a total of 152 nations, including eighteen from Europe, have signed relevant memoranda of understanding (MOUs) to participate in the BRI. A number of international bodies, including UN agencies, also now participate in its many forums. Of the European states, some twelve countries are EU member states and six, excluding Turkey, are aspirant states. One way of looking at this is that European countries are well represented in the BRI, while another is that China has been particularly successful in extending its global political influence far across Eurasia, beyond Central Asia.

Of the total BRI investment to date, 46 per cent has gone to energy projects and 25 per cent to transport, while the rest has been distributed between chemical engineering, construction, mining and other, smaller activities. The regional distribution of investment so far has been mainly to East Asia and the Pacific, which account for 34 per cent of the total, then Europe and Central Asia (Eurasia) with 32 per cent, South Asia with 19 per cent, the Middle East and North Africa with 13 per cent, and sub-Saharan Africa with 2 per cent. The biggest recipients have been the Russian Federation, Pakistan, Laos, Malaysia and Indonesia.[40]

The financing of BRI projects has become increasingly controversial, with accusations from many quarters, including the Trump White House, of 'debt-trap diplomacy'. This has become a setback in China's attempts to use BRI projects to build its soft power, an essential requirement for establishing leadership of an order. The median BRI investment is 6 per cent of a recipient's GDP, which the World Bank finds is 'not large' in view of the infrastructure financing needs of the countries involved, implying that some accusations against China may be exaggerated.[41]

The BRI has a number of antecedents, going back at least to early last decade when strategic planners began to address China's major vulnerability: its dependence on ships carrying oil, gas and other vital resources for its fast-growing industries going through the South China Sea and the Straits of Malacca. Then, as now, the US controlled these strategically sensitive shipping lanes and so it could at will deny China access.

By the time the BRI was announced, plans for major Eurasian pipeline projects, such as the Central Asia natural gas pipeline and the Kazakhstan–China oil pipeline, were well advanced. The Myanmar–China natural gas and oil pipelines were commissioned in 2013 and stretch from the Bay of Bengal to Kunming in Yunnan Province; the oil pipeline was completed in August 2014 and reached full capacity in 2017.[42] The upgrade and development of the Karakoram Highway into the CPEC was also well underway in 2006, as we have seen, although the official start date is given as 2008. The Hambantota deep-sea port, which is so often used as an example of the dangers of China's purported debt diplomacy under the BRI, actually began development in January 2008.[43]

The history of Pakistan's Gwadar Port serves to highlight both the earlier genesis of projects now badged as the BRI and how much disconnect there is in some cases between the imputed strategic motives of China's planners and the reality of how decisions are made. Gwadar predates the BRI by some fifteen years, and far from being part of a military strategy, at least initially, to establish potentially valuable naval assets in India's backyard along the Arabian Sea, it arose from bilateral considerations between China and Pakistan. The project was brought to the Chinese by Pakistan president Pervez Musharraf, who had recently installed himself in power through a coup. He went early in his term to Beijing to demonstrate his legitimacy to people at home, and to show India that China had a close friendship with Pakistan. The Chinese leadership were doubtful about the feasibility of the port, and concerns that it would prove to be a white elephant have been largely borne out. Construction was delayed by a decade or more by many issues, including attacks by the Balochistan Liberation Army. Meanwhile, in Indian and Western foreign and defence planning circles, Gwadar has become symbolic of the threat of Sino-Pakistani strategic cooperation. Had it been left to the Chinese side, it probably would never have been built.[44]

Pakistan has served to keep pressure on India, with which China has ongoing border disputes; it was an even more important strategic partner when India for decades was closely aligned with the Soviet Union. Pakistan has also been the agent through which Beijing has kept in touch with Afghanistan and West Asia, especially before it was able to exercise direct influence in the area. This has been of major security importance for Beijing because of its vulnerability to the movement of Islamic populations across its borders in Xinjiang, which run for hundreds of kilometres along the high Pamir and Kunlun mountains. The frontier lands are potentially porous and to this day absorb massive internal security resources.

As the BRI policies became more fully articulated by Beijing following Xi's Astana speech, so local officials started to formulate more ambitious plans for the CPEC. At this time, the entire infrastructure across the vast reaches of thinly populated Xinjiang was being transformed—improbably—by high-speed railway lines, six-lane expressways, and massive airports. The template of investment that was proving so successful in wealthier parts of China was being rolled out in Xinjiang. It had two main objectives. One was to serve domestic political security for the empire by promoting rapid economic growth through infrastructure investment and by removing transport constraints, lowering costs, and creating more integrated and hence efficient markets. The other was to position Kashgar as the transport hub for Central Asia and the portal to the Indian Ocean via Pakistan.

Kashgar has come to play an increasingly strategically important role in maintaining stability in China's western, Uighur-populated border area, and as a trading nexus. In 2010, local officials were discussing a vision of Kashgar as Central Asia's version of Shenzhen, China's first Special Economic Zone. By 2015, considerable manufacturing had been relocated from the more developed eastern parts of China to Kashgar.[45] Robert Kaplan, the realist strategist who emphasises the role of geography in China's grand strategy, observes that a 'place like Kashgar might normally be associated with the back-of-beyond travel writing. But, in fact, it could be the center of the world geopolitical order'.[46]

In the contest on China's western periphery, the BRI has supported Xinjiang becoming the economic powerhouse of Central Asia and extending Chinese influence over Eurasia in direct competition with Russia, while tying Pakistan ever more closely to China. As with the pipelines across Myanmar, a domestic economic imperative—which would have been addressed with or without a wider geopolitical calculus—actually served multiple purposes. It promoted economic development in Xinjiang, which it was hoped would not only produce wealth but political stability, on the assumption that the large ethnic Muslim Uighur population would be coopted into a Han economy by higher living standards. The widespread internment camps across Xinjiang suggest that the latter, if not also the former, policy objectives have been a cruel, dismal failure.

The trans-Myanmar pipelines are another example of how BRI projects can serve multiple policy objectives for Beijing, both domestic and external. When oil and gas started to flow through the pipelines, it was the first time that China could receive those resources without having to transit US-dominated shipping lanes in South-East Asia. It also was to solve a practical domestic economic problem. As explained by the chairman of the National Energy Authority and vice chairman of the National Development and Reform Commission (NDRC), Zhang Guo Bao, it would bring oil and gas to the rapidly developing south-west of China under the State Council's 'Go West Strategy', which was intended to even up the levels of economic development between the fast-growing provinces of China's littoral regions and the lagging interior. It served a geopolitical end, but it was primarily envisioned to address domestic economic imperatives.[47]

Some BRI lending has been criticised for leading recipient countries to higher levels of debt than they would otherwise have had. Fault may be found on both the borrower and lender sides, but China is increasingly taking a more narrowly commercial approach to BRI financing. Some countries that have experienced heavy indebtedness as a result of reckless borrowing policies were doing so long before the BRI was thought up. Moreover, whether or not there is a BRI, China, with its massive foreign exchange (forex) reserves, a function mainly of its high savings rate, will increasingly be the source of capital for such projects around the world.[48]

Despite the BRI's execution problems and increasingly negative perception, its core connectivity project offers substantial economic benefits. The World Bank estimates that if the foreshadowed projects are all implemented among the seventy-one corridor economies, and accompanied by the necessary policies, such as deeper economic reform, greater transparency and greater trade liberalisation, it could add up to 2.9 per cent to global real income, or about as much as a multilateral round of trade negotiations. In the corridor economies, the World Bank estimates that real incomes could increase by an order of two to four.[49]

China's Bounded Order

Since the early 2000s, China has been fashioning an order that reflects its overall weight in the world. Stuenkel argues that, consequently, China is crafting a 'parallel order' of international institutions and norms, rather than directly challenging existing ones, or what John Mearsheimer has called a 'bounded order'.[50]

China is not seeking to replace existing global or regional institutions where it sees them serving its interests, or where prospects exist for them to be shaped to China's advantage. China, for example, actively participates in UN bodies and is the largest contributor to UN peacekeeping. It wants bigger roles in the International Monetary Fund (IMF) and the World Bank, supports the G20, and is strongly committed to the WTO, Asia-Pacific Economic Cooperation group (APEC), and the various ASEAN-plus forums. In these bodies, China behaves more like an 'established great power than a revisionist one'.[51]

China has been building and strengthening relations through initiatives that place it at the centre of networks of countries. In 2003, it created the SCO with ambitions to be something of a Eurasian North Atlantic Treaty Organization (NATO). In November 2006, the first-ever Sino-African summit was held. During this event in

Beijing, president Hu Jintao hosted the inaugural meeting of the Forum on China–Africa Cooperation, at which the China–Africa Development Fund was created, with, by today's standards, a modest contribution of US$1 billion from the China Development Bank. The summit was preceded by ministerial-level meetings that began as far back as 2000. It continues to meet and oversee joint development projects, with the most recent forum taking place in September 2018.

Cheekily, in 2012, together with eleven existing and five aspirant EU members, China formed the Central and Eastern Europe Countries Plus One Forum, which has regular ministerial meetings and summits. Brussels has little option but to grin and bear it, as what is now the 17 + 1 grouping (Greece joined in 2019) can and will weaken EU unity, tenuous at the best of times, on foreign policy issues. Hungary, for example, as it has become more authoritarian, has shown itself more sympathetic towards China. And in March 2020, early in the COVID-19 pandemic, the President of EU aspiring member, Serbia, Aleksandar Vučcić, declared that only China could help his country—it was intended as a sharp rebuke of Brussels.

China's ever closer relationship with Russia, however, may hinder how far it can push relations with some members of the forum at the expense of Brussels. Poland has a tense security relationship with Russia and is unlikely to be comfortable with Russia and China's deepening security relationship. Meanwhile, the Czech Republic may have begun losing interest in the BRI, which is seen as over-promising and under-delivering.[52]

In 2015, after a decade of diplomacy around extending and deepening relations with Latin America, the China–CELAC Forum was convened. The Community of Latin American and Caribbean States (CELAC) was formally established in 2011 in Caracas, Venezuela. By then, the government of Hugo Chávez was in open confrontation with the US, with the Venezuelan president positioning himself as something of an ideological figurehead among a number of left-wing leaders in the region. China's interest in CELAC, besides extending its geopolitical influence in a distant part of the Western Hemisphere, was natural resources. This engagement came on the heels of more than a decade of Chinese firms investing in the region's resources.

China has largely funded the New Development Bank, which was established in 2014 as the BRICS Development Bank and headquartered in Shanghai. The countries that lent their initials to the original acronym—Brazil, Russia, India and China—began meeting informally from 2006. The first summit was held three years later, and has taken place annually since then. In 2011, when the summit was held in the city of Sanya on Hainan Island, South Africa joined the group.

When the EU and US refused to support material changes to the operations of the Bretton Woods institutions of the post–World War II era—the World Bank and the IMF—to reflect the shift of economic power to the newly emerging economies of East and South Asia, China led an international response by establishing the AIIB. This marked a new and important stage in China's global institutional statecraft. China could have unilaterally achieved all of its economic objectives, such as recycling its forex reserves and providing a vent for its surplus infrastructure construction capacity, but instead Beijing chose to create a new multilateral institution, open to all countries, and in doing so bound itself to act within a set of agreed multilateral rules and disciplines. This marked a bold bid by China for leadership of the new order, and so it is not surprising that the US has resisted joining and encouraged its allies to do likewise.

India was among the first to join the AIIB and is the bank's second-biggest contributor, yet because of the position it holds that the CPEC transgresses Indian territory, it has not joined the BRI. Led by the UK, a slew of European states soon joined the bank too, eventually followed by one of the US' closest allies, Australia. Australia's joining marked a rare triumph of interests over friendship. It was a near thing, with the Australian Cabinet, on and off, spending the best part of six months agonising over it. The US has had more success in keeping Australia in its camp on the BRI and Huawei. The AIIB, BRI and Huawei's involvement in 5G systems have all become defining issues in terms of where states stand in the new order.

China is now a highly capable, protean actor on the world stage, engaging with established multilateral institutions while creating new arrangements when it finds the existing architecture wanting in terms of its own interests. China is both a status quo power and a disruptor. It participates in the rules-based system while working with others to create new rules. This is what the new order increasingly will look like.[53]

Australia and the New Order

The Australian Government's hackneyed call that China must abide by the 'rules-based system' is missing the point. The international order already comprises many rules-based suborders—various UN obligations, legally binding WTO commitments (the only such binding obligations), IMF and World Bank rules and procedures, and various regional arrangements. China has ratified the UN's Law of the Sea Convention, while the US has not. As Mearsheimer observes, great powers 'write the rules to suit their own interests' and equally ignore them if on specific issues the rules do not advance their interests. The US invasion of Iraq in 2003 is a case in point.[54]

China refused to submit itself to the jurisdiction of the International Court of Arbitration in The Hague, to which it was a signatory. This became the focus of sustained criticism from prime minister Turnbull and foreign minister Julie Bishop. It was something of an eccentric position for Australia to take, since its closest ally, the US, had not ratified the Law of the Sea Convention and so was outside this particular set of international rules. Criticism of China was legitimate, but Australia had the loudest and most strident public voice on the issue, to nil effect except considerable harm to our relations with China.[55] As Professor Hugh White, former head of the Australian Strategic Policy Institute, said at the time, 'no regional leader—not even Japan's Shinzo Abe—has gone this far before'.[56]

In international relations, the unpleasant reality is that great powers do what they wish and the rest do what they can. As the Athenian ambassadors said to the citizens of Melos, impatient with their pleas for justice, 'Justice is found only between equals in power, as to the rest the strong do as they will and the weak suffer as they must'. Global rules are a core element of the international system but, as the US by its actions has shown over and over again, adherence will always be tempered by national interest.

Australia and the BRI—the Trust Deficit

Australia has adopted an ambivalent approach to the BRI. Recognising its central role in organising China's outward investment priorities, Australia has been largely noncommittal publicly, but it has joined only one of the BRI's several MOUs, and in 2017 its trade minister only perfunctorily attended the Chinese Government–sponsored BRI conference. In 2018, the Victorian Government broke ranks with the Commonwealth and signed memoranda of association with the BRI. It is not clear what all these documents amount to beyond affirmation of support for aspects of the BRI—they certainly do not carry any treaty-level, legally binding obligations. Victoria's association with the BRI has, however, caught the attention of US Secretary of State Mike Pompeo. He felt compelled to threaten to cut off 'information exchanges with Australia' over this. The US ambassador was forced to make an unseemly correction to his boss' remarks.[57]

Australia's reluctance to endorse the BRI and engage with China on related activities, including in other countries, is driven by broad geopolitical considerations. It is likely that Australia's disinclination to be party to the BRI has cost it Chinese investment. In the longer term, however, missed investment may well prove to be less consequential than the more diffuse but nevertheless significant costs of basing the bilateral relationship on strategic mistrust, rather than cooperation.

Since Australia joined the AIIB in 2015, the lines of US–China strategic competition have hardened, and Australia has aligned itself more closely with the US in this rivalry. It is most unlikely that Australia would join the AIIB today if it were just being established. Rather, some strategic analysts are urging that Australia find a new strategic equilibrium in the Indo-Pacific. The assertion that 'Australians can have little appetite for China's Orwellian vision of a "Community of Common Destiny for Mankind"' is probably true.[58] It is not at all clear that, even if political convergence were in the mind of Xi, as the only possible way to make the world secure for China and allow the CPC to retain power, this could ever occur.

So far, there seems to be little evidence that the BRI has led to the convergence of political systems or values, as some have expected.[59] The 2020 Economist Intelligence Unit Democracy Index report shows the lowest level of 'democracy' since the report was launched in 2006, but no correlation with the BRI, not least because many BRI states were either 'authoritarian' or 'flawed democracies' before the BRI existed. It is more likely that China's banded order will evolve as a broad church that can accommodate a full spectrum of states with their individual forms of political and social organisation.

In the past, Australian diplomacy has supported multilateral institutions, seeking to participate actively to ensure they do not develop in ways inimical to our interests. The BRI is a reality. China's leadership of it is a reality.[60] But Australia has instead opted to embrace enthusiastically US-led competitor arrangements. It has become a champion of the Quadrilateral Security Dialogue (the Quad), involving three of China's strategic competitors—the US, Japan and India—and ourselves, even though we are more dependent on China economically than any of the other participants. Australia has signed up to the US-led Free and Open Indo-Pacific Strategy, which has elements such as the Blue Dot Network (BDN) that compete directly with the BRI, and has also materially deepened military interoperability with the US. Australia has now based its foreign policy towards China on strategic mistrust.

A Regional Hegemon?

China's grand strategy has been to build a network of relationships with many different states with a wide range of systems of political and social organisation. It has not set out to remake the world in its image—that is, not universalist—but to create an international environment that provides stability, minimises threats and challenges, and does not seek to undermine the CPC's claim to be the sole government and source of power in China.

The contest is often misunderstood as zero-sum: either one group prevails or not. In the extreme universalist form of Pax Sinica, this is the case, but for the pluralistic interpretation of the Community of Common Destiny, this is not the case.[61] The latter simply accepts multiple forms of social and political organisation that will exist from state to state.

China's grand strategy has been executed through the agencies of geo-economics and international institutional innovation. Based on its insecurities about maintaining territorial integrity and regime continuity, over the past twenty years, Beijing has built a bounded order which continues to attract states. The strategy has evolved progressively, incrementally and disjointedly. It will continue to do so and, as it is modified, will attract additional states. States that are part of China's bounded order also participate in the international order through trade and investment outside the BRI corridors and within existing international institutions. Greater connectivity under the BRI, if implemented well, which means accompanied by policies that support greater economic reform and transparency, offers substantial economic gains to participants. These are likely to outweigh the criticisms of, and pushback against, both specific BRI projects and lending practices in certain countries.

China cannot replicate the Monroe Doctrine in East Asia to become the local hegemon, as the US did in the Western Hemisphere, however much it may like to do so. Japan is too big and too powerful to allow it, and China needs the US presence to help manage Japan and the Korean Peninsula. It would like to diminish US influence, and to some extent it has been successful, but it has singularly failed to win hearts and minds, from Jakarta to Manila to Hanoi, Hong Kong, Taipei, Seoul and Tokyo.

Furthermore, China's assertiveness in the South China Sea in peremptorily claiming disputed reefs, rocks and shoals through its building program, and militarising some of these, has led to a backlash in the region and confirmed suspicions in Washington, Brussels and Canberra about its military intentions.

The historical analogy with the Monroe Doctrine breaks down over the vast differences in historical conditions between then and now, and the powerful states China confronts in East Asia. Nor is it a question of China as the ascendant power replacing the dominant power. Regional security was once based on hub-and-spoke arrangements between the US and its allies and friendly countries in East Asia. Now there are networks of relationships or 'multiple coalitions, some involving the United States and many others exclusively within the region itself'.[62] Some of these China participates in, and others not, such as Japan and Vietnam, Japan and India, the Quad, and other security and military arrangements such as the Malabar naval exercises. All countries in the region are engaged in a continual process of adjusting and modifying their positions in response to China's rise.[63]

China is, however, the dominant regional power, a status derived from its massive economic weight, BRI activities, and statecraft in all of its dimensions. All local countries are more dependent economically on China than China is on them, few more so than Australia. China participates in most regional political, economic and security forums; it has bilateral and plurilateral free-trade agreements with most states in the region; it hosts expansive academic and other intellectual exchanges. The list could go on. The point is that China is deeply integrated at every level in East Asia due to its absolute size, its economic power, its openness, and its lengthy historical and cultural ties and relationships across the area. While it confronts the US at many points in the region, none more so than the South China Sea, it is the dominant influencer and shaper of East Asia. That will not change, no matter how much other major powers may wish to push back.

Robert Blackwell and Jennifer Harris, in *War by Other Means*, argue convincingly that China is the world's leading practitioner of geo-economics to project power. In doing this, China has been the major factor in returning regional or global power projections back to a largely economic (as opposed to political–military) exercise. This, of course, is precisely what a militarily constrained great power would do.[64]

Beijing's grand strategy is in reality a limited strategy. Unlike that of the US, it is not universalist, nor based on a belief in exceptionalism. To the extent that a Community of Common Destiny attempts to define the strategy in terms of values, it is more likely about non-interference, about states with different forms of political and social organisation getting along with each other, rather than envisaging a most improbable convergence towards a China–centric authoritarian market order, as some China alarmists assert.[65]

China's strategic objectives have not changed over the past half-century. It seeks security for its borders and respect for its territorial integrity, and, of equal importance, it seeks to protect at every point the party that gathered together the shards of a broken empire and imposed a modern nation-state on them.

PART II

PROMETHEUS BOUND

CHAPTER 2

THE TIES THAT BIND CHINA
GEOGRAPHY AND HISTORY

China faces vastly different conditions than did the US in its rise to become the dominant world power in the twentieth century. Compared with the US and its unrestrained capacity to project power globally, China is Prometheus bound. It is an economic giant, but by virtue of its geography, history, its utter dependency on international markets for all the resources and energy it needs to sustain its economic growth, and the limits on its use of soft power stemming from its party-state political system, the circumstances of its rise could not be further removed from those of the US during its ascendency to global pre-eminence. Since the Manchu expansion of Ming China's territories from the early seventeenth century, the constraints of geography and history have been major influences on China's grand strategy, and will continue to be so.

The US had no hostile borders to secure and no internal threats to its territorial integrity. In contrast, China has the longest land borders in the world and still has unsettled boundary disputes with neighbours. Internally, China remains an empire with big areas of unresolved territory that, when viewed from Beijing, are not secure. Externally, China has fourteen states adjacent to it and 22 383 kilometres of land borders to defend. The ties that bind East Asia's Gulliver are its Eurasian geography and its history of empire.

The Revenge of Borders and Empire

Yu Men Guan, or Jade Gate Pass, is today a crumbling ruin on the
edge of the vast, boulder-strewn but otherwise empty expanse of
the Gobi Desert. A rusting iron fence, keeping tourists at a distance,
suggests historical significance. Indeed, Jade Gate Pass once marked
a departure point from the 'civilised' world for merchants embarking
on journeys from China to the south and west. After passing through
the gate, the Silk Road soon bifurcates into its major northern and
southern arterial arms.

Just beyond Jade Gate Pass, at the outer reaches of the Han empire,
are sections of the city walls of Hecang Cheng, a Han outpost built
in 101 BCE, and the ruins of what once was a massive commissary
used for provisioning troops engaged in the worthy task of protecting civilisation from the barbarians. To the troops stationed at that
remote garrison at the edge of the Chinese known world, the seemingly empty lands beyond were full of threats and dangers. Sentries
gazed into a desolate vastness, alert for signs of dust indicating the
approach of caravans to be taxed or armies to defend against. It was
literally life on the edge.

From here, skirting the Taklamakan Desert, the southern arm of
the Silk Road continues towards Pakistan and India. It was via this
route that Gandharan Buddhism travelled from Hellenistic Peshawar
throughout western China, as far as present-day Gansu Province.
The Dunhuang cave paintings in Gansu attest to the vibrancy of the
culture until the establishment of Islam across western China during
the cosmopolitan Tang Dynasty. Later, Lamaist Buddhism spread
throughout the region during the Tibetan occupation to become
the dominant form of Buddhism in China. The northern arm,
meanwhile, divided into many Silk Roads across Central Asia, with
the most important leading to the oasis trading centre of Kashgar
and beyond to Persia, the Middle East and the Mediterranean.

Until the westward expansion of the Chinese empire began
under the Qing Dynasty in the seventeenth century, the territory
named by the Qing as Xinjiang (which meant 'New Frontier') was
occupied by successive waves of tribal and nomadic people from
Tibet and Central Asia. Attesting to centuries of different peoples

washing over the region, today Xinjiang has some twenty-two ethnic groups, of which the Turkic Uighurs are the biggest, accounting for some 40 per cent of the autonomous region's population. The Qing expansion extended China's borders to an unprecedented size, encompassing Xinjiang, Inner Mongolia and, with dominant influence, Tibet. Effectively, the China of today is the result of these mighty Central Asian conquests.[1]

Xinjiang has occupied a special strategic role for Beijing, as it borders three of the five Central Asian states: Kazakhstan, Kyrgyzstan and Tajikistan—the others being Uzbekistan and Turkmenistan. Beijing has long feared succession in Xinjiang and loss of influence in the wider region. More recently, the threat of Islamic terrorism has been directed at the majority Han population. There was a series of terrorist incidents in 2014, including one in Tiananmen Square which struck at the heart of Beijing's sense of security.

In the Xinjiang city of Yili, near the Kazakhstan border, a large mosque stands as a crude reminder of the anxieties that the eighteenth-century emperor Qianlong held over his control of the hearts and minds of his recently subjugated people in the far west. On the outside, the building is in the Chinese style, with exposed beams and cantilevered tiled roofs. Inside, it is brightly decorated in the garish colours of the Qing, with lots of bright greens, blues, reds and yellows, in contrast to the spare, plain interiors customary in mosques. According to the resident imam, Qianlong was so insecure about his grip on the territory that he decorated the mosque in this way so that worshippers would think of Beijing when they were praying.

Other than a brief period in the early twentieth century when, with the help of the Russians, the independent state of East Turkestan was declared, the local peoples have had little sense of a national identity. The region's ethnic diversity, open borders and distance from Beijing meant it was only loosely part of the Qing empire. Lacking obvious boundaries to demarcate Xinjiang from the rest of Central Asia, the Qing tended to see it as a buffer zone and consequently of immense strategic importance.[2]

The neighbourhood is not a happy one for Beijing's rulers. China suffered massive losses in the Korean War, which began in 1950 when Mao lent support to his ally, Kim Jong-il, the leader of the Korean Workers' Party, only to end three years later in an armistice— neither victory nor peace—and with the US gaining a permanent presence through major military bases in South Korea, effectively on China's borders. China's longest border is with Russia, with which it nearly fought a war in 1969. Relations were not normalised until 1989, but tension remained high until the Soviet Union collapsed in 1991; a Treaty of Friendship was eventually signed in 2001.[3] It has a longstanding border dispute with India, with whom it fought a war in 1962. More recently, in 2017, a military skirmish occurred between the two nations on the Doklam Plateau near Bhutan, a country with which China still does not have diplomatic relations, despite sharing a common border. A fracas in June 2020 in Ladakh saw the first fatalities along the border in nearly fifty years. China invaded Vietnam in 1979 but was forced to withdraw its regular forces soon after without having achieved its strategic objectives. Away from its land borders, China and Japan have unresolved historical issues, including the contested Diaoyu/Senkaku Islands. China faces a formidable, highly technologically capable military in Japan—in 2020, Japan was estimated to be able to project some 50 per cent of China's power, despite China's vastly greater number of personnel.[4]

Yet internal security challenges command the largest share of resources. Xinjiang has an area four times that of California. Tibet has an exiled government and advocates a high degree of regional autonomy, if not independence, for large areas of China, including the province of Qinghai, and large parts of Sichuan and Yunnan provinces and Inner Mongolia. Taiwan is another major outstanding historical issue. China requires a massive commitment to arms to back its threat to reunify by force were Taiwan unilaterally to declare independence. This also brings China directly into conflict with the US. Furthermore, with the half-year-long demonstrations in Hong Kong in 2019, a new challenge to the territorial integrity of China emerged, with a younger generation showing little affinity for the mainland, preferring to rule themselves rather than be ruled by Beijing.

Defending the Empire from Threats Within and Without

China's defence expenditure (see figures 2 and 3) has grown rapidly over the past twenty years, to the point that other countries in the region feel threatened. However, this has been outpaced by the growth in expenditure on domestic security.

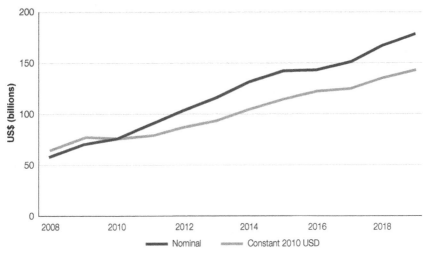

Figure 2. Official Chinese Defence Budget
Source: China Power Project, 'What Does China Really Spend on Its Military?', Center for Strategic and International Studies, 2020, https://chinapower.csis.org/military-spending/ (viewed June 2020)

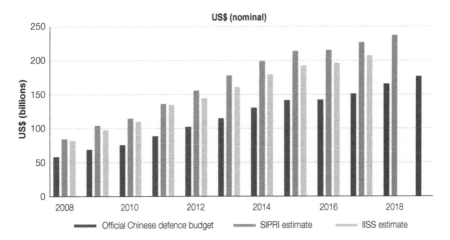

Figure 3. Estimates of Chinese Defence Spending
SIPRI = Stockholm International Peace Research Institute
IISS = International Institute for Strategic Studies
Source: China Power Project, 'What Does China Really Spend on Its Military?', Center for Strategic and International Studies, 2020, https://chinapower.csis.org/military-spending/ (viewed June 2020)

In 2019, China's official defence spending was US$177.5 billion, an increase of 7.5 per cent in nominal terms compared with 2018 and GDP growth of 6.6 per cent.[5] China's official numbers may understate the actual expenditure. Adjusted figures from the Stockholm International Peace Research Institute suggest it was over US$200 billion in 2018, compared with the officially reported figure of US$167 billion. China spends about 2 per cent of its GDP on defence, compared with 3 per cent for the US and 1 per cent for Japan.

In terms of regional expenditure, East Asia as a whole spends about the same as Western and Eastern Europe combined, or about US$340 billion. China accounted for 71 per cent of East Asia's total expenditure in 2018, whereas in 1990 it accounted for just 23 per cent.[6]

Official figures on internal security expenditure from the Ministry of Finance and the National Bureau of Statistics are available only up to 2017. In that year, spending on internal security was US$183.5 billion, 19 per cent higher than that year's official defence budget of US$151.5 billion. This internal figure excludes security-related urban management and surveillance technology initiatives.[7]

Over the decade up to 2017, when the latest data are available, domestic defence expenditure relative to external expenditure rose from 98 per cent of external expenditure to 119 per cent. It rose 7 percentage points during president Hu Jintao's second term in office, from 2007 to 2012, while it rose 12 percentage points during President Xi's first term. Measurement uncertainties apart, this does suggest greater attention to domestic security and hence greater concern over internal stability in the Xi era.

Per capita domestic security spending indicates that the Tibetan and Xinjiang autonomous regions spend several times the national average (as shown in Figure 4, where the dotted line indicates estimates).

The costs of keeping the empire together are a major drain on China's security resources. Xinjiang security expenditure, for example, has shot up in recent years. The sudden surge from 2016

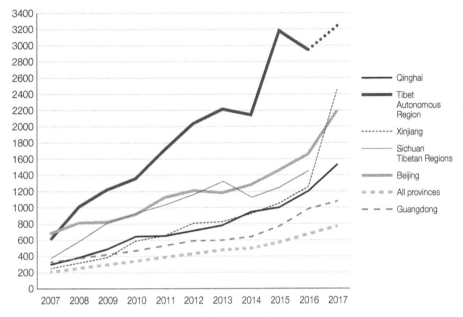

Figure 4. Domestic Security Spending in RMB Per Capita
Source: Adrian Zenz, 'China's Domestic Security Spending: An Analysis of Available Data',
China Brief, vol. 18, no. 4, 2018

probably reflects the policy to intern some million or more ethnic Uighurs and Kazakhs in what would seem to most observers to be, in the long run, a self-defeating attempt to turn them into 'loyal' patriots of China as defined by the CPC's narrative.[8]

Geography Matters

Mackinder, in his highly influential 1904 study *The Geographical Pivot of History*, argued that whichever state controlled Central Asia, which he called the 'heartland', would be the centre of world power: 'who rules the heartland, commands the world'.[9] Things did not quite turn out that way for the Soviet Union, which controlled not only the heartland but also Eastern Europe—which in Mackinder's hierarchy was the key to controlling the heartland.[10] The global geopolitical centre of the world remained with Europe until the Soviet Union collapsed, leaving the US as the unipolar power. Nevertheless, Mackinder and Central Asia still resonate among strategic analysts.[11]

A 1990 National Security Strategy for the George HW Bush administration stated that 'for most of the century, the United States has deemed it a vital interest to prevent any power or group of powers from dominating the Eurasian landmass'. Two years later, a 'leaked' Pentagon document returned to the same theme:

> Our first objective is to prevent the reemergence of a rival that poses a threat on the territory of the former Soviet Union ... and requires that we endeavor to prevent any hostile power from dominating a region whose resources would, under consolidated control, be sufficient to generate global power ... Our strategy must now refocus on precluding the emergence of any potential future global competitor.[12]

Geography matters still for great land-based powers like Russia and China. Central Asia has been and remains a key area of strategic concern and competition. As Kissinger argued in his book *On Order*, Russia historically sought its security by territorial expansion to ensure buffer areas between it and potential aggressors.[13] To Russia's east, Moscow has long sought to keep the Chinese hordes at bay by holding scarcely populated territories in Mongolia and Manchuria.

Kaplan notes that Chinese diplomats over the past two decades have been busy settling outstanding border disputes with Central Asian republics.[14] This has been one of the major but little noticed strategic developments in Asia. Despite these efforts, China still has unresolved territorial issues with India, Myanmar, Nepal, North Korea, Pakistan and Russia, while in the South China Sea it faces an increasingly acrimonious dispute with Vietnam.

The Indian Wedge
Viewing Pakistan, Bangladesh and much of South-East Asia as generally well disposed towards China and accommodating of its

interests, India sits like a 'blunt geographical wedge' in the sphere of influence to China's south.[15] In June 2017, China and India confronted each other at Doklam on the Sino-Bhutanese border. As has been the case since the 1962 Sino-Indian War, yet another border skirmish was resolved without further escalation. Both India and China have shown consistent strategic restraint for the best part of sixty years. Nevertheless, for this to have worked has required substantial military assets to be kept on the disputed borders. This broke down in June 2020 when violent skirmishes occurred in Ladakh's Galwan Valley on the Line of Actual Control, recognised by both China and India. These events mark the most dangerous escalation since the 1962 Sino-Indian War.[16]

Fraternal Enemies

China's last major war on its borders came when it invaded Vietnam on 17 February 1979. In just one month, the fierce fighting claimed tens of thousands of military and civilian lives on both sides before China's military withdrew.[17] While China had consistently and strongly backed Hanoi during the long years of the war with America and its allies, including Australia, in the ensuing peace Vietnam was drawn more closely into the Soviet Union's orbit and joined the Soviet-dominated Council for Mutual Economic Cooperation (COMECON). China then pilloried Vietnam as the 'Cuba of the East'.[18]

Subsequently, a series of border clashes between Vietnam and China-friendly Kampuchea (now Cambodia) were followed in 1978 by Vietnam's military incursion into Kampuchea to remove the murderous Pol Pot regime. Meanwhile, the Soviet Union continued a massive build-up of forces on China's northern border. As threatening to China's security as this may have been, it was also early in Deng Xiaoping's ascendancy after overthrowing the Gang of Four. War with Vietnam may then have fulfilled an important domestic political imperative as well.[19]

At least half-a-dozen clashes occurred throughout the 1980s, before bilateral relations were normalised in 1991. Hundreds of thousands of troops were tied up on the border during this period, representing major resource commitments for both sides in what were then, by any measure, poor countries.[20]

The China–Vietnam war is often assessed by foreign analysts as a Chinese failure as it did not lead Vietnam to divert troops from Kampuchea and so relieve pressure on Pol Pot. But it served another purpose for the Beijing leadership, which was to demonstrate that the Soviet Union, which did not intervene as expected by Vietnam, could not be relied on despite their military pact.[21] China's security was threatened only indirectly by Indochina. It was the threat coming from the Eurasian landmass which was of most concern, that of the Soviet Union.

Despite Hanoi's efforts to prevent historical animosities from unsettling contemporary relations, China's behaviour in the South China Sea has inflamed public resentment in Vietnam, bringing a chill to Beijing–Hanoi relations. Vietnam, which defeated the US in a long war that ended in 1975, has embraced its former foe and allowed itself to be embraced in return, as both countries seek to find common cause in balancing China.

From Beijing's perspective, greater engagement with Vietnam diplomatically, economically and militarily by the US and its allies, such as Japan and Australia, is a direct provocation in an area where historically China has expected and received strategic acquiescence. The fact of Vietnam drawing much closer to the US to balance China, as with its earlier alliance with the Soviet Union, is a threat to Beijing that it feels it needs to address.

One's Enemies' Enemies

Beijing has no allies and few friends on its borders, or in its region for that matter. Apart from North Korea, Pakistan is the only one. In recent years, Russia has become another, as these two authoritarian states have found common purpose in resisting and challenging the US, and the West more generally. For both Beijing and Moscow, this is an historically uncomfortable but necessary accommodation.[22] While it serves their strategic purposes for the present, it is transactional. Either could seek to balance the other and align itself more closely with another state—Europe in the case of Russia, and the US in the case of China, as has happened before. For now, though, balance in the new order finds these neighbours, once so suspicious of each other, displaying high levels of mutual trust and cooperation.

Russia's closer relations with China offer it one way of managing its strategic impasse with the West. As Mark Smith argues, in his study of the West's Russian 'anxiety', most Russians 'probably see themselves as Europeans—bruised and unwelcome, second-class, but Europeans nonetheless'.[23] One consequence for international relations, he suggests, is that Chinese respect for Russian nationalism and Eurasianism may lead to longer-term, closer, more stable relations between Russia and China.[24]

Despite what mutual suspicion lurks beneath the surface, for Russia in particular, the China relationship has become more comfortable than that with the West. NATO 'has defined itself against Russia'.[25] In the Xi–Putin era, cooperation has taken on far-reaching military dimensions, including a sophisticated arms trade. Closer relations between China and Russia have occurred as each country's relations with the US and the West have become much more tense.

Russia and China also have a common weakness. They have both sought to challenge the past order from positions of relative inferiority in recent times. Now they have pivoted towards each other in ways that Mackinder would have understood a century earlier[26]—'Eurasia is all about geopolitics. The thing about geopolitics is that they can change, and sometimes quickly …'[27]

China sees an increasingly close and cooperative military relationship with Russia as a response to what it regards as the US' determination to contain China's rise and undermine its security.[28] Since 2005, various forms of joint military exercises have occurred under the aegis of the SCO. Since 2017, China and Russia have held joint naval exercises in the Mediterranean and the Baltic, and in July 2019 their first joint patrol using long-range bomber aircraft was held over the Pacific.[29] Military cooperation in areas such as strategic missile defence, hypersonic technology and the construction of nuclear submarines are mutually beneficial, while posing minimum risk to the national security of either country.

However, Russia and China's geographical proximity also means that they each require large armies with different capabilities to maintain security should their relations deteriorate at some future time.[30] Improved relations with Russia, then, do little to lighten the burden on China's military to guard its longest border, one of over 4000 kilometres.

History's Ties that Bind

In the twenty-first century, China is alone in the world as an empire with unresolved territorial issues inside its borders. Russia, the great Eurasian expansionary power, has few remaining unsettled issues following the collapse of the Soviet Union. Seen this way, China is something of an anachronistic modern state, pinned down by the weight of the Qing Dynasty's imperial ambitions. Ethnically Mongolian, those Manchurian rulers of Ming-era China expanded the empire's borders through relentless conquest.[31] Xinjiang and Tibet are the imperial legacies that today drain vast security and political resources from Beijing, while costing China international acceptance and prestige, and undermining costly efforts to project soft power.

Just as Xinjiang and Tibet trace different historical paths to the present and present different challenges to Beijing's security order, so it is with Taiwan and Hong Kong. Their historical experiences are also completely different, but they are, unlike Xinjiang and Tibet, ethnic Chinese territories with—to a greater extent in Taiwan's case and since the imposition of the National Security Law in July 2020 to a much lesser extent in Hong Kong's—political systems outside of Beijing's authority.

Peripheral Security

It was not until after 1949, with the communists securely in power, that Xinjiang was brought under the firm control of Beijing, which could now set about exploiting the region's rich agricultural resources. Although short, the summers are intense and help produce a cornucopia of fruit, nuts and vegetables. Initially, however, the main cash crop was cotton.

For the Qing emperors from the eighteenth century, when Xinjiang was formally integrated with China, the area was to be a firm border protecting against Russia. But it has also been an area of sustained instability and turbulence.[32] The CPC imposed a novel development model on China's remote western frontier, establishing large commercial projects producing cash crops run by the military. The semi-secretive *bing tuan* system was effectively a state within a state—a commercial cooperative, but with its own security forces, employment arrangements, and welfare and medical systems, and with a responsibility to secure China's borders and internal stability wherever it operated. These projects have continued to the present day without reform and are the major producers of cash crops such as cotton, grapes and tomatoes.

Xinjiang has always been viewed suspiciously by Beijing. Its Muslim population is seen as potentially disloyal, a latent incubator of anti-state terrorism and harbouring ambitions for an independent East Turkestan. Long ago it was courted by the Russian tsars and Soviet communists as an integral part of a Russia–dominated Central Asia. So Beijing remains fearful of Islamic-led 'separatism', to use the Party's propagandists' term. Terrorist incidents and the international activities of the US-based East Turkestan independence movement, led by the exiled formerly wealthy businesswoman Rebiya Kadeer, stoke Beijing's deep anxieties about its security in this peripheral region.

In late 2017, the land crossing from Sary-Tash in Kyrgyzstan to Kashgar in Xinjiang, via the Tian Shan mountain range, required passing through three checkpoints. The first was on the border between Kyrgyzstan and China, while the next two were deeper inside Xinjiang. Once greeted with a cheery 'Welcome to China' at the border itself, I undertook a 5-kilometre walk through a no-man's-land edged by 4-metre-high, razor-wire-topped fences. At the next border post at the end of this corridor, my belongings needed to be unpacked and all items X-rayed, with considerable delay. This time there was no cheery welcome. When I was finally waved on, prearranged transport from Kashgar took me a further 10 kilometres to the perimeter for entry into Kashgar, where the whole procedure of unpacking and X-raying was repeated, with the same thoroughness as at the previous post. Finally reaching Kashgar, I found it was effectively under military lockdown, even though there had been no recent terrorist events.

I had visited the city on and off since February 1989, when I'd arrived there after an excruciatingly uncomfortable four-day trip by local buses that skirted the northern fringes of the Taklamakan Desert. It was indeed frozen in time, with its souk-like mudbrick centre of narrow winding lanes filled with donkey carts and children, and bordered by leaning crumbling-brick houses. Chinese communist modernity had already landed like an alien from outer space in the form of a new city across the Kashgar River, with multistorey apartment blocks, department stores, and an oversized 'people's square' with a massive statue of Chairman Mao, one arm raised, pointing grateful citizens towards the glorious communist future.

Then, the security and military presence was directed towards the grave external threat posed by the Soviet Union, not Chinese citizens. On that first trip, the only time the police presence had been obvious to me was when, on entry to the city, our bus driver had to pay a bribe. After another interminable day on the four-day road trip from Urumqi, we had arrived at the outskirts of Kashgar in the fading light to find we'd missed the curfew—vehicles arriving after 6 p.m. could not enter the city until sunrise the following morning. It became quite cold when the sun finally disappeared and the passengers were all exhausted from the days of travel, and hungry too. But our driver had clearly handled this situation before. He sauntered towards the police officers huddled smoking around a fire and after about twenty minutes, which seemed like ages, he returned to the bus. Without a word he passed around his hat, which quickly filled with crumpled dirty notes, though he would not take money from me. He then left the bus again and, without stopping or acknowledging the police, continued into the shadows behind an office building, followed by what appeared to be the senior officer. Soon the driver returned, the bus engine roared to life, and we were on our way into town.

Over three decades since, I had watched the transformation of Kashgar as the old mudbrick town was demolished and rebuilt in brick with mud veneer for tourists, along with massive shopping malls and tall hotels, the city's outskirts hemmed in by manufacturing plants bearing the names of east-coast, high-income provinces. For many years, as part of Beijing's efforts to develop Kashgar and other parts of Xinjiang, wealthy provinces have been required to relocate their manufacturing there. As a deputy mayor explained to me in 2010, long before the BRI policy, the plan was to re-create a Shenzhen in Central Asia. An entirely obvious comment about distance from markets, transportation costs and the relative poverty of the neighbours did not dampen the official's enthusiasm for the plan.

By late 2017, however, Kashgar had become a city under siege from its own government. Roadblocks manned by armed para-military troops, *wu jing*, interrupted traffic flow along the major roads, entry to and exit from all neighbourhoods was controlled, and the streets were patrolled 24/7 by armoured metal boxes on wheels with half-a-dozen police inside, and all manner of electrical equipment on the roof and dangling over the sides. Even throughout the night, these would patrol with sirens on and lights flashing at a distance of about 100 metres from each other. It was threatening and created a real sense of anxiety. I asked a local how he could put up with it. He replied that, like all things, one got used to it.

It has since been revealed that Beijing had in 2015 already authorised the mass detention of Uighurs and Kazakhs in re-education centres. More recently, it seems that large numbers of those detained are being channelled into the formal prison system, and that some of the camps may be closing, possibly in part due to international criticism.[33]

Tibet is similar to Xinjiang, but exceptional in that the Dalai Lama is the leader of a government-in-exile that fled China in 1959 after demonstrations against the occupying PLA, who had been stationed there since 1950. While the Dalai Lama still seeks some sort of rapprochement with Beijing, and occasionally there have been promising signs, under Xi Jinping the possibility of this seems to have retreated.

Tibetans also have a much stronger national identity than the Uighurs in Xinjiang, having claimed independent statehood at different times. For long periods, Tibet was ruled under Chinese suzerainty but effectively was a highly autonomous state, self-governing in all but name. Tibetans will point to historical periods when Tibet was in fact fully independent, a claim that, of course, Beijing rejects. The arguments run in both directions, as such things usually do. What is indisputable is that a symbiotic relationship long existed between Lhasa and the court in Beijing. Qing rulers in particular sought Lhasa's spiritual guidance and hence authority. Lamaseries were often joint projects between the emperor and the Dalai Lama, such as those in Yunnan Province.

Seldom visited by Western tourists, although roads greatly improved in recent years should change that, are the Eastern Qing tombs outside Beijing, where all but two of the Qing emperors are buried. Located with perfect *feng shui*, the long, declining entrances to the tombs and the high vaulted ceilings of each crypt are lined with hundreds of carved buddhas. Each tomb was blessed and consecrated by Tibetan lamas. It is impossible, when visiting the pavilions and museums of any of the Qing courts, the Forbidden City, or emperor Kangxi's summer court in Chengde, where foreign ambassadors were received, not to be impressed by the presence of Tibetan Buddhism and how deeply it was integrated with imperial court life.

The comparatively liberal but brief period under Party general secretary Hu Yaobang, from the early 1980s until the violence in Tiananmen Square in 1989, saw Tibet officially opened to foreign visitors. Still in April 1987, Lhasa felt like a city under military occupation. Outside the old quarter in which sits the Jokhang Temple, one of the most significant holy places in the Tibetan religious world, a modern communist town was starting to spread out along the valley. The stark but cheaply built functional buildings contrasted with the traditional Tibetan buildings. The latter had been designed with the local harsh elements in mind and were made of thick brick walls, their small doorways and windows decorated with heavy cantilevered lintels and brightly coloured, geometric cotton blinds and curtains.

A year earlier, a Holiday Inn had opened in Lhasa, the first Western hotel in Tibet and something of a symbol of the profound change occurring throughout China. It was a statement of China's new openness that such a remote, inaccessible and hitherto sensitive place was starting to welcome foreign tourists. In a sign of those progressive times, each hotel room was fitted with oxygen devices to help visitors deal with the, at times, debilitating effects of high altitude.

Since then, over the course of a series of bloody clashes in the laneways of Lhasa and other centres across Tibet, repression by China's security forces has only increased. Tibet has become another peripheral border security nightmare for Beijing, made worse by nearby India's hosting of the government-in-exile, in Dharamshala. In 2008, when all international eyes turned to Beijing for the Summer Olympics, another major riot occurred. When I returned to Lhasa in 2010, it was still locked down under tight military occupation. Heavily armed paramilitary troops patrolled the streets on foot, and on top of many buildings, snipers sat ever watchful in their nests. Access to the old city was through checkpoints, even on the smallest laneways. The holy Jokhang Temple area itself had been largely cleared of pilgrims. Only a few were prostrating outside its entrance, and it was mainly tour groups of wealthy Han who were permitted inside—it was now effectively a museum piece. The resources and effort required to sustain this level of control were clearly enormous.

The Golmud–Lhasa railway, with its heated pylons sunk into the permafrost, was a remarkable engineering achievement, as the world has come to expect from China. It is breathtaking in its technical audaciousness. Completed in 2006, it has since been extended to Shigatse, the home lamasery of the Panchen Lama, and will most likely one day be extended under the Himalayas themselves, all the way to Kathmandu. Returning to Tibet in 2013 by the train from Golmud, it was clear to me that control had been reduced, but tension remained, particularly the sense of being held under a tight security regime. The museumification of the whole place was now entrenched. Enigmatic, mysterious, romantic Lhasa had been changed thoroughly, and forever.

Still, and herein is the enduring problem for Beijing in regards to both Tibet and Xinjiang, despite the most invasive security penetration of these places, at huge financial cost and also in terms of China's international standing and soft power, it can never feel secure with these territories. Correctly, it knows that it cannot relax control, lest anti-Han, separatist elements return and great instability ensues. The irony is that Beijing's own unrelenting policies of repression and control, in both Xinjiang and Tibet, have created precisely the problems they were meant to avoid. Beijing knows the apparent stability in these areas is not security. It is ephemeral.

Treasure Island

'Treasure Island' was an informal code word used for Taiwan inside the Australian Government in the 1980s. In those days, Taiwan, despite its lack of official status, was a far more important economy and market in the region for Australia than was the mainland, being a major buyer of coal, iron ore, wheat and wool. Interest in mainland China then was still largely a boutique preoccupation. And so a policy debate raged in Canberra over how Australia could deepen its formal relations with Taiwan in the face of Beijing's staunch opposition to such moves. Countries started to open quasi-diplomatic posts with this in mind, and so, correctly, Australia gradually came to the view that we should too.

For Beijing, Taiwan is one of a number of 'core' interests, but it is much more than that emotionally and symbolically. Taiwan represents unfinished business from 1949, when the Communist Party took control of China. The Kuomintang (KMT) led by Chiang Kai-shek fled to Taipei, after emptying the Forbidden City of its treasures and the Bank of China in Shanghai of its gold. In Taiwan, it set up a US-backed government and imposed martial law on the island's indigenous inhabitants. In the early decades of the People's Republic, it was a base from which US propaganda and threats could be directed against the communist mainland. For its part, Beijing to this day has threatened and harassed Taiwan with displays of military aggression and economic bullying.

Nonetheless, over the past two decades, the changes in relations that have occurred would surprise many. Direct flights, direct postal services, a burgeoning direct tourist trade, investment in both directions, a bilateral FTA, a formal bilateral meeting held in 2014 in Singapore between each country's respective leaders—all of this at one time seemed improbable. Yet by the end of the first decade of the twenty-first century, these things had become the norm (except of course the leaders' meeting, with the election of the pro-independence Democratic People's Party, or DPP), weathering major ructions. The relationship between Beijing and Taipei has alternated between accommodation and tension, but so far it has not swung to military conflict.

Some may argue that cyberwarfare is Beijing's new preferred instrument of intimidation. But if one looks at the results of the January 2020 presidential election in Taiwan, where Beijing was accused of engaging in cyber-aggression to influence the outcome, then if true, it would have to be one of the most unsuccessful examples of an attempt to sway a democratic election. The DPP won an historic majority. It was a complete rejection of the KMT and its accommodating policies towards Beijing. The young voters in Taiwan emphatically declared that they saw no future with China.[34]

The massive demonstrations in Hong Kong throughout 2019 would have reinforced these attitudes. Indeed, before those demonstrations, Tsai Ing-wen's DPP was behind in the polls and a KMT victory was a possibility. The Hong Kong protests seem to have galvanised opinion around issues of identity, taking the focus away from the lacklustre economy.

Beijing really has few options when it comes to Taiwan. Western strategic analysts suggest the game plan would involve either a military invasion of some sort, or mass interference through cyber-attack and economic disruption, or an attempt to force the Taiwanese Government to capitulate and agree to begin discussions leading towards eventual reunification.[35] With the US' continuing support for Taiwan through congressional legislation, which has recently been strengthened, it is difficult to imagine the circumstances in which China could prevail. It would not wish to risk war with the US, which could escalate, on the first option, and the second option would invite the imposition of similar, economy-crippling, US-led sanctions on China itself; it could readily be denied access to crude oil supplies, for example. However, the third option of applying pressure to enter into reunification talks could be executed without necessarily attracting direct US intervention. China certainly has the economic means and leverage and the cyber-interference capacity to do so. With its typical 'united front' tactics, it also has a cadre of influential business, media and political supporters within Taiwan. Moreover, it seems as if it increasingly has the will to take this path.

In his speech at the closing session of the National People's Congress (NPC) in February 2018, President Xi significantly upped the ante over Taiwan by declaring that reunification was an essential part of what since 2013 he has been promoting as the Chinese Dream.[36] He said this question could no longer be left to future generations to resolve. In other words, it is to be addressed on his watch as president. The Chinese Dream, of a rejuvenated and united China taking its place as a leading nation in the world, is to be Xi's historical legacy, to be fulfilled by 2049, the centennial of the founding of the PRC. Xi has now set a clear timeline for the reunification of Taiwan.[37] In doing so, he has stripped much of the ambiguity out of how China and Taiwan have been able peacefully to manage their relations for the past fifty years.

In however many years Xi has left in power, it would probably be sufficient for him to begin the process of negotiating for reunification. But since the recent Taiwanese elections, and considering the experience of Hong Kong's long demonstrations, Beijing must now seriously consider that massive civil disobedience in Taiwan would likely bring down any government that even contemplated such negotiations.[38] In 2014, demonstrations and riots occurred, including an attempted invasion of the Taiwanese Parliament, when the then ruling KMT hastily concluded an FTA agreement with China.

History continues to weigh heavily on Beijing, and as more time passes, its strategic options are narrowing despite its economic development and massive, recently acquired military capacity.

Hong Kong—a Problem of Beijing's Own Making

In July 1997, Hong Kong officially returned to China to be governed under the Sino-British Basic Law and Joint Declaration for the next fifty years. It was a moment for celebration. Apart from the truculence of the last British governor of Hong Kong, Christopher Patten, everything ran smoothly and according to plan. At the time, young people were full of joy at the prospect of the return to the mainland, of regaining their national identity and ridding themselves of the British colonial rule that had been neither democratic nor egalitarian. At midnight on 1 July, despite a torrential downpour, the night sky was lit up by a spectacular fireworks display across the harbour.

Twenty years later, for six months, the streets of Hong Kong were full of demonstrations and much of the island's downtown and Kowloon were shut down. The demonstrations were prompted by the hated Extradition Bill that Hong Kong's hapless Chief Executive, Carrie Lam, had signed into law. This bill would have allowed Hong Kong residents who faced charges on the mainland to be extradited there to stand trial.

Concern already had been rising over Beijing's increasing interference in the territory. The disappearance from Hong Kong's streets (and in one case, from Bangkok's) of publishers who regularly printed gossip and scandals about China's senior leaders and their families alarmed citizens regarding their security and rights. This was heightened by the publishers' subsequent appearance in mainland courts on trial for patently spurious reasons.

Demonstrations against the extradition law began in June 2019, with some million or so people protesting in central Hong Kong. They began peacefully, but over subsequent months the level of violence escalated on both sides, especially between more extreme groups of protestors and the police. The demonstrators were predominately young, including a remarkable number of high school children who felt they had little future in Hong Kong, worried as they were about their freedoms under Chinese rule. Essentially, the demonstrators wanted a Hong Kong Government that would represent Hong Kong's interests to Beijing, not Beijing's to Hong Kong.

On the mainland, the demonstrators found very little support. Mainlanders looked at Hong Kongers as privileged and spoilt. They were horrified by the riotous instability in the territory, what with anarchists attacking banks and ATMs, vandalism in underground railway stations and shopping malls, and violence directed at the police. Were Beijing to have cracked down using its military, the protesters would have received little or no sympathy from the mainland—Beijing had successfully set up a narrative through its domestic propaganda to prepare the way for that. Instead, Beijing managed this crisis more adroitly.

It was widely anticipated that Beijing's patience would soon run out, especially as the important seventieth anniversary celebrations of the founding of the PRC, to take place at the start of October, were going to be a major propaganda exercise for Xi Jinping. It seemed unlikely that he would allow Hong Kong to rain on his parade. But he did. Apart from some gauche displays for the evening television news and social media of the troops at the PLA's Hong Kong garrison and in Shenzhen, the military were kept in their barracks. It was left to the Hong Kong police eventually to restore order. Beijing's restraint was probably attributable to how limited its military options were to conduct operations in the narrow, twisting, hilly streets and lanes of Hong Kong, an urban topography that could not be further removed from the wide flat boulevards of the Chinese capital. Beijing also would have been mindful of the massive international opprobrium it would have brought down on itself had it intervened violently.

After the handover, Hong Kong was largely allowed to run its own affairs under a mainly pro-Beijing Legislative Assembly led by a Beijing-appointed CEO. The economy had been growing strongly with China's resumption of reform and open-door policies in 1992, finally ending the post–Tiananmen Square policy hiatus.

The handover was viewed positively within and outside Hong Kong. Confidence was buoyant and foreign capital flowed in, as the city was seen as the most convenient gateway to the rapidly growing mainland market. Not even the Asian financial crisis that occurred not long after the handover could disrupt Hong Kong's rising prosperity.

Hong Kong became the destination of choice when China's already massive state-owned enterprises (SOEs) began their decade-long period of raising vast amounts of capital by listing on the Hong Kong Stock Exchange. The wealthy scions of China's ruling elite and well-to-do businesspeople also gravitated there to enjoy the benefits of an inherited British legal system—they were just out of the reach of the Beijing authorities, but near enough to the mainland to stay in touch and work at their relationships, keeping their valuable *guanxi* (strong personal relationships) current.

But Hong Kong itself increasingly has been run by a cabal of five wealthy families, which control much of the local property market, quite apart from major businesses such as ports. Despite strong economic growth, income inequality has continued to rise and housing has become inaccessible to many local residents. This has fuelled popular dissatisfaction which was manifest during the recent demonstrations.

Street protests have become an important means by which Hong Kong residents compensate for the democracy deficit in their political system. In 2003, demonstrations saw the then chief executive replaced. In 2013, as part of the global Occupy Movement, students and young people began occupying the CBD. This grew into the Umbrella Movement, so-called because umbrellas became a symbol of resistance. The protests finally dissipated after several weeks, and many arrests followed, but young Hong Kong people were becoming schooled in the art of street protests and older residents were supporting them. The 2019 protests were markedly different, not only in their scale, but also in that they directly challenged Hong Kong's return to mainland control and extended to calls by some for independence.

At the time of the handover, people in Hong Kong and the West were optimistic that China would continue to reform and liberalise.

Realists had little or no expectation that the CPC would reinvent itself and adopt a competitive political process and the rule of law, but there was a sense that China might become more like Hong Kong in terms of protecting the rights of its citizens against the state, rather than the other way round. This has not come to pass. Xi Jinping's increasingly authoritarian rule in China has been gradually extended into Hong Kong. This growing interference by Beijing, with its seeming disregard for the Basic Law, its refusal to allow more democratic electoral processes, its efforts to exert direct influence in everything from social commentary (disappearing publishers off the streets for embarrassing China's leaders) to the appointments of university professors, have created an unbridgeably wide chasm of mistrust between large numbers of Hong Kong people and Beijing.

As in Taiwan, over the past twenty years, Beijing has lost the younger generations in Hong Kong. While Taiwan's older generations looked towards the mainland, and those in Hong Kong who were refugees from communism looked askance, the younger generations in both places began looking to independence, to national self-identity, and to the West—in particular, the US.

By its own actions, as much as anything else, Beijing has added to security challenges within its borders. Hong Kong will never be allowed to be the same again after the demonstrations of 2019 and early 2020. Beijing will set about further reinterpreting the Basic Law to permit it to interfere more and more in Hong Kong's internal affairs.[39] It will also seek to change the liberal character of Hong Kong through such things as further interference in academic appointments and the media, and by flooding the universities with 'patriotic' students from the mainland. It has now made its intentions crystal clear with the introduction of the National Security Law in July 2020. 2047, when the Basic Law was scheduled to end has been collapsed into 2020, twenty-seven years sooner.

Beijing will endeavour to subsume Hong Kong into the Greater Bay area of Guangzhou and Shenzhen along the Pearl River. Hong Kong will gradually become less distinguishable from its mainland counterpart cities. Population movements are already substantial and continuing to grow, with Chinese families in Shenzhen daily sending their children to school in Hong Kong, for example, and with Hong Kong identity card holders living in Guangzhou, where real estate values are lower, and commuting to work across the border. All of this is a far cry from when Shenzhen was first created as a Special Economic Zone in 1979 as an open-door policy experiment and had to be fenced off from the rest of China, along with an almost impenetrable border with Hong Kong.

Having lost significant numbers of the next generation in Hong Kong, people who are now seasoned protestors, some violently skilled, and who understand their power on the streets, Beijing is on notice that without the significant betterment of people's daily lives, an end to corruption and privilege, especially in the property sector, and respect for the Basic Law, Hong Kong's streets could erupt again.

The risk for Beijing is that Hong Kong has become a flashpoint that could be set off at any time by the former's efforts to meddle in and control the internal affairs of the latter. Beijing can never acknowledge matters as being 'internal' to Hong Kong as it is an integral part of China's sovereign territory. So Beijing now has one more historical problem to add to Xinjiang, Tibet and Taiwan, one more challenge to its territorial integrity that it will see as another opportunity for Western adversaries to divide and weaken it. Beijing will see in every move by its enemies an attempt to exploit the disenchantment of the people of Hong Kong. This being the case, Hong Kong will require much more high-level attention and time than it previously did, and will command more resources for security and running political interference. Vigilance will have to be ramped up.

For Beijing, the trends in Hong Kong, as in Taiwan, are all moving in the wrong direction. The peoples in these places have enjoyed relative material abundance for decades and now take it for granted. They have increasingly internalised the norms of more open societies and the protection of the rule of law. These things they do not want to change. Beijing now knows this, which means that its existential anxieties over territorial integrity will continue to dominate its security priorities. As much as China looks outward, it will need, more than ever before, to look inward.

CHAPTER 3

RICH COUNTRY, POOR COUNTRY
RESOURCE CONSTRAINED

It was never meant to be this way.

In 1978, when Deng Xiaoping launched the economic reform and open-door policies, China was poor, isolated and fearful of the outside world. Deng had just returned to power following a palace coup against the late Chairman Mao's estranged radical wife and her group of high-level supporters—the so-called Gang of Four. Reinstalled in the central leadership, Deng was quickly able to gain support for modest reforms in agriculture and the gradual opening up of the economy to international trade. That December, the Third Plenum of the Eleventh CPC Congress officially adopted those policies.

Reform policies had been tried on and off for some years in rural areas of China, far distant from Beijing. As an old saying in China goes, 'The mountains are high, and the emperor is far away'. Concerned with improving the living standards of the peasantry, local and district Party leaders such as Zhao Ziyang and Wang Li, both of whom eventually rose to be national leaders during the 1980s, had cautiously pioneered experiments to lift the tent flap on central planning and let in the market.[1] As China's economy began to recover from the stagnation of the Cultural Revolution, it became apparent that individual incentives stimulated production, with the result that incomes were rising and consumer choices expanding.[2] Still, after the reforms of 1978, it would take another six long years for the inner-party arguments to play out and for Deng Xiaoping to consolidate his hold on power before even these limited market-based reforms were extended to the industrial sectors of the economy.[3]

The Party's fear of losing control meant strong resistance to market reforms in a Leninist political system with a Stalinist command economy. Indeed, since that time, China's political system has changed little, while the economy is unrecognisable. It is one of the great historical curiosities that this should be so, and the Party remains firmly in control.

The Bird Escapes the Cage

The urban reforms introduced by Deng at the Third Plenum of the Twelfth CPC Congress in October 1984 seemed audacious at the time. The 'Decision on Reform of the Economic Structure' was explained as having been derived from 'basic Marxist principles' together with analysis of China's 'current situation'. The new policies reflected the 'necessity and urgency of speeding up the reforms of the country's entire economic structure, with special attention devoted to the urban economy'.[4]

Initially, the urban reform did little more than introduce elements of, by then, the rural Household Responsibility System to the industrial sector, mainly in the form of relaxed physical quotas and some price flexibility for 'non-essential' parts of the industrial economy. The definition of 'non-essential' in those days was broad. Only gradually were some of the most egregious inefficiencies in the economy being ironed out. The early years of reform inched forward through trial and error.[5] Even two years after the urban reforms began, many areas of the economy had not yet been touched by markets of any type, with all the ongoing resource misallocation and waste that entailed.

In 1986, when I visited a vertically integrated woollen textile factory in Hohhot, the capital of the Inner Mongolia Autonomous Region, it was evident that nothing had changed. The central planner's preferences still ruled. In this enterprise, the raw materials were allocated centrally and comprised mainly coarse wool from hairy sheep raised primarily for meat. The local wool was better suited to carpets than tailoring. It was then mixed with some Australian fine wool, also centrally allocated, which had been imported using scarce foreign exchange. The final product, after the full process of washing, carding and spinning was completed, was worth less than the small portion of Australian fine wool that went in at the beginning. This, then, was a value-reducing enterprise, not a value-adding one. Such examples could be found in their hundreds of thousands across China.

In August 1987, in a surprising announcement, the Chinese Government said it would begin a reform of the labour system. This foreshadowed greater labour mobility, which was sorely needed to raise productivity and hence incomes. Soon after the announcement, when I attended a massive, state-owned steel-making enterprise in the north-eastern city of Shenyang, originally built by the Soviet Union, at first it seemed as if nothing at all had changed. No sackings were permitted. All staff were still allocated to enterprises by the Shenyang Labour Bureau. Wages were fixed by the Shenyang Planning Commission. It was not obvious what had contributed to the impressive rates of productivity growth that management was proudly showing off in a series of graphs. It felt like a propaganda exercise for the foreigner—until it was gleefully explained that, since the reform, management had been able to move labour around to different jobs within the enterprise. Previously, the Shenyang Labour Bureau had allocated workers not just to the company but to specific roles within it. Management were not permitted to move staff from areas of even temporary redundancy to areas of shortage without the approval of the bureau. The slow overnight steam-train ride back to Beijing provided plenty of time to reflect on what even modest reforms could achieve in terms of higher productivity and, in turn, economic growth.

As much as was possible in China's party-state system, something of a public debate occurred between reformers and those resisting reforms. Party elder and erstwhile revolutionary colleague of Deng Xiaoping, Chen Yun, chairman of the Party's Central Advisory

Committee, himself a professionally trained economist, promoted the 'bird cage' theory to keep reforms in check. The market was said to be a bird that was inside a cage representing the state planning system. Reform was about how big the cage should be, not whether the bird should be let out of the cage.[6] In these early years of reform, the policy arguments on the extensiveness of change and how open China should be to the outside world were about power, and the existential threat to the Party's control that markets posed.

The mass demonstrations from April 1989, following the untimely death of the deposed but popular liberal-inclined leader Hu Yaobang, through to the denouement of the military crackdown in Tiananmen Square on 4 and 5 June that year, stoked conservative elders' worst fears that the reforms had gone too far. Even though the protests had dwindled by the start of June, Deng ordered the military to attack the remaining demonstrators in Tiananmen Square, take charge of the capital, and arrest Party general secretary Zhao Ziyang.[7] Suddenly, it was all over.

Three years of repression followed, with arrests, internal Party reviews, re-education in Marxism-Leninism, and the inevitable paralysis of China's vast bureaucracy. The reform hiatus ended when an ageing, frail Deng made a much-publicised trip to the Special Economic Zone of Shenzhen, which had by then become a globally recognised symbol of China's reforms, and to Guangzhou, with its long tradition of international trade. This was an attempt to end the post-Tiananmen debates inside the Party, while he still had the physical stamina and political weight to do so.

From then on, market liberalisation advanced far beyond what had been, or could have been, envisaged in the early years of reform. Ideological influence over policy retreated until it finally disappeared, replaced by pragmatism in pursuit of economic growth. The post-Tiananmen implicit social compact essentially required the Party to deliver on the promise of continually rising material living standards and withdrawing from interfering in the details of people's daily lives, while the people were to accept unquestioningly its monopoly on political power. This has since underpinned social and political stability in China.

The incremental approach to reform based on trial and error persisted well into the 1990s, a decade when incomes rose rapidly based on annual average productivity increases of an astonishing 10 per cent. Personal wealth jumped as a private property market quickly emerged. A massive transfer of state assets, and thus wealth, to private owners occurred at low historic cost.

Until then, China's economy, as with those of the Soviet Union and the centrally planned economies of Eastern Europe, had since 1949 been characterised by shortages of consumer goods. In the mid-1980s, a typical household's ambition was to have the 'three things that spun'—a bicycle, a watch and a sewing machine. The bicycle was a particularly desired good that could only be acquired with ration tickets. Although foreigners had access to the most desirable brands, such as Flying Pidgeon, Phoenix and Forever, they could buy them only at a special state-run department store, and delivery took several months. A popular book among economists in Beijing at that time was *The Economics of Shortage* by the Hungarian economist Janos Kornai. Scarcity was such a pervasive feature of centrally planned economic systems that Kornai had been able to base an entire economic theory on it.[8]

In the second half of the 1990s, however, the supply side of the economy responded massively to incentives and market-based prices. In one of a number of major transformations of the reform period, the Chinese economy shifted from one of shortage to one of previously unimagined abundance. The materialism and pragmatism of the times were captured in the newly emerging Chinese contemporary art movement known as Cynical Realism. This linked the traditions of Propaganda Art, inherited largely from the Soviets, to the Pop Art of New York and Absurdism, to create a Chinese contemporary international style that dealt with themes of consumerism, corruption, breakneck economic development, and the resultant alienation.[9]

By the start of the 2000s, runaway economic growth was changing the face of China's cities. New infrastructure was crisscrossing the entire country, at first six-lane freeways, with bridges suddenly spanning massive steep-sided gorges where previously there had been only donkey tracks—these would be followed a decade later by high-speed trains. Ports of staggering scale popped up using the most advanced heavy equipment from Japanese and South Korean suppliers. Cities with existing airports modernised them, and smaller cities and towns began drawing up plans to have their own. Power stations and major steel mills, such as Baosteel near Shanghai, were built on the coast, where they could be serviced more cheaply by foreign suppliers of raw materials and energy than operations in the interior, and have better access to foreign markets.

Efficiency was the order of the day. Economic growth at almost any cost was embraced, including great damage to the environment and massive social dislocation as migrant workers flocked into the newly industrialising areas from the surrounding countryside.

Throughout its history, China had been a rich country with abundant supplies of natural resources. Its tradition of insularity could be sustained by this resource base. But this was to change in the second half of the 1990s. China went through a series of tipping points, from being mainly self-sufficient to becoming increasingly dependent on world markets for key inputs into its rapidly indus-trialising and surging economy, to becoming the world's biggest importer. This was especially the case with crude oil and iron ore.[10]

China's great transformation was about to stoke the greatest commodity super-cycle ever seen. Its appetite for energy and min-eral resources grew far more rapidly than the domestic economy could possibly supply. From 2003, markets globally for all major commodities snapped tight and prices skyrocketed.[11]

From Resource Abundance to Resource Scarcity

In 1985, in the early days of the reforms, a surge in China's tin exports wrecked global tin markets. It forced the closure of the last tin mine in Australia, in Tasmania, and the collapse of the London-based Tin Council, which had been established in 1947 to support prices of the metal. China has the world's largest tin reserves, almost twice as much as the country with the next biggest, Indonesia.[12] Under its reforms, China had begun relaxing export controls of selected commodities. The state-controlled domestic tin price under the central plan was well below world prices. Suddenly, huge quantities of Chinese tin flowed out of the country, collapsing global prices. China then was seen as a potential major threat to world markets because its huge supply capacity would depress markets for commodities if these were sold overseas. The main constraint at the time on China's exports of resources and energy was its woefully inefficient and inadequate transport system.

Also in the 1980s, and the early 1990s, Australia viewed China as a serious threat to its traditional markets for coal in Japan, South Korea and Taiwan. China has huge reserves of coal, which are located in the middle of the country in provinces such as Inner Mongolia, Shanxi, Hebei and also Shandong and Hebei on the coast. The coalmines in the city of Tangshan in Hebei Province were built by the British in the 1890s and the surface infrastructure is still there today, having been among the few structures to have survived the catastrophic Tangshan earthquake in 1976. A young Herbert Hoover, who would go on to become the thirty-first US president, worked as an engineer at the mines at the turn of the twentieth century; before that, he also worked in the goldfields at Coolgardie, Western Australia.[13]

Early in the 1980s, Japan had begun major development aid projects in China, many of which were intended to support the modernisation of China's coal sector to supply Japan, helping it diversify from its heavy reliance on Australian coal. Japan had long pursued government-led strategies to diversify sources of raw materials and energy on the grounds of national security, and China seemed an ideal opportunity for this. Such investment in China's coal-exporting capacity would also underpin closer bilateral relations with its big neighbour, with which it shared a bitter and fractious past.

Shanxi was opening up for exports and attracting foreign capital and expertise at the same time. Long a strategic industry to be protected, it was a measure of Beijing's reform agenda that the coal sector was being considered for international opening. The US resources magnate Armand Hammer, a legend from his dealings with the early Soviet Union and its first leader, Vladimir Lenin, had met Deng Xiaoping when he visited the US as a guest of president Jimmy Carter. In 1985, Hammer's company, Occidental Petroleum, invested in the An Tai Bao coalmine in central Shanxi, taking a 30 per cent share in the US$650 million joint venture. It was among the earliest major foreign investments in China and would result in the country's first open-cut coalmine, producing 15 million tonnes per annum.[14] Writing about the project in 1985, Hammer said: 'The best strategy [for China] is to tap into and utilise [its] abundant natural resources. China is rich in reserves and lacks only the know-how and capital to develop them'.[15]

This was fairly typical of assessments of China at the time. The country had rich resources and a completely underdeveloped and unsophisticated manufacturing sector. Much of its population was tilling the soil. China's economic future was viewed by some foreign commentators, like Hammer, as being an exporter of raw materials and energy.

Meanwhile, Japan had begun building China's first automatic coal-handling facility at Qinhuangdao Port in Hebei Province, just south of where the Great Wall plunges into the sea at Shanhaiguan. The terminal was to receive coal from Datong, a transport hub in the heart of the vast Shanxi coalmining area. Complementary to the port's construction, Japan was also building China's first-ever electric railway line, which would be dedicated to coal freight. Until then, all train engines in China were either locally made steam or East German diesel locomotives.

Rather than North-East Asian markets, as Australian officials fretted about, the main destinations for coal exports using the new Japanese facilities at Qinhuangdao became China's southern ports, where energy was emerging as a major constraint on growth. This was another spectacularly wrong call based on the customary lack of informed policy in Australia regarding China. China did not swamp Australia's North-East Asian thermal coal markets with product from Shanxi. As it grew, China consumed more and more itself.

In 1993, China became a small net importer of crude oil for the first time; imports accounted for just 12 per cent of total consumption (see Figure 5). By 2000, this had risen to one-third

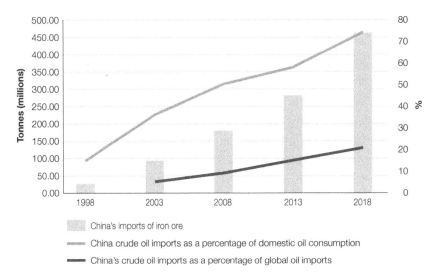

Figure 5. China's Crude Oil Imports
Sources: The General Administration of Customs of the People's Republic of China (GACC), National Bureau of Statistics of China (NBS) and BP (2018)

of total consumption; by 2005, imports accounted for 45 per cent of domestic consumption; and by 2018, this had risen to 65 per cent.[16] Today, China is the world's biggest importer of crude oil. In 2014, China also became the world's biggest importer of petroleum and liquid fuels.

By 2030, China's dependency on oil and petroleum imports is expected to have risen to 80 per cent, far exceeding the US' maximum import dependency of around 60 per cent in the late 1990s.[17] As China's dependency on foreign suppliers has continued its inexorable rise, the US has become largely self-sufficient in energy.[18] In terms of strategic resources vulnerability, over the past fifteen years, the tables have been turned significantly against China in favour of the US. Since 2019, the US becoming largely self-sufficient in crude oil has 'fundamentally shifted the global energy landscape'.[19]

The Iron Ore Wars
Small quantities of iron ore were imported by China during the 1980s. By 1990, the annual volume was 14 million tonnes; by 2018, it was one billion tonnes (see Figure 6). China's own deposits

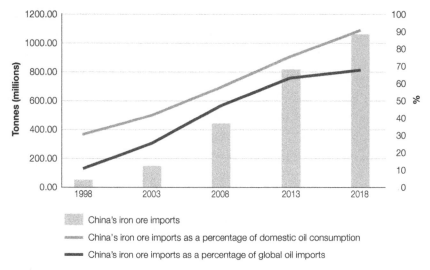

China's iron ore imports

China's iron ore imports as a percentage of domestic oil consumption

China's iron ore imports as a percentage of global oil imports

Figure 6. China's Iron Ore Imports
Sources: Worldsteel and the GACC (2018)

were often remote and mainly magnetite, which requires more expensive beneficiation, or processing, before being fed into blast furnaces, compared with hematite, of which Australia has abundant resources. Much of Australia's iron ore is in the north-west of Western Australia and can be shipped within ten days to China's main ore-receiving ports.

From the mid-1980s, the Australian Government and Hamersley Iron, which was to become a subsidiary of Rio Tinto, began to discuss with the Chinese Government the possibility of China taking part in a project to develop a greenfields site at Mt Channar in the Pilbara region of Western Australia, on the basis of an offtake arrangement. The Channar Iron Ore Joint Venture between Hamersley Iron (CRA Limited) and the Ministry of Metallurgical Industry was China's first major overseas investment since 1949.[20]

Within the senior levels of the Chinese Government, foreign capitalists were viewed with suspicion, and trusted personal relationships between leaders were vital to successful outcomes. A high level of personal trust was established between Australian prime minister Bob Hawke and Party general secretary Hu Yaobang.[21]

The Channar mine, which opened in 1990, was designed to yield 10 million tonnes per annum, with China taking a 40 per cent share.

Australia's ambassador to China at the time of the Mt Channar negotiations, Ross Garnaut, was highly regarded by the Ministry of Metallurgical Industry for having helped it find a way out of the old autarchy and into a future in which high-quality imported raw materials could support a much more productive steel industry, capable of underpinning the plans for accelerated modern economic growth. At a lecture at the Wuhan Iron and Steel University in 1988, Garnaut suggested that by 'the end of the century [China] will be using 100 million tonnes per annum of high-quality imported iron ore, much of it from Australia'. A week or so later, the Xinhua News Agency reported premier Li Peng as saying: 'Some foreigners think that we will one day be importing 100 million tonnes per annum of iron ore, but those foreigners don't understand the Chinese situation'.[22] In 2010, China imported 618 million tonnes of iron ore.[23]

China's sudden and soon-to-be-insatiable appetite for natural resources hit global commodity markets across the board, but none more so than that for iron ore, putting Australia at the forefront of Beijing's sudden anxieties about its newly acquired strategic vulnerabilities. The resources super-cycle was, more than anything else, an iron ore story, one that went to the core of China's leaders' sense of national security.

Within a few years, iron ore prices more than doubled, rising from US$18 per tonne, where they had been languishing for much of the 1990s, to US$37 per tonne in 2005. On the eve of the GFC in 2008, prices shot up to US$83 per tonne, peaking three years later at US$148 per tonne (see Figure 7). In a little over a decade, prices had increased more than seven-fold. Thereafter, supply rapidly caught up with China's demand and prices subsided.

The market snapping tight in the mid-2000s alarmed China's leaders. Evidently not understanding international commodity markets and their inherently cyclical nature, Beijing searched for ways in which to intervene. The Chinese Government's first instinct was to assume that the Australian Government was somehow

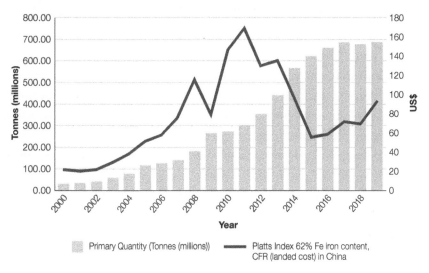

Figure 7. Australia–China Iron Ore Trade and Prices
Source: Global Trade Atlas (GTA), various dates

complicit in price gouging. It had convinced itself that it was facing a price-fixing cartel between the three major producers: Rio Tinto and BHP from Australia, and Brazil's CVRD (Companhia Vale Do Rio Doce, later Vale).[24] Beijing's victim mentality was on full display when China's ambassador to Australia, Fu Ying, began telling prime minister John Howard and foreign minister Alexander Downer that, to demonstrate it was a 'friendly' country, Australia had to get the companies involved to lower their prices. She also became a regular visitor to the major mining companies' boardrooms, warning them that their pricing behaviour threatened the long-term cooperation of China and access to its market.

Ever the suave, erudite and fashionably well-groomed diplomat, with an unusual playfulness for a Chinese official, Fu Ying surprised both government ministers and senior business figures with the aggression of her representations over iron ore prices. She was evidently under great pressure to have something done to reduce them. On one occasion, she confronted Downer so forcefully that he later said despairingly to his senior officials that he'd 'thought that she was such a nice woman'. One official pointed out that she was just doing her job.[25] Still, she could not have picked two less promising targets to lobby in prime minister Howard and Downer. They were both firmly philosophically opposed to government intervention in the economy. China's 'wolf-warrior' diplomacy—the name derived from a popular Chinese movie about the fictional defeat of American mercenaries—existed long before the bruising exchanges and accusations over COVID-19.[26]

The reaction by Beijing at this time was instructive on two levels. First, it showed how utterly unprepared Beijing was for this price shock, which dramatically highlighted China's strategic vulnerability to the disruption of supplies of raw materials and energy. Second, it drew attention to how reliant China was on a single supplier such as Australia. At the time, Australia accounted for about 70 per cent of all of China's iron ore imports.

Until 2011, iron ore prices had been set via annual price negotiations on 'contract' volume and price. This system worked reasonably well for decades, led on the importers' side by Japanese steel mills, until markets spiralled into disequilibrium. In 2007, when negotiations began for the 2008 contract, iron ore contract prices had risen for five consecutive years. At the same time, prices for non-contract product sold on spot markets had risen to heights never seen before. For much of 2007, it ranged between US$180 and US$200 per tonne.[27]

By then, in view of its big share of global iron ore consumption, China had replaced Japan in leading the annual contract price negotiations. On the Chinese side, annual steel price negotiations had initially been led by Baosteel, a major state-owned steel mill based outside Shanghai and a symbol of China's new modern industrial capacity. In time, as negotiations became more fractious and prices kept rising, the China Iron and Steel Association (CISA) took an increasingly leading role. The negotiations gave CISA power and influence within the central organs of government, and the government some residual, though rapidly diminishing, control over the industry. But the industry had become so deregulated within China that mills were free to trade on the spot market. To emphasise China's unhappiness with Rio Tinto, BHP and CVRD,

CISA broke a long tradition and did not invite them to the annual peak steel industry conference in 2008, instead inviting FMG, which had shipped its first ore to China only in May of that year.[28]

Markets in disequilibrium, escalating prices, the involvement of strategic industries and resources, and bureaucratic turf battles all made for a febrile atmosphere. Into the midst of this stepped a tall, boyish-looking South African, Marius Kloppers, newly appointed as BHP's CEO and with a big agenda to reform the iron ore trade. He wanted to get rid of the annual contract system of negotiations and replace it with a market-based index pricing system. He also wanted to stop the 'transport' discount Australian exporters had long been giving China's customers, which effectively removed the freight cost advantage that Australian miners should have enjoyed by virtue of its proximity to China compared with Brazil.[29] Effectively, Australian companies had been handing back to China part of the value of the iron ore trade.

Kloppers had an even bigger agenda, however, which would dominate the Australia–China relationship and the iron ore business for the next eighteen months, setting both governments against each other. On 8 November 2007, BHP announced a hostile takeover bid for Rio Tinto. This threatened China with unprecedented concentration of market power on the supply side. The EU too was concerned about this and referred it to their Competition Commission to review. From early December, media speculation suggested that Baosteel or Chinalco might also bid for Rio in order to block BHP's move. On 1 February 2008, Chinalco announced that it had taken a 9 per cent stake in Rio and was entitled to one seat on the board. Five days later, BHP's formal takeover offer for Rio was announced, and for the rest of that year, both companies struggled with each other, Rio resisting and BHP pressing as hard as it could. The governments in China and Australia were involved too, although they tried to keep out of the public discussions. For both, national security concerns were paramount.[30]

Rio tried to increase its value by selling 10 per cent of its contracted iron ore on the spot market at greatly higher prices than under the contract arrangements. This incensed China's steel industry and its government. Contract arrangements had a force majeure clause that permitted 10 per cent flexibility in the volumes supplied. Rio's exercising of this to take advantage of higher spot prices, to boost revenue and hence the price of its stock, was seen as reprehensible by the Chinese Government.[31]

Then, in November 2008, as the GFC started to unwind stock valuations, and uncertainty over the outlook for the global economy took hold, BHP withdrew its bid. Rio still had a huge debt burden from its US$38 billion acquisition of the Canadian company Alcan in 2007, which industry analysts have described as the 'worst mining deal ever'.[32] Rio was now in serious difficulty, its share price sinking 50 per cent as the GFC washed over global markets. In February 2009, Chinalco made a bid to raise its holding in Rio to 18 per cent and gain an additional board seat. Chinese media were delighted by this, claiming it would increase China's control over the market. CISA claimed it would influence iron ore prices.[33] BHP was alarmed about China becoming an insider in the Pilbara and lobbied the Australian Government to resist the deal. Similarly wary of Beijing, the Australian Government actively engaged with BHP behind the scenes to ensure this would not happen.[34]

By May 2009, China's massive GFC stimulus package had changed market sentiment and recovery was already underway. Rio's share price rebounded strongly. In June, with the Rio board deeply divided, the company's shareholders rejected Chinalco's bid to increase its holding. The announcement could not have been crafted more ineptly if Rio had any regard for its relations with China. Not only was the investment rejected when Chinalco had every reason to believe it would go ahead, having been directly encouraged by Rio's chairman and CEO, but at the same time, Rio and BHP announced an agreement on an infrastructure joint venture in the Pilbara. China was furious that the proposed venture would result in precisely the concentration of market power that the Chinalco investment was intended to mitigate.[35]

Prime minister Kevin Rudd was keen to ensure that China did not hold the Australian Government accountable for what had now become a major debacle, and to avoid lasting harm being done to the bilateral relationship. He instructed me, as Australia's ambassador to China, to stress to the chairman of the NDRC that it had been a purely commercial matter, with no involvement from the Australian Government, and that markets had moved dramatically in support of Rio's share price in response to much more positive sentiment over the previous couple of months. The NDRC vice chairman, Zhang Xiaoqiang, took my call. Having listened carefully to all of the prime minister's points, he replied that he hoped the Australian prime minister might understand that China had lent Rio a 'helping hand' as a friend, but when it no longer needed it, Rio had 'slapped China in the face' with the infrastructure joint venture. He concluded by saying that there would be 'consequences'.[36]

In July, Rio Tinto's Shanghai-based representative, Stern Hu, an Australian citizen of Chinese heritage, was arrested on charges of dealing in state secrets and corruption. This led to another major fracture in the Australia–China relationship.[37] Stern Hu was subsequently tried and, in 2010, found guilty of the charges. He spent over nine years in prison. Putting questions of guilt or innocence concerning Stern Hu to one side, his tragedy is that he, and his three fellow co-accused and sentenced, were the human faces of the iron ore wars that erupted as China's demand ran far ahead of supply, confronting the country's leaders with massive vulnerabilities that their own policies had created. The wars were less about the prices paid for the material and much more about the insecurity of being utterly dependent on foreign suppliers for strategic resources.

Markets at Work
Over time, markets stabilised and prices fell. Supply expanded not only in Australia but in other countries, especially Brazil. Part of the supply response in Australia involved Rio Tinto and BHP adding substantial new capacity. It also gave rise to new entrants, the most notable of which was Fortescue Metals Group (FMG), led by the charismatic and mercurial ex-investment banker cum recently minted mining entrepreneur Andrew Forrest. He understood the potential of the China market probably much better than

the Chinese leadership themselves at the time understood their inevitable future dependency on imported ore.

Forrest made a massive bet on the Chinese economy and won many times over. Until FMG's first shipment to China in the Summer Olympics year of 2008, BHP and Rio Tinto held a duopoly over iron ore mining in the Pilbara, a business that had grown out of Japan's industrialisation in the 1960s and 1970s. These companies had built long, trusted relations with their Japanese customers, and later with South Korean and Taiwanese steel mills. China was just another of the 'flying geese', in the phrase of the popular economic theory of the time about 'catch-up' in industrialisation in East Asia.[38] Neither company controlled all the iron ore deposits in the Pilbara, only the best in terms of the quality of the ore. Lower grade, more remote or more expensive deposits were to be found there, but it would require prices and a demand well beyond what prevailed before 2003 to develop these. Neither of the majors understood the potential of the Chinese market. Forrest did, seeing it as a way of breaking their control over Australia's valuable iron ore trade. Importantly, it provided the chance to build new relationships with new customers, which had been blocked in Japan and elsewhere in North-East Asia. To drive home the point, FMG labelled itself 'The Third Force in Iron Ore'. This was an appeal to the Chinese, and other potential customers, to welcome competition in the trade.

FMG quickly built its first mines, with annual production by the end of the 2000s of 44 million tonnes. In 2011, with China's enormous GFC stimulus package running through its economy, FMG again rolled the dice, borrowing a breathtaking US$10 billion to build the Solomon's Hub mine in the Pilbara and take annual production to 166 million tonnes by 2014. In 2011, the price per tonne had reached its highest level ever: US$149 per tonne. By then, BHP and Rio were also investing heavily to expand production to meet China's demand.

The new FMG mine was built on time and on budget. But before it was finished, supply finally caught up with demand and prices fell to US$97 per tonne, though this was still highly profitable for producers. Thereafter, with slower growth in China as the post-GFC stimulus eased, and with supply expanding quickly, prices fell to the mid US$50 range, where they remained for the next two years, only to recover strongly following supply-side shocks from Brazilian company Vale's tailing dam catastrophes and China's sustained high rates of economic growth.

By the time of the post-GFC spike in iron prices, Beijing had developed a good understanding of how global commodity markets worked and it adopted a much more relaxed approach than in the mid-2000s, when its vulnerability and utter dependence on foreign suppliers were fully recognised. A market-based index pricing system was implemented, as BHP's Marius Kloppers had sought, and the fractious annual contract price negotiations were abandoned. Rio set about successfully rebuilding its relations with Beijing. Stern Hu stoically served his time. The iron ore wars were over.

China's 'Going out' Policies

Resources and energy security were behind China's 'going out' or 'going global' policies. In the second half of the 1990s, 'going out' was occasionally referred to by general secretary Jiang Zemin in speeches and Party documents. As China was preparing to join the WTO in 2001, premier Zhu Rongji stated it as policy in his annual report to that year's NPC. After that, a series of state decrees and regulations was issued.[39] This was the precursor of the much more geopolitical, expansive and ambitious BRI policy that now underpins China's grand strategy.

Initially, before the resources boom, China's outward investment had been predominantly in Asia, with about two-thirds in Hong Kong and Macau. It was mainly in services to support its exports of manufactured goods. As China became increasingly dependent on the global supply of raw materials and energy, so its outward investment turned toward securing overseas sources of supply.[40] By 2006, 'mining, quarrying, and petroleum' accounted for over 40 per cent of the country's total outward FDI.[41]

The surge in China's outward investment was accompanied by what was called 'resource diplomacy', whereby diplomatic activity was 'designed' to enhance China's access to resources and energy as part of its national security policies.[42] China began to mobilise other elements of its statecraft around ensuring energy and resource security from this time. Military doctrine, for example, began to shift from being concentrated solely on the near abroad to recognising gradually the necessity of protecting far-distant sea lanes carrying crucial supplies of oil.[43]

Perhaps lulled into complacency by its long history of resource self-sufficiency, and overwhelmed by the speed with which it had become dependent on foreign markets, in the early years of 'going out', Beijing did not actively pursue a policy of diversifying foreign suppliers. For a time, Australia was the second-largest destination for China's outward FDI, which went mainly into Australian iron ore, and other resources such as coal. In effect, its outward investment was making China more, not less, dependent on a single supplier, namely Australia.[44]

Between 2006 and 2012, Australia accounted for 13 per cent of China's total outward direct investment, or US$50 billion, almost equal to its investment in the US over the same period (US$50.7 billion) and substantially greater than any other destination; for example, Canada (US$36.6 billion), Brazil (US$25.3 billion), Russia (US$12.5 billion), the UK (US$11.8 billion) or South Africa (US$8.2 billion).[45] During this period, mining accounted for 73 per cent of total Chinese FDI in Australia, oil and gas 18 per cent, renewable energy 4 per cent, and 'other' (mainly agriculture and real estate) 5 per cent.[46] Investment flowed into projects that went way over budget and would not be commercially viable without SOE involvement. On occasions, China's major investments ran into regulatory issues and prompted clashes with local partners, such as the long-troubled CITIC Pacific investment in Clive Palmer's Sino Iron magnetite project in the north-west of Western Australia. The project, begun in a blaze of publicity and flush with optimism and Chinese cash, ended up five years late and cost US$12 billion compared with its original budget of US$2.5 billion.[47] With a name-plate capacity of 22 million tonnes per annum, it was nearly eight times as costly per tonne of iron ore mined than FMG's Solomon's Hub, and took twice as long to build.

A number of mine projects have yet to begin operations, such as Sinosteel's US$2.5 billion investment in the Mt Weld Iron Ore project in Western Australia, which has been on hold since 2014 over an inability to finance the Oakajee rail and port infrastructure, and iron ore prices that no longer support such investments.[48] Anshan Steel's multi-billion-dollar Karara magnetite project with ASX-listed Gindalbie Metals is another case in point—by 2017, the asset value had been written down to zero.[49]

In the resources sector, and in regards to iron ore in particular, markets have worked as they should have, with supply eventually expanding and equilibrium restored. In the 2000s, however, huge sums of money were wasted by China because of a deep mistrust of foreign companies and a misunderstanding of markets, and heightened anxiety over the strategic vulnerabilities that a lack of resource security implied.

China's major vulnerability, when total share of world trade and imports as a share of domestic consumption are taken together, continues to be iron ore, which greatly exposes China to Australia, one of the US' closest allies in East Asia. In 2018, China imported 90 per cent of its needs and consumed some 68 per cent of global trade. A year later, 64 per cent of those imports came from Australia. Over the past decade, China has attempted to diversify supply away from Australia by investing in Brazil, Africa, Kazakhstan and elsewhere, but Australia enjoys a big advantage by being close to the market, having a range of higher quality to lower quality ores suitable for blending, and having highly experienced and efficient companies that have built world-class infrastructure to supply the China market.

Brazil's Vale did plan to remove most of the transport margin that has worked in Australia's favour, by building a fleet of Valemax very large ore carriers (VLOCs) with a capacity of between 380 000 tonnes and 420 000 tonnes, or about a third greater capacity than the next-biggest VLOC: the capesize ships (so named because they were too big to go through the Suez Canal). Yielding a 20–25 per cent saving in costs, Valemax ore carriers reduced but did not remove Australia's freight cost advantage.

With higher-quality iron ore and therefore lower processing costs for the mills in China, Brazil was to have become a price-competitive, large-volume competitor to Australia. Brazil is also a member of the China-led BRICS Group, and sourcing iron ore from it would be a further geopolitical consideration. But two major tailings dam failures, one in 2018 and one in early 2019, temporarily put an end to that challenge to Australia's dominance of the market and China's quest for competitive alternative sources of supply of iron ore. Brazil also has been badly affected by COVID-19, which is likely to delay substantially its return to the market. These setbacks have again highlighted to the leadership in Beijing China's acute vulnerability to supply-side shocks.

The Boot on China's Throat

Former president Hu Jintao reportedly described the Straits of Malacca variously as the 'boot on China's throat' and as China's 'Malacca dilemma'.[50] Hu was troubled by how a 'certain power', the US, which the PLA was at least twenty to thirty years away from being able to challenge in terms of naval clout, 'had all along encroached on and tried to control navigation through the Straits'.[51]

The Straits of Malacca, the shortest sea route between the Persian Gulf and China, linking the Indian Ocean with the South China Sea, is second only to the Strait of Hormuz (which connects the Persian Gulf and the Gulf of Oman) in terms of the volume of crude oil and petroleum products passing through it.[52] In 2016, 16 million barrels per day went through the Straits of Malacca compared with 18.5 million barrels per day through the Strait of Hormuz.[53] The U.S. Energy Information Administration estimates that, if the Straits of Malacca were blocked, almost half of the world's crude oil tanker fleet would have to be rerouted around Indonesia. Were this to happen, it would 'tie up global shipping capacity, add to shipping costs, and potentially affect energy prices'.[54] The Straits of Malacca are similarly an important route for liquefied natural gas (LNG) being transported from the Persian Gulf to China and elsewhere in North-East Asia. All of Australia's iron ore passes through the South

China Sea. Far from China seeking to restrict maritime transport, its interests require open shipping lanes.

China is most exposed to a denial of supplies in crude oil and iron ore (see Table 1). Between 2003 and 2018, China's dependency on imported crude oil doubled to 73.6 per cent, and its dependency on foreign-supplied iron ore doubled to over 90 per cent. For coking coal, the increase was just 13 per cent, but for bauxite it was 55 per cent and LNG 86 per cent (see Table 2). China's resources insecurity is also obvious from the share of total world trade in key commodities for which it accounts. In 2018, China's imports accounted for 20 per cent of the world trade in crude oil and 68 per cent of that in iron ore. While steaming coal still comprised a relatively low share in view of China's rich endowments of coal, the country's imports of coking coal used for steel making accounted for 10 per cent of world trade. The figure for LNG was 17 per cent (see Table 3).

Year	Crude Oil	Iron Ore	Steaming Coal	Coking Coal	Bauxite	LNG
1998	26.80	51.77	1.37	0.10		0.04
2003	91.13	148.13	4.63	2.60		0.00
2008	178.89	444.13	10.29	6.86	25.79	3.34
2013	281.95	820.31	113.05	75.40	70.70	18.03
2018	461.90	1064.47	76.50	64.90	82.62	53.78

Table 1. China's Imports of Major Commodities (in Millions of Tonnes)
Sources: The GACC and Worldsteel

Year	Crude Oil	Iron Ore	Steaming Coal	Coking Coal	Bauxite	LNG
1998	15.41%	30.85%				
2003	36.56%	41.63%				
2008	50.39%	57.68%	1.95%	3.57%	50.60%	
2013	57.95%	75.51%	3.79%	11.91%	58.38%	86.21%
2018	73.55%	90.33%	2.38%	12.70%	54.71%	85.66%

Table 2. China's Imports of Major Commodities as a Share of China's Total Consumption
Sources: The GACC, Worldsteel, NBS, and BP

Year	Crude Oil	Iron Ore	Steaming Coal	Coking Coal	Bauxite	LNG
1998		10.98%			na	
2003	5.15%	25.41%			na	
2008	9.08%	47.58%	5.37%	16.35%	na	1.96%
2013	15.01%	64.28%	5.23%	12.97%	na	7.53%
2018	20.41%	68.07%	3.50%	10.20%	na	17.04%

Table 3. China's Imports of Major Commodities as a Share of World Trade
Sources: The GACC, Worldsteel, BP and World Coal Association (WCA)

China is highly susceptible to supply-side shocks in crude oil. Hence, its Middle East policies have sought to support regional peace processes and diplomatically navigate between the two main protagonists: Saudi Arabia and Iran.

China also has sought to diversify sources of supply away from the volatile Middle East to its BRICS partners. In 2019, Russia and Brazil accounted for nearly a quarter of all of China's crude oil imports (see Table 4).

Country	Value (US$)	Share of total imports (%)
Saudi Arabia	40.1	16.8
Russia	36.5	15.3
Iraq	23.7	9.9
Angola	22.7	9.5
Brazil	18.5	7.8
Oman	16.4	6.9
Kuwait	10.8	4.5
UAE	7.3	3.1
Iran	7.1	3
UK	6.3	2.7

Table 4. China's Top Ten Sources of Crude Oil Imports in 2019
Source: Daniel Workman, 'Top 15 Crude Oil Suppliers to China', *World's Top Exports*, 28 May 2020, http://www.worldstopexports.com/top-15-crude-oil-suppliers-to-china (viewed June 2020)

China's overseas investment and the BRI

Several other factors have combined to influence China's outward foreign investment in recent years. Resource and energy security no longer dominate as they did in the 2000s, when China was coming to terms with the security implications of its foreign resources and energy dependency. China's economy has changed as manufacturing has moved further up the value-added chain, and so advanced manufacturing knowledge and technology are more sought after. The growth of China's services sector, which now accounts for some 55 per cent of GDP, is also reflected in the composition of its outward investment, especially in the area of financial services.

Australia has become less prominent with the shift in the structure of China's economy and what would seem to be Beijing's greater understanding of international markets for resources and energy. In terms of the stock of Chinese investment in Australia, in 2015 China accounted for 3 per cent of the total, compared with 24 per cent for the US, 14 per cent for the UK, 10 per cent for Japan and 4 per cent for Singapore.[55] In 2017/18, China was the second-biggest source of investment after the US—the first time China had not been the biggest investor since 2012/13. Also in 2017/18, China's investment in Australia fell by 50 per cent to $23.7 billion.[56] It is likely that tighter regulatory control by the FIRB and political difficulties in the bilateral relationship contributed to such a steep fall.

China's overall level of outward investment also has been trending down since 2016 and China is once again a net capital importer, which is more consistent with its per capita income than being a substantial net capital exporter, as in the previous decade. China's outward investment fell 18 per cent between 2016 and the end of 2018.[57] The decline was particularly big in relation to China's traditional major destinations: Europe, Asia (particularly Japan and Singapore), North America and Oceania. A recent study has concluded that this was in response to increasing political concern in more developed countries over China's investments.[58]

The BRI has also had a big influence on the direction of China's outward investment. Developing BRI countries have seen the biggest growth, with total Chinese investments in these countries increasing

by 8 per cent, lifting their share of total Chinese outward investment from 17 per cent to 22 per cent between 2016 and 2018.[59]
China's investment in the BRI countries surged from 2013 when
Xi Jinping launched the initiative (see figures 8 and 9). It accelerated for the next two years, but then fell following the tightening of
capital controls in 2015.

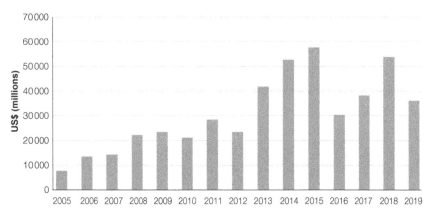

Figure 8. China's Investments in BRI Countries by Year (2005–19)
Source: China Global Investment Tracker and American Enterprise Institute, various dates

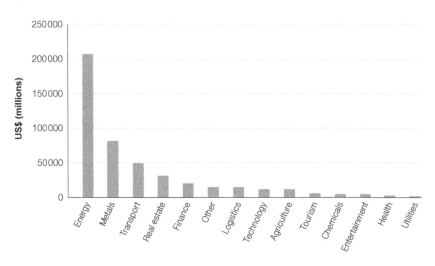

Figure 9. China's Aggregate Investments in BRI Countries by Sector (2005–19)
Source: China Global Investment Tracker and American Enterprise Institute, various dates

Despite the attention that China's outward investment attracts in popular media coverage and strategic discussions, it is small compared with China's share of global GDP. In 2019, China's GDP accounted for around 18 per cent of global GDP, while its outward investment comprised about 5 per cent, suggesting that it had considerable room to expand if and when domestic economic conditions permitted, and developed countries again became receptive to it.[60]

China's Biggest Strategic Vulnerability

Compared with the US' historical experience, China's ascendency has been constrained by resource and energy insecurity. During its ascendency, the US had all the raw materials, energy and food it needed to sustain continued economic growth. It lacked only people, which it sucked from Europe in large numbers. Many who came had also been educated at the expense of European states.

From the late 1990s, China rapidly became dependent on international markets to sustain its own economic growth, both to consume its products and fuel its industries. Far from shielding it from the world, China's economic development and the rising prosperity of its people created a greater dependence on the outside world and hence greater strategic vulnerability. Growth in incomes over the past twenty years has made China's own consumers much more important for sustaining GDP growth, but foreign resource dependency is greater than ever.

It was never intended that China integrate into the international economy on the basis of Ricardian principles of comparative advantage. Reform was based more on mercantilist ideas of building national treasure and strength. Trade was seen then as zero-sum—my gain is your loss—and import substitution was a central policy objective.[61] For natural resources and energy, however, few possibilities exist for import substitution other than exploration. China has pursued this vigorously, and the modernisation of the resources sector has seen great success in expanding domestic production of some commodities, especially crude oil and natural gas in Xinjiang. In the ten years from 1998, China's crude oil production increased nearly four-fold, and it did so seven-fold between 2012, from when numbers are available, and 2018.[62]

Of course, when the opening of China's economy began, the international economy looked nothing like it does today, with its highly integrated global production supply chains. The policies were intended to raise China's living standards and strengthen its economy and military, but the vision was independence from the international economy as far as that could be achieved, consistent with maintaining strong economic growth.

China's resource dependency is a nightmare for its strategic and defence planners. It is not difficult to imagine that at some time around the mid-2000s, someone in the leadership compound at Zhongnanhai in Beijing woke up in the middle of the night and screamed at the ceiling, 'What have we done!?'

CHAPTER 4

SOFT POWER, SHARP POWER
WHEN CHINA'S HARD POWER IS NOT ENOUGH

An early distinction between soft and hard power in China was made by the former revolutionary leader and subsequently vice premier Bo Yibo, whose son, Bo Xilai, was Party secretary in Chongqing and challenged Xi Jinping in 2011 for leadership of the Party. Commenting on US secretary of state John Foster Dulles' theory of 'peaceful evolution' to engineer over time, through a patient strategy and without war, the collapse of the Soviet Union, the elder Bo observed that 'imperialist countries' were inclined to adopt 'soft' methods in support of the deployment of 'hard' policies.[1]

Although the CPC has long been aware of the importance of using soft power to complement hard military power, its exercising of soft power is constrained by its political system. The party-state, authoritarian, political organisation of China inevitably means that soft power is shaped by the CPC's political narrative. Whether in media, culture, the arts, education or, increasingly, private business, the Party's narrative prevails. It has been said, 'The Party is like God. He is everywhere. You just can't see him'.[2]

Writing a decade ago on how other countries would respond to China's emergence as a great power, the noted strategic policy academic and commentator Wang Jisi, who was then dean of the School of International Studies at Peking University, said:

> China will have to invest tremendous resources to promote a more benign image on the world stage. A China with good governance will be a likeable China. Even more important, it will have to learn that soft power cannot be artificially created: such influence originates more from a society than from a state.[3]

China has invested massively over the past decade in soft power, but the party-state has not understood Wang's insight.

China's authoritarian political system is afflicted with a poor human rights performance; the stifling of non-government organisations, including religious organisations; the suppression of individual rights in favour of the state; the absence of the rule of law; a tightly controlled and scripted media; and an obsession with peripheral security in Xinjiang and Tibet. All this hardly makes China a model that many would wish to emulate.

Yet the Party does not see it that way. It sees the Chinese Government's performance as an exemplar: sustained economic growth over forty years and the concomitant lifting of hundreds of millions of people out of poverty in that time, reforging national power and pride; military strength; technological advancement; almost double the world's total high-speed train track length; and on it goes. The Party's achievements are truly astonishing and need to be recognised as such. Many outside China will ask, 'At what cost?', but many will also say, 'If only our political systems could perform so well'.

Within China, the government's response to COVID-19 has been projected as a major achievement. The Party's narrative of fighting as one against the disease and getting it under control, and the invidious comparisons drawn with the American and European responses, have been seen by many to vindicate China's model. While Xi may have been criticised earlier in the crisis for tardiness, later he was seen to have steadied the ship in comparison to the chaotic responses in the US and parts of Europe. This may have strengthened Xi's grip on power. Foreign criticism of China by the Trump administration has rallied strong nationalist sentiments within China in support of the party-state.[4]

The problem for the party-state is that what works in terms of propaganda within China seldom works outside it. China's struggle with projecting soft power can be seen in international surveys of attitudes towards it, and the problem is becoming worse.[5] The challenge of soft power is another major constraint on China's capacity to exercise power and influence globally, in addition to its geography, history and resource dependency.

The Party has always feared that its grip on power will be undermined by foreign ideas coming into the country through culture and foreign media. During the first decades of reform and opening, campaigns against 'spiritual pollution' and 'peaceful evolution' were conducted on a regular basis. 'Ideological work' has always been among the Party's highest objectives. Official recognition of the importance of soft power occurred in 2007 at the Seventeenth National Congress of the CPC, when president Hu Jintao said that the 'great rejuvenation of the Chinese nation will definitely be accompanied by the thriving of Chinese culture'.[6]

The democratic uprisings of the so-called colour revolutions of the mid-2000s, in which specific colours were used as symbols in civil protests, and then the Arab Spring of 2011–12 were seen as examples of foreign influence through the media, and as evidence of the Party's need to double down on its propaganda work. As the Arab Spring began to subside, a confidential document prepared by the Party's General Office was circulated, discussing the threat of liberalism from the West. It rejected Western liberal values on the basis that they could undermine 'national rejuvenation', introduce 'constitutionalism' (that is, enforce citizens' rights against the state, as set out in the PRC constitution), and create space for an independent civil society. The document also demanded that the media serve the Party.[7]

Then, in January 2013, the Guangzhou-based *Southern Weekly* was told to replace its Chinese New Year editorial, which was on constitutionalism, with text written by the local propaganda department that extolled the Party's virtues. Staff at the newspaper, supported by bloggers and human rights lawyers, protested this, but to no avail. So began the decline of China's most liberal newspaper of the previous forty years. It ceased publication in 2014.[8] Constitutionalism was supressed.

Speaking to the Thirteenth National Committee of the Chinese People's Consultative Conference in March 2019, Xi called on 'writers, artists and theorists to strengthen cultural confidence and serve the people with fine works, and guide the public with high moral standards'.[9] He went on to urge more writing about and 'praising [of] the New Era'. The New Era, of course, is Xi's own doctrine, inscribed into the Party's constitution in 2017 as 'Xi Jinping Thought on Socialism with Chinese Characteristics for a New Era'.

François Bougon, in his book *Inside the Mind of Xi Jinping*, says that Xi strongly believes that the Soviet Union was destroyed by a strategy of cultural subversion led by the US together with other Western powers. According to a reviewer of Bougon's book, paraphrasing the author, this belief has led to

> the jailing of historians; crackdowns on internet personalities, human rights activists, feminists, and labor organizers; censorship in literary journals, newspapers, and Chinese social media; an all-out assault on Chinese Christianity; and the labyrinth of detention centers in Xinjiang … It is also … the impulse behind the coercion and surveillance of activists, students, dissidents, former officials, and Chinese-language media outlets outside of China's borders. Culture and ideology spill across borders.[10]

China's 'culture wars' are not aimed solely at the West, and foreign interference more generally, but also at the Party itself and wider society, seeking to strengthen resolve and unity around nationalism, traditional Chinese culture, and the Party's definition of a consumer-driven 'techno-modernity'.[11] In the hands of the Party, these become the face of China projected onto the outside world.

Soft, Hard and Sharp Power

Soft power is often defined by what it is not—as the opposite of coercion, or hard power. It is the ability of a country to persuade others to do what it wants without force. The concept is mostly associated with former Harvard International Relations professor Joseph Nye, who said that 'the currency of soft power is culture, political values, and foreign policies'. Updating the concept for the social media age, Nye suggested that 'the best propaganda is not propaganda' because 'credibility is the scarcest resource'.[12] Therein lies China's problem with soft power. With the Party controlling the narrative, propaganda prevails over expressions of authentic Chinese voices, values and culture.

Soft power also involves governments directly. The role of public diplomacy in the West is often all too underrated, a point Joseph Nye made about the US in 2004 at the onset of the 'War on Terror'. He quoted a leaked secret memo from 2003 from then secretary of defence Donald Rumsfeld, a well-known sceptic regarding soft power, in which Rumsfeld asked: 'Are we capturing, killing or deterring and dissuading more terrorists every day than the madrassas and the radical clerics are recruiting, training and deploying against us?'[13]

This, of course, was pre-ISIS (the Islamic State of Iraq and Syria). Its global attraction may have answered his question and changed his views on soft power.

Nye argues that successful states need both hard power and soft power. Soft power is difficult for states to direct to achieve specific foreign policy objectives. He observes the paradox that 'societies often embrace American values and culture but resist US foreign policies'.[14]

While hard power is easily understood and clearly distinct from soft power, comprising military and state-sponsored cyber-power, together with intelligence and surveillance reach, the more recent concept of 'sharp power' is much murkier and has become associated more with authoritarian and quasi-authoritarian states like China and Russia.[15] Narrowly defined as information warfare, it actually extends beyond that to agents of influence—mobilising patriotic students, businesses and community groups resident in other countries. Social media is one of its major vehicles. It also involves many traditional forms of exerting influence, including state-supported financial donations to political parties, or individuals in politics, the media and entertainment industries, and education institutions. The Central Intelligence Agency (CIA), for one, has been involved in this particular element of statecraft throughout its existence.[16]

Until around 2016, China had been making considerable in-roads in Australia through soft power. Then its use of sharp power was exposed, drawing a strong negative reaction and setting back its previous efforts considerably.[17] It led to the passing into law of legislation aimed at limiting foreign influence in politics and government. While the legislation was ostensibly aimed at all countries on a non-discriminatory basis, it was clearly prompted by China's sharp power and intended to restrain it.[18] The then prime minister, Malcolm Turnbull, made it abundantly clear, as if Beijing needed to be told, when he gratuitously said in poor Chinese, paraphrasing Chairman Mao's purported statement in announcing the formation of the People's Republic, that the Australian people had stood up.[19] Never mind that Mao didn't actually say this.[20]

Confucius Controversy

Confucius Institutes have been controversial since their inception in 2004. While ostensibly a way of promoting China's soft power through the teaching of Chinese language and culture, they are closer to the exercise of sharp power.

Universities and colleges around the world have gratefully accepted funding from the Hanban (the National Office for Teaching Chinese as a Foreign Language), which was set up to run the global network of Confucius Institutes using direct funding from China's Ministry of Education. But while university administrators welcome the money, academics have objected to politically slanted subject matter in their curricula; for example, how the events in Tiananmen Square in 1989, or the Falun Gong, or Tibetan independence are glossed over, or rather are not mentioned at all. One of the earliest critiques of Confucius Institutes was made in 2007 by Jocelyn Chey, who cautioned that if the institutes' activities went beyond teaching Chinese language and culture to promoting Chinese studies and research, 'then it is fundamentally flawed because of its close links with the Chinese government and Party. At best, it will result in a dumbing down of research; at worst, it will produce propaganda'.[21]

Concerns also have been raised over a broader encroachment on academic freedom, where Confucius Institutes have sought to sway on-campus activities of which the Chinese Government may not approve. This situation has never been clear-cut. Examples can be found of announcements of lectures with views contrary to Beijing's having been posted on Confucius Institute websites.[22] Regardless, foreign institutions have become increasingly sensitive to their activities and have sought to put protocols around them to preserve academic freedoms.

Confucius Institutes blur the distinction between soft and sharp power. The cat was let out of the bag in 2009 when Li Changchun, a member of the Politburo Standing Committee and in charge of propaganda, said that the institutes were 'an important part of China's overseas propaganda set-up'.[23] Increasingly, they are seen as belonging to China's arsenal of sharp power.

In 2019, 550 Confucius Institutes were operating globally, but this fell far short of an earlier target to have 1000 established by 2020. In fact, from 2018, some US colleges started closing down their Confucius Institutes in recognition of their sharp-power role on behalf of the Chinese party-state. Many closures also may have been in response to legislation passed that year by Congress which prevented institutions that host Confucius Institutes from participating in certain Defence-funded programs—in 2020, the University of Maryland cited this legislation when it closed its own Confucius Institute, which had been America's first when it opened in 2004.[24] A number of other US universities, however, including Chicago, North Carolina State and the University of Massachusetts Boston, have closed or have announced they are closing their Confucius Institutes over concerns about compromising, or actual interference in, academic freedom.[25]

As part of China's 'going out' strategy in the early 2000s, Confucius Institutes must have seemed like an inspired idea to those in Beijing who were worried about how to build China's soft power. Today, if anything, Confucius Institutes might be seen as counterproductive. The US-based Human Rights Watch has called on universities not to accept any more and to close existing ones. In 2019, Human Rights Watch proposed a twelve-point code of conduct aimed at 'Resisting Chinese Government Efforts to Undermine Academic Freedom Abroad'; point 7 is to 'Reject Confucius Institutes'.[26] The code was based on surveys conducted during 2015–18 in Australia, Canada, France, the UK and the US.

All the World's a Stage, but No-one's Watching

Judged by international surveys, China has a big problem with its soft power, but even more so when judged by the billions spent on promoting China's image abroad through numerous channels. Of China's many wasteful, state-led investments, the funds devoted to building its soft power would probably be among those yielding the poorest returns.

Over the past decade, China has invested heavily in an expanded global media network. By 2017, its traditional official news agency, Xinhua, had 170 foreign bureaus, the *China Daily* and *Global Times* each published English-language editions distributed internationally, and the big, cash-burning CGTN was broadcasting on six channels—two in English and the others in Arabic, French, Russian and Spanish—and had bureaus and reporting teams in seventy countries. According to the US Council on Foreign Relations, China Radio International broadcasts 392 hours of programming a day in thirty-eight languages from twenty-seven overseas bureaus.[27]

Although it is notoriously difficult to estimate what China actually spends on global media efforts, it has been suggested that by 2014 it may well have been in excess of US$10 billion per year, compared with US State Department expenditure that same year of US$666 million.[28] The money China spent on the creation of the China Global Television Network (CGTN) in 2017, to compete with CNN, BBC, Al Jazeera, Sky and other broadcasters, would add considerably to that figure.[29]

Reliable numbers for audience size and composition for CGTN are not available, but what work has been done suggests only a small number of Western viewers. It may have more reach in regions such as Africa, but still, the audience sizes are believed to be slight.[30] This would likely also be the case for the numerous Beijing-funded newspapers, journals and websites directed at international audiences.

A recent study of CGTN has concluded that the lack of attractiveness of its programming to international consumers can be attributed to the network's bureaucratic structure, office politics, low rewards and morale, and the deep divide between local employees and foreign experts. The study points to how state-owned media in other countries, such as the BBC, operate independently of the government—the BBC has 'independence' written into its charter, and also operates in a setting of vigorously free media that hold it to account. Within China, different media businesses can, and do, operate with a degree of individual discretion, although they are still heavily circumscribed. The national broadcaster, however, stands apart from other media. Xi Jinping, on a visit to the network in 2016, told staff that it was their duty to support the Communist Party.[31]

Each day at CGTN, editors receive guidance on the main stories, being told what to cover and what not to touch. The leadership's overseas travels usually lead the stories, with setpiece shots of them meeting and greeting foreign dignitaries. Explicit directives for each program are not required, as the presenters know well the limitations. The most Westernised and famous anchors, such as Liu Xin and Tian Wei, as with the recently retired Yang Rui, are strongly nationalist and personally feel that the Western media is out to get China. Many of the same foreign commentators feature over and over again on their programs, as the views of these people, without any coaching, are reliable. In effect, content passes through the prism of the propaganda authorities, not that of the marketing people. The constraint is structural, and content inevitably will support the Party's narrative at home and abroad.

The money and activity involved are dizzying. David Shambaugh attributes this to Beijing having the same attitude towards soft power as it does to building high-speed train infrastructure: 'spend money and expect to see results'.[32] In turn, this is due to Beijing's command-and-control mentality, which derives from the rigidly vertical structure of decision-making in the authoritarian party-state.

In other words, the constraints on China's projection of soft power through the media are systemic and as such cannot readily change, if at all.

Pew Research Center global opinion poll results from 2020 show that China's soft power problem is becoming greater, notwithstanding the resources ploughed into it. Compared with 2019, those in the US who hold an unfavourable view of China increased by 6 percentage points to a record high of 66 per cent, while those who hold a favourable view remained at 26 per cent. Significantly, polls held before and after the COVID-19 pandemic was declared in March showed no change, suggesting that the sharp deterioration in China's approval rating in the US was not influenced by the virus.[33] Subsequent polling may well change in view of the heightened international controversy over what Beijing knew about the virus and when.

The expulsion of four *Wall Street Journal* reporters in March 2020, for what is believed by most foreign media to be their coverage of Beijing's under-reporting of data on the virus in its early stages, will do little to assist China's image abroad, no matter what the facts are on the ground in China itself. Beijing has launched a massive information and disinformation campaign against the democracies, but principally the US, over their own bungled initial responses to the virus and lack of preparedness. While President Trump has given China's propagandists fecund material with which to work, Beijing's unsubtle efforts to play the 'politics of generosity' have been called out by leaders in Europe and elsewhere, such as Australia.[34] In a recent poll in Italy, however, both China and Russia were seen as more friendly countries than either Germany or France—although intra-European budgetary tensions may be more at play here than Chinese soft power.[35]

Going Downhill since Xi

All of the Pew time-series data show an abrupt change in the trend of unfavourable ratings from when Xi Jinping took over as CPC General Secretary in 2012. Beforehand, favourable and unfavourable ratings were both at 40 per cent, but between 2012 and 2013, negative views increased to 52 per cent, continuing to the high of 66 per cent today.[36]

Older Americans have always held more negative views of China than younger ones. But since Xi's ascendency, the number of young Americans who hold negative views of China has doubled, compared with a 50 per cent increase in older Americans. The 2020 survey was the first time in the fifteen years since the polling began that a majority of younger Americans (53 per cent) held unfavourable views of China.

This is reflected in markedly more negative views of Xi Jinping. In 2020, those holding unfavourable views of Xi increased to 71 per cent from 50 per cent, the level of the past two years. Meanwhile, confidence in Xi among the Americans polled fell from a high of 39 per cent in 2018 to just 22 per cent in 2020, which may reflect criticism of Xi's handling of COVID-19 in its early stages in Wuhan.[37]

Xi's muscular and assertive foreign policy, unsurprisingly, is reflected in an appreciable increase in respondents who see China as a significant threat. Some 90 per cent of Americans now view China as a 'major' threat. The two top issues of concern are 'China's impact on the global environment' (91 per cent) and cyber-attacks (87 per cent).[38] Presumably this is consistent with sharp increases in younger people's negative views of China.

Such results serve to highlight the failure of China's soft power projection. It remains publicly a major supporter of the Paris Agreement on climate change, from which the US under Trump has walked away. In these circumstances, China should have been able to make itself more appealing, not less, to young people who accord a very high priority to environmental issues. But under Xi Jinping, this has not happened.

Human rights behaviour has also reinforced the more critical perspective held by young people towards China. For all age groups, the three top areas of concern are the environment, human rights policies and cyber-attacks. Noteworthy also are the falls in concerns with China over economic matters—worries about the trade deficit fell from 61 per cent in 2012 to 49 per cent in 2020, and uncertainty over losing jobs to China reduced from 71 per cent in 2012 to 52 per cent in 2020.[39] The rhetoric of President Trump over trade relations with China seems to have reassured people in the US.

Helpfully, in the interests of peace, US respondents show a great deal of renewed confidence in their country. The greatest risk of Thucydides' Trap becoming self-fulfilling is when the dominant power feels that the ascendant power threatens its security and therefore it must strike. In 2020, 59 per cent of respondents named the US as the world's leading economy, up from 49 per cent two years earlier. As for the world's leading military power, 83 per cent named the US, up 11 percentage points from 2016.[40]

These results for 2020 are just from the US surveys by the Pew Research Center. But in October 2019, the results of polls in twenty-five countries, while not as negative, also showed little return for China's massive investment in attempts to win friends and influence people. Pew found that a median of 45 per cent of countries had a favourable view of China, while 43 per cent had an unfavourable view.[41]

Of most concern for China should be recent polls of attitudes in its immediate neighbourhood. Polling of a sample of six Asian neighbours from May and October 2019 showed that despite President Trump, who is widely disliked, a median of 64 per cent had favourable views of the US. In Japan, South Korea, the Philippines and India, views of the US were overwhelmingly positive, with all at or above 60 per cent.[42] Sentiment was highest in the Philippines (80 per cent) and South Korea (77 per cent). At the same time, views towards China were sharply negative in Japan (85 per cent), South Korea (63 per cent), Australia (57 per cent), the Philippines (54 per cent) and India (46 per cent).[43] Whatever the degree of imprecision of such surveys, those promoting China's soft power clearly have a lot more work to do.

China's global reputation on press freedom is abysmal. The 2020 World Press Freedom Index, compiled by Reporters without Frontiers, ranked China fourth lowest in terms of press freedom, just above Eritrea, Turkmenistan and North Korea—hardly company with whom China's internationally exposed middle classes would normally think of themselves associating.[44]

China's massive soft power investments offshore have not only come to little, its position on nearly all measures is worse than it was in 2005. Yet billions of dollars have been invested to promote China's image abroad. Xi's ascendency marks a break in trends in nearly all the polls which is consistent across all issues and age groups in most countries. Xi's rule has been characterised by a return to more authoritarian methods of governing, especially involving the greater repression of borderland minorities, non-government organisations (NGOs), and individuals and groups advocating for greater protection of citizens' constitutional rights.

Xi is facing a dilemma in that his use of greater hard power at home is making it more difficult to exercise soft power abroad. The ineffectiveness of the latter, as judged by the polling, may also partly explain the rise in China's use of sharp power. The dilemma for Beijing, however, is that this will only further harm China's exercise of soft power.

Authoritarian Creep

China's problem with soft power stems from its authoritarian system of political and social organisation. It is the nature of these systems to be highly sensitive to public criticism of the government or ruling political party. Under Xi Jinping, the party-state has become even less tolerant of public criticism. It has reintroduced greater ideological guidance across the cultural fields while monitoring, restricting and seeking to shape social media to its advantage.

Authoritarian systems achieve a high level of social and cultural control by having ill-defined boundaries, or 'red lines', which tend to have a chilling effect on creativity. Over the past decade in particular, dullness and conformity have been creeping back into cultural spheres, just as more money and technological wizardry have been applied. Some years ago, Xi Jinping warned against designing 'strange'-looking buildings.[45] Since then, Beijing's new architecture, as impressive as it may be for its sheer scale (another authoritarian touch), has been all straight lines and rigid symmetry.

Over the past four years, the back lanes of the Sanlitun bar and restaurant area—previously a melting pot of hip local Chinese and foreigner cultures—have been stripped of their snack stores, bars, DVD shops and pop-up cafes, to be replaced by planter boxes and fussy tiled pedestrian walkways. Grunge is out, and with it the frisson of challenging authority, no matter how innocent it may have been.

The Hegezhuang artists' village on the outskirts of Beijing has been given an expensive Potemkin makeover, with brick facades, needlessly broad sidewalks and the ubiquitous oversized flower boxes. It all has a communist aesthetic that's straight out of a 1950s playbook. The state can nurture and nourish cultural development, but it should not direct nor seek to lead it. The state's objective is always political, whereas cultural development derives from personal and individual expression.

The structure of the CPC's methods of governing, with Party officials embedded at every level of decision-making, the role of the Party schools in training senior cadres and ensuring that each and every one is always 'on message', and the education system more broadly, deliberately foster conformity and standardisation. As Richard McGregor says of the teaching of history in China, 'it is not enough for the Party to control government and business in China. To stay in power, the Party has long known that it must control the story of China as well'.[46]

The same is true in cultural life. Xi Jinping set it out in his usually blunt manner, lest there be any misunderstanding of his intentions:

[The Party] will devote more energy and take more concrete measures in developing a great socialist culture in China, cultivating and observing core socialist values, and promoting the creative evolution and innovative development of fine traditional Chinese culture …[47]

China's cities, which largely have been rebuilt over the past fifteen years, in one of the world's greatest bursts of urban redevelopment, have followed a similar plan—wide multi-lane roadways, green median strips (with flower boxes!), overhead lighting, rows and rows of storeyed apartments, parks, and, at the centre of it all, thrusting upwards, the CBD with its copse of high-rise office towers. China's bright, new, clean and safe cities are hardly distinguishable from each other. The achievement is both astonishing in its scale and deeply flawed in its uniformity and conformity.

In the late 1990s and early 2000s, China started to be noticed around the world as an exciting, lively, creative place. This was concentrated in the early days in Beijing, despite the city's grey, generally staid bureaucratic atmosphere. Nothing captured this as much as the huge international success of China's contemporary artists and filmmakers. Foreigners were attracted to the idea of living in China to be part of this new, fresh, internationally recognised, creative force that was building impetus.[48]

Red lines appeared to be dissolving. The opportunities and potential seemed boundless. The Party may even have been easing its grip. Political boundaries began to be extended with the rights lawyers' movement, and the spread of NGOs and environmental activism. The 2008 Olympics in Beijing won foreign journalists the right to travel to any part of China they wished to visit without prior approval. And then in the same year came the crackdown on the Charter 08 democracy group and the tide turned.

Famous Chinese film directors are an example of how the state ultimately stifles soft power. In the 1980s and 1990s, like their painting and sculpting counterparts, directors such as Chen Kaige and Zhang Yimou, with authentic movies such as *Yellow Earth* and *Raise the Red Lantern*, captured an international audience and an enthusiastic following. But over time, they were coopted by the party-state's propaganda machinery and accordingly lost their overseas audiences. The much-touted first Chinese movie to be made in Hollywood was Zhang Yimou's extravagant state-supported *The Great Wall*. It was a lavish, expensive, commercial flop, rated his worst movie.[49]

The tennis star Li Na is an instructive case. She was the first player from an Asian country to make it to a Grand Slam singles final. That was in Melbourne in 2011, before she won the French Open in the same year. Earlier in her career, she parted company with the state-controlled All China Women's Tennis Federation, feeling that she was being held back and that her prospects would improve if she based herself privately in the US. She rose to the top of her sport despite, not because of, state-managed professional tennis in China. However, even if you are the world number one, it is still difficult—probably impossible—to remain apart from the state system.

When Li Na returned to Beijing from Melbourne in 2011 as runner-up in that year's Australian Open, as the Australian ambassador, I invited her and her husband to what was planned to be a small, private lunch at the St Regis Hotel. On entering the lobby to greet her, I found that a TV sports channel crew was there to film her arrival, and about a dozen representatives of the All China Women's Tennis Federation had invited themselves to lunch. It became a media event, and discussion over lunch was dominated by the officials. The subtext was that if Li Na wanted to make her home in China and have a family there, which she did, she had no choice if she were to continue competing but to submit to the suffocating embrace of the state. On her part, the lunch had a strong feeling of resignation about it.

Li Na for a moment did capture the hearts and minds of tennis-loving Melbournians, and indeed many people in Australia. She had pluck, courage, a wicked sense of humour, and she was a winner. It was the best of Chinese soft power on display. She was authentic. Officials in Beijing could not understand her attraction, but they knew they had to hold her close.

Brittle Diplomacy

At times, the behaviour of Chinese officials overseas is totally counterproductive. In 2009, the Melbourne International Film Festival, in normal circumstances an unremarkable event, shot to global prominence due to attempts by local Chinese consular officials to prevent the screening of *Conditions of Love*, by the prominent, exiled, US-based Uighur activist Rebiya Kadeer. Not only did this ensure the movie attracted a much larger audience than it ever would have without the helpful intervention of China's Melbourne consulate, it set back China's soft power efforts considerably. The consulate then further damaged China's image by threatening Melbourne's lord mayor, Robert Doyle, with ending the longstanding and productive Melbourne–Tianjin sister city relationship, if he did not prevent the film from being shown at Melbourne Town Hall. Ironically, the town hall had only been selected as a venue at the last minute because demand for seats had increased greatly as a result of the controversy created by the consulate. As anyone with even a passing knowledge of Australia would have known, Doyle refused to intervene and did so in a most public way.[50]

Examples of this type of behaviour have occurred over and over again, most recently the threat of economic retaliation over Australian Prime Minister Morrison's proposal that an international investigation be launched into the origins of COVID-19 and China's actions in the early days of the pandemic, in terms of notifying the WHO and alerting other countries to the potential risks of contagion. Whatever the merits of the idea at issue, threatening economic retaliation does enormous harm to China's soft power.[51]

China needs to develop a more mature foreign policy that reflects its recently acquired status of a great power, not an immature, insecure power.[52] Instead, Beijing seems to have set its officials on heavy-handed autopilot. And the polling suggests that this is inimical to China's aims. The engagement of agents of influence, bribery, and the coopting of patriotic students, are all forms of sharp power. That these are the main instruments at hand for the party-state in Australia suggests that Chinese soft power is badly wanting.[53]

In 2010, China was accused by the US of imposing restrictions on the export of rare-earth elements to Japan in response to the Japanese arrest of a Chinese fishing boat captain. This led to an international reaction against China. In fact, Beijing had taken the decision to cut worldwide exports of rare-earth elements two months before the trawler incident, on environmental grounds.[54] Whatever the motivation for and exact timing of the decision, views hardened against China as a dependable supplier. It encouraged Japanese and US investors, and non-Chinese consumers, to look for alternative sources of supply, such as the ASX-listed Lynas company, which mines these elements in Australia and processes them in Malaysia.

At times, Beijing has tried to conceal its actions through 'plausible deniability'. In 2012, when it wanted to pressure the Philippines during the Scarborough Shoal stand-off over who controls the area, it announced new quarantine restrictions on fruit imports from the Philippines. It did this again in 2019, this time in regards to Australia's exports of wine and coal, thereby delaying goods at the ports.

One of China's most high-handed efforts at coercion occurred in 2017, when Beijing tried to pressure the Republic of Korea (ROK, or South Korea) into withdrawing from an agreement to permit the US to deploy locally its anti-ballistic missile system, the Terminal High Altitude Area Defense (THAAD). Beijing's efforts caused considerable economic damage, including a 50 per cent drop in Chinese tourists visiting South Korea, and the exiting of the Lotte Department Store from China.[55] While harming South Korea, Beijing managed to achieve the worst of all outcomes. THAAD was still deployed, and China's standing in South Korea fell while that of the US rose. Before the THAAD sanctions, 33 per cent of South Koreans saw China as a 'reliable partner', compared with the 60 per cent who favoured the US. After China's actions, South Korean confidence in it collapsed, with less than 14 per cent of citizens viewing China as reliable, compared with a 78 per cent rating for the US.[56] Another own goal for China's soft power had been scored.

This deterioration in South Koreans' trust in China has since continued, while trust in the US has kept rising. Immediate post-THAAD trust was at the lowest level since polling began in 2014. By 2019, it had fallen to only 13.6 per cent, while trust in the US had risen to an all-time high of 80 per cent.[57] This is all the more remarkable since it occurred under Trump, whose policies towards the Democratic People's Republic of Korea (DPRK, or North Korea) have been erratic at best. He unilaterally changed the game plan by meeting directly with North Korean dictator Kim Jong-un and suspending the annual US–South Korea military exercises. But far from one of China's most important long-term strategic objectives being advanced, that of loosening the ROK–US alliance, and at one of the most propitious of times thanks to Trump's presidency, South Koreans now hold the US in an even tighter embrace.

Beijing may be reckoning that actions today will discourage other states from defying China's wishes on certain key foreign policy matters in the future. Mao Zedong and Deng Xiaoping both relied on the old proverb, 'Kill a chicken to scare the monkey'. But their policies of deterrence evinced a woeful misunderstanding of how democracies work. Actual or threatened economic coercion will lead to popular support for staring Beijing down, which will embolden politicians to stand up to China, rather than the reverse.

The Asian Institute for Policy Studies has concluded that:

> Chinese economic retaliation for South Korea's decision to allow the deployment of THAAD appears to have had an enduring psychological impact on South Korean perceptions of the United States as a preferred security partner and of China as an uncertain neighbour.[58]

It should also worry Beijing that, in South Korea, as in Taiwan and Hong Kong, it is losing the youth more quickly than the older generations.

China's fierce reaction against Scott Morrison's call for an international investigation into COVID-19, which clearly targeted China's early response, held the implication, communicated through China's ambassador in Canberra, that Australia's actions could harm wine and beef exports, as well as the numbers of students and tourists coming to Australia. Beijing then doubled down on that with the unexplained withdrawal of export licences from four Australian abattoirs and the application of punitive tariffs on Australian barley exports, while simply saying these were, in the case of barley, longstanding issues and normal responses by China. These have been followed by the Chinese Government's warning to Chinese tourists and students of risks to their safety from supposedly anti-Chinese racism in Australia.

Predictably, the response from Australia was swift and robust, and it achieved the remarkable result of uniting the government and opposition parties against Beijing. Of course, it also provided a gift to those within Australia who look for any opportunity to attack China and steer Australia's foreign policy closer to the US' antagonistic position.[59]

Over 1.5 million people in Australia, around 5 per cent of the population, are ethnic Chinese—people who comprise a longstanding, integrated and welcome part of Australia's highly successful multicultural society. It is not the Chinese face that is not being embraced, but rather the face of the CPC. As a senior political correspondent wrote of Beijing's reaction to the call for an independent inquiry into the origins of COVID-19:

> It laid bare what those in political, diplomatic and foreign affairs circles have always known about the nature of the regime in Beijing. It was a glass-jaw bully that viewed bilateral relations as a one-way affair that should be skewed to Beijing's interest.[60]

While many in the West may feel that China, with its wealth and power and the hubris that accompanies these, does not care how it is perceived globally, Beijing understands that its image abroad is an essential part of statecraft. Historically, China has had immense soft power in its arts—painting, calligraphy, ceramics, poetry, music, food and much more. But foreigners' age-old attraction to these endeavours does not belong to the Communist Party. Rather, it is inherent in Chinese traditional culture. Again, it is authentic, not propaganda.

In 2012, when he was still active as a blogger, the popular Han Han observed that 'the restriction on cultural activities makes it impossible for China to influence literature and cinema on a global basis or for [Chinese] culture to raise our heads up proud'.[61]

As Nye said, while all cultures can attract and influence others, for China to succeed, 'it will need to unleash the talents of its civil society. That does not seem about to happen soon'.[62]

Soft Money for Soft Power

It was not so long ago that China itself was a recipient of overseas development assistance (ODA) and concessional lending. The clumsiness of some of its efforts in these areas is as much attributable to China's having arrived relatively recently on the scene as a technical assistance donor and substantial creditor, as it is to necessarily ill intent. China's aid and BRI activities have at times triggered domestic political arguments in recipient countries.

China's Overseas Development Assistance

In the same way that the first decade of the new millennium saw an abrupt break with previous decades in terms of China's economic growth, demand for imported resources and outward investment, so it was for China's ODA. With burgeoning forex reserves and recognition of its growing strategic dependence on imported energy and mineral resources, China's ODA grew rapidly.

Understanding the direction and economic impact of China's ODA is challenging in the absence of published consistent data. Moreover, China's aid comprises mainly concessional finance rather than grant aid, or rather, the grant component is low relative to the total flows. It is also delivered largely via China's major policy banks: the China Export-Import Bank and China Development Bank. The continuing opaqueness of China's ODA and its close alignment with China's search for energy and mineral resource security has led to unease about who ultimately benefits from it. Seeking political support for China internationally is a major consideration as well and has led to longstanding concerns over feeding corruption in recipient countries.

According to RAND Corporation estimates, China's ODA rose from US$1.7 billion in 2001 to US$12.5 billion in 2011, a seven-fold increase over the decade, albeit from a small base. This estimate may be on the high side, as China's 2014 white paper on foreign aid showed that aid, administered by the Ministry of Commerce, at about US$4.6 billion per annum. But with the BRI launched in 2013, it is likely to be higher, although most BRI lending is on commercial terms.[63] Pledges are very much higher than the actual aid delivered because of time lags in implementing projects. Pledges for 2011 were estimated by a RAND study to be US$125 billion. Of the total amount pledged for the ensuing decade, 42 per cent was for 'resources', 40 per cent for infrastructure—much of it for supporting resource projects—and 18 per cent for a variety of other purposes, including debt forgiveness. Reflecting the resources and energy bias in China's early ODA, Latin America received the biggest share, followed by Africa and the Middle East—although by 2014, Africa would begin to attract the largest share.[64]

While resources, energy security and infrastructure all feature highly in China's ODA activities, the motivations and decision-making overall remain opaque. China's ODA has been largely indiscriminate, driven more by demand and opportunity rather than 'supply-driven by a Chinese master plan'.[65] Political considerations are prominent. ODA is seen by China's leaders as a means of 'consolidating friendly relations' to assuage fears of China's rise and foster support for China's positions internationally.[66]

Foreign policy priorities are at the forefront of China's ODA in the Pacific, for example. Initially, Beijing's interest was drawn by Taiwan's dollar diplomacy that sought to retain diplomatic recognition and support from numerous Pacific island states. More recently, China has seen the Pacific as another area of geopolitical competition.

China's ODA both in the Pacific and elsewhere has at times been problematic for its foreign policy. It has received much criticism in the West for being a 'rogue donor' and for 'debt-trap diplomacy', being a form of neo-colonialism that is environmentally damaging and fosters corruption in recipient countries.[67] China's ODA in the Pacific, however, is also welcomed. In addition to the specific projects funded, for the island states it has drawn competition from Australia, New Zealand and the US.[68]

In 2018, Beijing established a new central coordinating agency for ODA, the China International Development Cooperation Agency (CIDCA). Previously, ODA was under the authority of the Ministry of Commerce, which coordinated many other departments, including the ministries of Foreign Affairs, Agriculture, and Education, and the State Administration of Foreign Exchange. The sheer size and negative perceptions of China's ODA, and the emergence of the BRI as the central organising principle of China's foreign policy and state-led international commercial engagement, require stronger central control of the program.[69]

CIDCA is directly under the State Council and is the responsibility of the minister for foreign affairs. ODA will presumably now be more deliberately used as an instrument of statecraft. China has pledged substantial aid packages to each of the Solomon Islands and Kiribati, for instance, which switched diplomatic relations from Taipei to Beijing in September 2019.[70]

CIDCA also confirms an influential political message of China's ODA, that it is conducted within a framework of south–south cooperation, distinguished by China itself being a developing country and so claiming particular insights and empathy with the developing world, a key constituency of China's bounded order. In this way, China is further positioning itself to have the developing world as a 'cornerstone of [its] diplomacy'.[71]

Displaying considerable sensitivity to the accusations of laying debt traps, and concern over deepening trade imbalances and neo-colonialism in Africa, China has tried to rebuild its image through debt forgiveness for the most heavily indebted African countries. In fact, it will face increasing pressure to do this from developing countries in the BRI as a result of COVID-19. China also has tried to claim some moral high ground by suggesting that developed country donors follow its example.[72]

In acknowledging that it has a soft power problem in Africa arising from ODA and the behaviour of state-owned companies, Beijing has introduced social corporate responsibility guidelines, including on environmental management, for enterprises investing in that continent. In 2017, China banned the ivory trade, and it is following international trends on 'green financing' and emphasising renewable energy projects. Although traditionally providing most of its ODA bilaterally, China has shown an increased willingness to work with UN agencies such as the United Nations Development Programme (UNDP), and even trilaterally with third–country partners.[73]

China's challenge in using its huge ODA program to strengthen its international attractiveness and influence is also that its appeal is limited by the nature of its domestic system. A lack of transparency and accountability, and an almost exclusive focus on economic wellbeing, to the exclusion of other rights, such as protecting individual freedoms, stand in the way of exercising real influence as distinct from attracting short-term opportunistic support.

As with much else in China's reform and opening-up period of the past forty years, its ODA has been an ongoing process of trial and error, summing up experiences and trying new policies. China is now entering a new phase where it is sharing its own experiences in development and basing aid decisions on the transfer of that experience. The BRI is the framework within which this is being done. BRI projects offer short-term benefits and contributions for creating jobs and relieving poverty, while major infrastructure investments lay the foundations for long-term development.[74]

Belt and Road Vision

President Xi's vision for the BRI is far greater than a means of fortifying China's energy and resources security and finding a vent for its ever-growing forex reserves beyond purchasing US Treasury notes. It includes the longer-term strategic goal of building a 'Community of Common Destiny'. Speaking at the BRI Leaders' Roundtable in Beijing in 2017, Xi put it this way:

> We need to make joint efforts in addressing challenges in the world economy, create new opportunities for development, seek new driving forces for development, and explore new space for development, so as to realize mutual complementarity, mutual benefit, and win–win solution[s].[75]

Following the Nineteenth CPC Congress in October 2017, the BRI has been written into the Party's constitution, enshrining it as a core political objective and beyond public criticism or debate within China.

Foreign critics see China's BRI as an attempt to create a China-centric world order.[76] Certainly, the BRI attempts to offer a vision of an alternative new order based on cooperation rather than competition. This is a narrative derived from a position of relative weakness compared with that of the US. However, the constraints on China exercising hegemonic power leave it no choice other than forms of cooperation with other states.

Governance issues around debt keep arising in the recipient countries of BRI projects. Corruption is seen as a major problem, and countries along the Belt and Road corridors are responding to the initiative more circumspectly.[77] These concerns have reached Xi Jinping who, at the second BRI Forum in Beijing in April 2019, said his government would strengthen oversight over infrastructure projects, support only high-quality projects, and have 'zero tolerance' for corruption.[78] But the BRI is a spaghetti bowl of bilateral deals in which Chinese financial institutions lend money mainly at commercial rates for projects in partner countries, and contracts are awarded to mainly Chinese firms. Chinese companies therefore receive most of the short-term benefits of the loans and the host country carries the debt.

Beijing has acknowledged it has a problem with some domestic resistance in BRI countries, and it has started to involve more multilateral agencies. At the 2017 BRI Forum, the IMF agreed to set up a China–IMF Capacity Development Centre in Dalian, in Liaoning Province. The UN has also offered support and advice. If poor financial behaviour is to be avoided and greater transparency achieved, and the international community's misgivings addressed, Beijing will need to involve more multilateral oversight of BRI projects. It has started achieving this with the AIIB, but it could do more by joining the Paris Club, a group comprising representatives of major creditor countries and which oversees international lending practices. Full membership would provide that much-needed greater transparency and help with debt-relief coordination.[79]

China has been able to square the circle with the AIIB, so there is potential to work in multilateral frameworks. The AIIB has been given the highest credit rating by the 'big three' rating agencies: Moody's, Standard & Poor's, and Fitch.[80]

The challenge for Beijing is the compatibility of the original geo-economic conception of the BRI, as an alternative vision of the world order, in linking with transparent multilateral organisations and processes. As with China's soft power deficit, governance problems with BRI projects also begin at home, where SOEs lack accountability.[81] Faced with slower growth, shrinking forex surpluses, pushback from recipient countries and rising international criticism, Beijing could try to internationalise the BRI, making it open and transparent. Rather than its mishmash of hub-and-spoke bilateral deals, projects could be multilateralised.[82] In doing so, however, the BRI's geo-economic wings may well be clipped.

———————

China's ODA and BRI lending add to its soft power, but they also have introduced new sources of apprehension and cynicism around Beijing's motives. China badly needs to build substantially its soft power to complement its economic power, thereby sustaining and extending its global influence. It needs this in order to achieve its security objectives both within and without. The constraint, however, is internal. It arises from the structure of China's party-state system of government. So it is difficult to see how any amount of spending will address this deficit. Limited soft power, like China's geography, history and resources, will be an enduring constraint on its exercise of global power.

PART III

NAVIGATING AUSTRALIA'S DYSTOPIAN FUTURE

CHAPTER 5

AUSTRALIA'S DYSTOPIAN FUTURE

Australia now finds itself all at sea in the new world order, unable to gain its footing and pursue a consistent foreign policy that balances a range of competing interests—security, prosperity and values. Faced with the challenges of China's economic rise and increasing foreign policy assertiveness, in recent years Australia has cleaved ever more closely to the US with policies that look like the triumph of hope over experience.

As China has established itself as the dominant power in East Asia, able to assert territorial claims in the South China Sea unchallenged, and with each of the region's economies more heavily dependent on its own than on any other country's, Australia looks back to a time when the US led a liberal international order. Yet it now faces a dystopian foreign policy future. In a bounded order in which two superpowers prevail, Australia is tied to the US by virtue of shared experiences, values, and a mutual distrust of China. But the US, like any great power, is wilful and capricious and pursues its interests on occasion without regard to its allies' interests.

Nowhere is this more clearly seen than in the area of economic security, where the US seeks bilateral trade deals with its strategic rival at great potential cost to allies, undermining the global rules-based order in the process. China provides Australia with its economic security, but the values of the CPC party-state sit at odds with Australia's. The new order also comprises many other authoritarian states that are comfortable in China's framework, but with whom Australia must work to advance its own interests.

Over the past four years in particular, Australia often has made its strategic choices without public discussion or debate. Its foreign policy in the new order stands on three reinforcing legs, each of which relies on security from China. One is the ever-tighter alliance with the US, another is engagement with the Quad, and the third has the Indo-Pacific as a strategic concept that seeks to coopt India into balancing China.

All the Way with the USA

Canberra has closely aligned itself with the US position of strategic competition with China. Australia is joined to the US' hip in a way that hasn't happened since the Cold War. Having done so, it is important for Australia to consider how far down the path of competition with China it is prepared to go. The 2017 US administration's NSS, Vice President Pence's 2018 Hudson Institute speech, and the May 2020 White House report titled *United States Strategic Approach to the People's Republic of China*, which sets out the principles for a whole-of-government approach to confronting China, all reaffirm that China is a strategic competitor of the US that must be resisted and challenged on a wide front, from security to trade to values.[1] The dominant power is explicitly resisting the ascendant power.

These policy statements are Trump's doctrine of 'principled realism'. As realism is essentially to put a state's security and economic interests first, principled realism is nothing other than 'America First', including, as Trump has made clear over and over again, ahead of allies.[2] As Trump himself has said, 'he is the President of the United States, not the world'. This is another way of stating 'America First' or 'principled realism'.[3]

Each of these major policy statements from the Trump administration reaffirms a shift in US policy that has been underway over the past decade, beginning well before Trump's election—a shift to strategic competition and increasing confrontation. The presentation of this policy may change to some extent under a Biden presidency, but the substance will not change until such time as Washington judges that the costs of competition outweigh the benefits of accepting China as a co-equal power. For the time being, a 'tolerance of greater bilateral friction' has become conventional wisdom.[4] Basing future foreign policy on the premise of conflict is what is to be expected from the dominant power which is being challenged. But it is quite another thing for a country like Australia, which is not a strategic rival of China's, and which is so utterly dependent on China for its economic wellbeing, to do so.

It is an act of faith, then, by Australia's foreign and security policy establishment, that following the US into strategic confrontation with China is in Australia's interests. It may well be so for the US, but it has not been demonstrated that it is equally so for Australia. China neither threatens Australia militarily nor its values. It has different values, but this is not in itself a threat to Australian values. Indeed, as seen from Chapter 4, on soft power, the CPC's efforts to project its values have proven counterproductive, not only in Australia but in most liberal democracies. At the same time that Beijing has had little or no success in undermining Australia's values, norms and institutions, its economic engagement has made an overwhelmingly significant contribution to Australia's security. Economic security is a cornerstone of national security.

Australia has willingly become a proxy strategic competitor to China, and the US position has broad support among Australia's security community.[5] It has also been argued that this could become the 'new, new normal' of Australia's relations with China. This would see a permanently adversarial association, with bilateral and multilateral cooperation severely limited and parts of the economic relationship regularly at risk.[6]

Unlike the US, China is overwhelmingly our biggest export market and trade partner, although contrary to popular views, it is still a relatively small investor when measured by the stock of FDI in Australia. In the new order, the US will deal with China more through bilateral negotiations than multilaterally. The US–China Phase 1 trade deal is a return to old fashioned managed trade. In the 2020 *United States Strategic Approach* document, the deal is welcomed as marking 'critical progress toward a more balanced trade relationship and a more level playing field for American workers and companies'.[7]

This is entirely outside of the rules-based international order under the WTO. No mention is made of multilateral processes or of respecting the interests of third countries such as Australia, who also happen to be staunch allies of the US and who will likely suffer loss of market access as a result. The WTO order was created to prevent managed trade such as this, which prevailed in the 1980s when the US was challenged economically by a rising Japan. Tellingly, the architect of the Reagan-era managed trade deals between the US and Japan, Robert Lighthizer, is the US Trade Representative.[8]

The US, through its refusal to join a consensus to appoint new members to the Appellate Body, the WTO's paramount dispute settlement adjudicator, has brought the system to its knees. It is a great irony that twenty-five years ago in the Uruguay Round of multilateral trade negotiations, it was the US that was the most active proponent of establishing an enforceable rules-based dispute settlement mechanism. Despite misleading information from the White House, the system has worked well for the US, which has had a 90 per cent success rate regarding 595 cases brought to the Appellate Body.[9]

A rules-based, multilateral trading system is the cornerstone of Australia's prosperity and therefore Australia's security. China will feel released from its obligations if the US disregards the rules and uses its own power to settle disputes, as it has done already with the unilateral imposition of steel and automobile tariffs, including on its Japanese, South Korean, Canadian and European allies. Weakening the rules-based trading order exposes countries to politically motivated exercises in economic coercion, in which China also has engaged with increasing frequency in recent years.

The contrast between the US and EU strategies for dealing with China are stark. Whereas the US approach is largely based on unilateral actions and confrontation, the EU emphasises bilateral and multilateral cooperation. Where there are challenges and concerns, many of which overlap those of the US in areas such as SOEs, industrial subsidies, predatory investments, forced technology transfer and cybersecurity, the EU's strategy focuses on how to strengthen its own domestic regulatory environment, hardening its own defences while identifying ways of working with China cooperatively.[10]

As an indicator of things to come in the new order, to protect the multilateral system from the unilateral exercise of power, Australia has joined with twelve other countries, including China, the EU, Japan and Canada, to put in place a new process for settling disputes in the WTO: the multi-party interim appeal arbitration arrangement (MPIA). The US is not a member.[11] It is another example of the bounded order that now prevails.[12] It meets the definition of having one great power in and one out of a multilateral grouping. The MPIA is based on an agreed set of rules and a vision that trade should be conducted within the framework of enforceable multilateral rules and disciplines.

On this occasion, Australia worked with a group of like-minded countries, which included China. This points to possibilities for future areas of cooperation to address common global problems. More usually, however, Australia has taken both a high profile and sometimes a leading role in confronting China. It had the most strident voice in the region over condemning China's rejection of the International Court of Arbitration's ruling over the South China Sea dispute.[13]

Although Australia has yet to support publicly US requests for it to join freedom of navigation operations (FONOPs) involving sailing within 12 nautical miles of reefs and atolls claimed by China in the South China Sea, regional neighbours including Japan, Singapore, New Zealand and India have made it clear that they will not participate in the US assembling an armada.[14] On this issue, Australia's position has been nuanced. It has been diplomatically coy about its intentions but has signalled to the US its reluctance to join in. Reports of the joint exercises in the South China Sea in February 2020 involving the HMAS *Parramatta* and USS *America* Expeditionary Strike Group did not mention FONOPs occurring. Joint FONOPs would be complicated to manage and involve considerable risk of accident if challenged. An Australian asset would be a softer target than a US one.

The implication for foreign policy of seeing China as a geo-political competitor is that Australia's relations with China are based on strategic mistrust. The tardiness with which Australia joined the AIIB; its refusal to participate formally in BRI activities; its strident position on the South China Sea; which is well ahead of like-minded countries in the region; it being the first of only a few countries to put a blanket ban on all aspects of Huawei's involvement in a local 5G network; its call for an international investigation into the origins of COVID-19, which was clearly directed at China and in which initially Australia had no company—all flow from an 'official' foreign policy assumption in Canberra that China is a strategic competitor. It is now ingrained in Canberra's world view that China does bad things and needs to be held accountable. Certainly, when China does behave badly, it should be held to account. However, Australia needs to be sure that China's bad behaviour goes against its own interests, and to then consider how best to levy a cost on this. Seldom, if ever, will that be by us acting alone or in the company of only the US. If we regard China as an enemy, it most certainly will become one.

The absence of a coherent policy framework saw Australia make a mess of its response to the China-initiated AIIB. China's proposal to create the AIIB grew largely out of its frustration at being unable to reform the Bretton Woods institutions of the IMF and World Bank, which reflected the distribution of economic power at the end of World War II, not as it was in the second decade of the twenty-first century, post the GFC. Australia was among the first developed countries China approached to seek support for the AIIB. Initially, the indications from the Abbott government were that Cabinet would support Australia's membership, but then the Obama administration took a hostile position to the AIIB and leant on Australia, as it did on Japan and Canada, to dissuade it from joining.[15] Former Obama administration assistant secretary of state for East Asia, Kurt Campbell—much admired by the Australian foreign policy and think tank establishment—believed Obama was wrong to have opposed the AIIB and advised that the US should itself join it.[16] So on matters of major strategic importance, when being guided by Washington, it is also necessary for Australian ministers to know from whom their instructions are coming.

Meanwhile, the UK and most other European nations soon joined the AIIB. Australia eventually did as well, after Luxembourg and before Norway, hardly big players in the Asia–Pacific region. In the process, we missed the early mover advantage that would have made us a much more influential member, one that could help shape the bank's early development. The weakness of Australia's position was caught in the contradictory argument that we did not want to join so as to ensure that the AIIB was well designed, as if not being on the inside somehow gave us more influence.

A similar situation arose in Australia's policy response towards the BRI. Despite the BRI's limitations, including difficulties in execution, local government and community backlash against debt and environmental concerns, overreach and an absence of policy coherence, and the associated corruption and lack of transparency, still it is viewed as a threat to US global leadership. Possibly nowhere more than in Canberra has this struggle been so emphatically joined.

In 2016, during Malcolm Turnbull's first visit to China as prime minister, President Xi said China wished to support the Australian Government's policy priorities for northern Australia and con-tribute to infrastructure there under the BRI. He was proposing cooperative projects that were aligned with Canberra's priorities. Extraordinarily, the prime minister's press release made no mention of this singular initiative to advance a key policy priority of the Australian Government.[17]

Most countries are sensitive about maintaining their independ-ence, and most have alternative sources of funding for infrastructure projects. A number of countries are re-evaluating and questioning various projects that are underway or being contemplated as BRI projects. Inevitably, as Australia should do, BRI projects will be assessed on their merits, particularly their commercial strengths.

Although much is said about China's 'debt diplomacy', it is more common for Beijing to renegotiate loans or scale back the size of projects as requested by recipient countries. A recent study of BRI debt renegotiations found only one case out of forty where a debt-for-equity swap occurred.[18] That was the Hambantota Port in Sri Lanka, which has received extensive media coverage and has been highly divisive within Sri Lanka, doing China no favours. The investment has become captive to local politics.[19]

In discussions of the strategic threat posed by the BRI, little attention is given to whether or not it is capable of being executed in ways that will deliver on its objectives and strategic intentions, be they real or imagined. We have seen that ill-conceived and hastily implemented investments have led to resistance and pushback in recipient countries, and accordingly, the BRI has done little to advance China's soft power. Research by Evelyn Goh on East Asia shows that China, like all states, brings to bear the full armoury of its statecraft purposefully to

> coerce, induce, or persuade others to behave in ways that help achieve Chinese goals. But whether and the extent to which it succeeds is determined as much by the political context and decision-making processes of the target states …[20]

Australian foreign and strategic policy needs to be better informed about the real capacity to implement, rather than jumping at shadows. In most cases, grand initiatives like the BRI can be expected to over-promise and under-deliver.

In its purposeful coolness towards the BRI, Australia has again demonstratively aligned itself with the US and Japan, as it initially did over membership of the AIIB. Like the AIIB, the BRI is another means by which China is attempting to shape the new order. It is perfectly rational for a rising power like China, especially given its immense economic weight and geographic position, to seek to do this.

Typically, the security realms in Canberra and Washington see the BRI's purpose as making 'China dominant in the Indo-Pacific and Eurasia, and a global power at least on par with the United States, perhaps even at the centre of a new world order'.[21] The BRI is central to China's grand strategy but is limited in its design and execution. As such, the purported threat to Australia's national interests is much overstated.

The Quad—Containment by Any Other Name

The second leg of Australia's foreign policy in the new order is the Quadrilateral Security Dialogue. The Quad is a strange entity. Until recently, its proponents hardly dared to speak its name, let alone explain its purpose and objectives, and they met only on the margins of other international forums. Now it has crept out of the shadows and taken on a more formalised structure, with senior officials and ministerial meetings, together with statements being issued.[22]

The Quad grew out of the capability and cooperation demonstrated by the four participating countries—Australia, the US, Japan and India—in response to the 2004 Boxing Day tsunami disaster relief efforts. As a grouping with geopolitical intent, it was first proposed by Shinzo Abe in 2005, during his campaign for the Liberal Democratic Party leadership, before he became Japan's prime minister in 2006. In its original formulation it was unambiguously about balancing China (if not 'containing' it) and was pointedly ideological, describing itself as a 'Dialogue of Democracies'. Abe had also referred to it as a 'concert of democracies'.[23]

Abe wanted to construct an 'Arc of Prosperity and Freedom' around the 'outer rim of the Eurasian Continent'. As observed by the *Hindustan Times*, 'in practice this arc—which [bore] no relationship to [Eurasia's] actual geometric shape—skirts almost entirely along the borders of China and Russia'. Earlier, the George W Bush administration began increasingly to speak of India as part of a 'values-based relationship' surrounding China.[24]

By 2006, the longer-term implications of the disastrous US-led invasion of Iraq and the failures in Afghanistan had not yet begun to sink in among the US' key allies. The White House under Bush and vice president Dick Cheney was smitten with hubris. Cheney, in particular, latched onto Abe's Quad proposal and prime minister John Howard quickly followed with Australia's support. DFAT was divided internally, with some arguing the proposal was disruptive, and being Japan-led it was clearly intended to be used as an instrument in that country's rivalry with a rapidly growing China. It was also curious that other robust democracies in the region, such as South Korea, the Philippines and New Zealand, were not included.

At the time, the secretary of DFAT, Ashton Calvert, a fluent Japanese speaker with three postings in Tokyo under his belt, including as ambassador, was staunchly opposed to the Quad and suspicious of Japan's motives. Once Calvert retired to take up highly prized directorships with Rio Tinto and Woodside, the department's view shifted to support the proposal, but still without a lot of enthusiasm. This was essentially the same as in Washington and New Delhi, where foreign ministries offered lukewarm responses but were being pushed along by the enthusiasm of their political masters.

The reluctant Indian position then, as it does today, underscores the complex set of considerations that New Delhi has to weigh up in balancing its relations with China and the US. At the time Abe first proposed the Quad, India was also attempting to become part of the Nuclear Suppliers Group, in order to obtain nuclear technology without becoming a member of the Non-Proliferation Treaty (NPT). For New Delhi, the stakes were high as it tried to balance several difficult and competing policy priorities. The Bush administration removed restrictions on sales of nuclear materials to India in 2008, and in 2011, under pressure from the US, the Gillard government in Australia removed the Labor Party's longstanding ban on selling uranium to India.[25]

The Quad was part of a wider conversation over how to manage China's rise, which was also, of course, of major concern to New Delhi. Aware of China's deep unhappiness over the Quad, but needing the US to support it joining the Nuclear Suppliers Group without joining the NPT, India indicated tepid support for the Quad while advising China of its reservations and doing as little as possible to support it.[26]

Following the inaugural meeting of low-level officials on the margin of an ASEAN-plus meeting in May 2007, China made firm representations to all participants about what it saw as an attempt to introduce 'ideological divisions' into the Asia-Pacific region.[27] In 2008, Indian prime minister Manmohan Singh conceded this, saying that India did not want to be part of the 'so-called contain China effort', adding that in any event the Quad 'never got going'.[28] Prime minister Singh then set out the unique circumstances in which India must develop its China policy, and explained why trying to enlist India in the cause of balancing China, let alone 'buck-passing' to it, is doomed to fail. He observed that 'China is [India's] largest neighbour and in many ways engagement with China is an imperative-necessity [sic]'.[29]

With the sudden end of Abe's short-lived first tenure as Japan's prime minister in September 2007, interest in the Quad quickly ebbed. Early in its term, the Rudd government quit the Quad. This was for substantive policy reasons: the group's strategic intent was unclear, and statements from Abe suggested a 'strategy of graduation' to higher levels of strategic cooperation; Japan's new prime minister, Yasuo Fukuda, had little interest in it and began a period of rapprochement with Beijing; as the Quad was directed at China as a form of external balance, Rudd did not want to make Australia's relations with China hostage to the future of Japan–China relations; and India and the US both evinced little interest in it.[30]

Unfortunately, the new and inexperienced but over-confident Rudd government made the announcement in the worst possible circumstances. Then foreign minister Stephen Smith stood next to Chinese Foreign Minister Yang Jiechi at a joint press conference in Parliament House and announced that Australia was leaving the Quad. The optics of the Australian Government having caved into pressure from China were terrible, notwithstanding the substantive merits of the decision. The government became an easy target for attacks by sections of the media and China-hawk think tanks, which maintained that it was soft on China. This impression was further compounded by prime minister Rudd's ill-judged decision to go to China on his first trip to East Asia and refusing to visit Japan. For the remainder of the Rudd government's term in office, great effort was directed at placating Japan and demonstrating that the government was *not* soft on China.

Ten years later, with Prime Minister Abe back in power and a hardening of geostrategic circumstances, the Turnbull government enthusiastically associated itself with the revamped Quad. Abe has consistently stressed the ideological element of the group, describing it in 2012 as 'the diamond of democracy'.[31] This time round, Quad 2.0 may well be 'more compelling' than Quad 1.0 in view of China's greater foreign policy assertiveness under Xi Jinping, especially in the South China Sea and in competition for influence via the BRI.[32]

In January 2018, in an interview with Angus Grigg of the *Australian Financial Review* as a preview of his forthcoming trip to Australia, Prime Minister Abe set out an expansive foreign policy agenda for the Quad which included regional infrastructure development and even maritime security, including naval cooperation.[33] Inevitably, such talk creates suspicion and leads to speculation. More likely, Quad 2.0, like its predecessor, comprises four partners in bed together, all dreaming different dreams.[34]

Apart from being 'one of the most poorly explained concepts in recent strategic memory', a key difficulty for Australia with the Quad is that three of the members are strategic rivals of China, whereas Australia, at least publicly, is not.[35] Two members—India and Japan—also have active border disputes with China. Moreover, other major democracies in the region, which also are not China's strategic rivals, such as South Korea, Philippines and Indonesia, are not included. It is therefore disingenuous to try to pass off the Quad as merely a discussion group of like-minded countries sharing views on common problems and not directed at China.[36]

Beijing was perplexed as to why Australia would be party to the Quad when it had been a leader in promoting deeper regional integration through APEC and was an enthusiastic supporter of the ASEAN Regional Forum and various ASEAN-plus mechanisms. Japan's motivation was clear to Beijing, while the US' was consistent with the neo-conservative voices in Washington urging containment of China. As ever, views in Washington differed, but vice president Cheney's prevailed in favour of the Quad.[37] India joining was also in keeping with its policy of opportunistically balancing China and the US to sustain multipolarity, on this occasion leaning against China.[38]

Australia seemed an unlikely front-running proponent. While demurring over the Quad's strategic intent, Australia is more dependent economically on China than other Quad members; it has no territorial or historical outstanding disputes with China; and in its public policy pronouncements, such as the *2017 Foreign Policy White Paper*, it says it seeks a cooperative relationship with China. Containment and cooperation seem oddly contradictory policies.

If Beijing's strategic planners were concerned about the Quad and its strategic intent to balance, not only did Abe's comments give them more cause for concern, but in 2007, Australia for the first and only time participated in the Malabar naval exercises with India, the US and Japan, in a specially convened operation also involving Singapore.[39] Since its one-time involvement in the exercises, Australia has been advocating to become a permanent participant of the Malabar exercises, thereby establishing the Quad's military dimension. India has consistently rebuffed Australia's efforts to join. While India is of course highly sensitive to Chinese anxieties, New Delhi also is still reluctant to send a message that the Quad has adopted a formal defence component to its activities.[40] This is more about strategic messaging than substance, as each Quad member's defence establishments interact bilaterally and trilaterally during the course of any one year.

Canberra nevertheless continues to dissemble on its strategic ambitions for the Quad. Early in 2020, the outgoing Australian high commissioner to Delhi, Harinder Sidhu, in a farewell interview with *The Economic Times*, said that while Australia would accept an invitation from India to participate in the Malabar exercises whenever that should be extended, four-power naval exercises 'should not be construed as a Quadrilateral military formation … it is quite unremarkable … we do military exercises in all kinds of permutations …'. The high commissioner had evidently been schooled in the Sir Humphrey Appleby art of dissembling, as portrayed in the British TV comedy *Yes Minister*.[41]

DFAT should update its talking points. Canberra has been seeking to elevate the Quad as a form of strategic signalling to Beijing. It has supported the upgrading of Quad meetings to the foreign minister level. It has been 'pushing hard to send a strong Quad military message to China'.[42] But no amount of spin will change Beijing's view that the Quad is inimical to China's interests and that Australia's behaviour is hostile towards China. The semi-official, bellicose *Global Times* has dubbed the Quad an 'Asian NATO', the implication being that it has been formed against the threat of China.[43] It may seem preposterous in Canberra, but Beijing does in fact feel threatened by the US. Japan's invasion and occupation of China are still in living memory. And China has a longstanding military conflict with India over disputed borders which in June 2020 resulted in the first military deaths in fifty years at the border point in the Galwan Valley in the high Himalayas.

India's reticence about including Australia in the Malabar exercises and elevating the Quad to a military arrangement, in addition to its existing activities, might have started changing after the Quad foreign ministers' meeting that was held on the margins of the UN General Assembly in New York on 26 September 2019. Statements from the participants reported on joint efforts to support infrastructure development in the region and cooperation on counter terrorism, development finance, maritime security and disaster response.[44]

A month later, US Secretary of State Mike Pompeo provided greater clarity on the Quad's purpose. He confirmed that the US was seeking not just to 'contain' China but to 'reduce its current global position'.[45] He affirmed that Washington viewed the Quad as a useful tool for achieving that policy objective.[46] As has become a characteristic of the Trump administration's policy unsteadiness, only a few months earlier, the head of the US Indo-Pacific Command had suggested shelving the Quad.[47] It is unlikely that other Quad members would have been consulted in advance of Pompeo's declaration of intent for the Quad. It may, however, have been a publicly undisclosed subject discussed in New York.

Pompeo has greatly added to Australia's difficulty in managing its relations with Beijing and Washington, and in sustaining the fiction that it does not view China as a strategic competitor. As one analyst recently argued: 'If Australia cannot completely and unambiguously disassociate itself from Pompeo's characterization of the Quad, and continues to participate in Quad meetings, then it is tacitly supporting its newly revealed purpose'.[48] This is occurring at a time when the US is hinting at the placement of strategic bombers and missiles on Australian territory.[49]

Australia also has been actively supporting the US-initiated Blue Dot Network, which it hopes will also become a Quad initiative that balances, to some extent, China's BRI in the region. The BDN was officially launched in November 2019 at the Indo-Pacific Business

Forum during the Bangkok ASEAN Summit, and currently involves only the US, Japan and Australia. The BDN is to provide a form of international certification for infrastructure projects in developing countries. But its public sector funding looks anaemic, with the US having committed US$60 billion, and Australia A$1 billion, mainly for South Pacific programs, alongside Japan having, since 2016, a regional investment fund of US$200 billion. It is hoped to leverage private–public investments, but the low level of private sector appetite in the region for infrastructure investment suggests that the BDN is unlikely to mobilise sufficient funds to compete with the BRI, the current commitments of which are estimated to be US$1 trillion.[50] The Asian Development Bank (ADB) estimates that Asia will need to invest US$1.7 trillion per annum over the next decade to support existing levels of development and to address climate change.[51] It has already been criticised for seeking to impose First World standards and approaches, which will only bring long-term benefits at a future time, when developing countries have more immediate needs.[52]

The BDN is presented as a market-based, transparent alternative to the BRI for identifying, certifying and funding infrastructure projects, but its real purpose is geo-economic. The BDN is unlikely to go beyond a vision statement, especially in a post–COVID-19 world where its donors will face unexpectedly massive fiscal budget deficits well into the future. Yet it is pitched in direct competition to the BRI and, as such, further heightens strategic tension with China.

China has responded predictably, with the *Global Times* declaring that the BDN is 'delusional' and 'doomed to failure', and is intended to 'divide the region' and 'force other countries to take sides'.[53] Presenting the BDN as being in opposition to the BRI—and the fact that it is led by three of the Quad members—is likely to 'turn countries off' engaging with it, as they will inevitably feel as if they are being asked to choose between China and the US.[54] India as a Quad member has itself proved difficult to attract to the BDN. Highlighting the strategic thrust of the initiative, President Trump, during his February 2020 visit to India, sought unsuccessfully to have Prime Minister Narendra Modi associate himself with the BDN.[55] India's caution, as it has exercised regarding the inclusion of Australia in the Malabar naval exercises, points to its ongoing ambivalence to being too closely aligned with other Quad members' activities that are directed too unambiguously against China.

Participating in the Quad also requires the heroic assumption that other members' relations with China will not change to Australia's disadvantage. Japan had warm relations with China throughout the 1980s. Indeed, at the time of the Tiananmen Square killings, among the developed countries, Japan was the most reluctant to apply sanctions, despite urgings from the US. It is an act of faith on the Australian side that the current tensions in the China–Japan relationship will continue, notwithstanding all the territorial, strategic and historical difficulties they share. A charm offensive by China, or a new Japanese prime minister, could see Japan quickly lose interest in the Quad—since 2019, in fact, Japan and China have been recalibrating their relations. Quad membership is also a long way down Delhi's list of priorities, and besides, it would hardly impact on its relations with China. The two countries' strategic competition in the Indian Ocean and their land border disputes transcend the Quad.[56]

In the case of the US, as the old adage goes, 'Big powers do what they will and the rest do what they can'. Membership of the Quad costs the US nothing, and is only as enduring as US interest in it. It is worth recalling that no US ally was consulted when Kissinger went to Beijing in 1971, including those like Australia whose troops were dying in Vietnam. As Trump has shown to allies in the Americas, Europe and East Asia. US foreign policy can turn on a coin. It is important for Australia also to recognise that the interests of others in the Quad can change unpredictably.

The danger with the Quad is that China will respond to what it sees as a potential threat, thus hardening Thucydides' Trap. This is the classic example of the security dilemma. The Quad elevates China's sense of strategic vulnerability and so, rather than encouraging China to step back, it is likely to achieve the exact opposite.[57]

It could be argued that, in the decade when the Quad was not meeting, China continued to assert itself in the South China Sea and rapidly built its offensive naval and air power capacities. But it also had other provocations, from Beijing's perspective, such as the Pivot to

Asia, associated troop deployments, extended and expanded military exercises involving regional states beyond traditional formal allies, and a shift in US doctrine from China engagement to containment.[58]

Proponents of the Quad long presented it as just another forum for dialogue between the participants. It was said to be one of any number of 'novel strategic dialogues' involving the US and regional interlocutors. It was asserted that the Quad 'is not about that much-abused word "containment"' and that '[n]o government advocates containment of China'.[59] Secretary of State Pompeo's ambitious and aggressive agenda for the Quad to be enlisted in containing China has finally put paid to that comforting assertion. Ambiguity about the Quad's reason for existence has now been replaced by Pompeo's directness.

Although Prime Minister Abe's original conception of the Quad was containment of China, neither Japan nor India will welcome being coopted into an arrangement with such pointed objectives as Pompeo has explained. Each country has its own complex calculations to make in weighing their long-term interests in relations with China. The clarity of purpose which Pompeo has brought to the Quad may see it dissipate, as none of the other participants would want to be seen to be actively working to contain China. Their complex, multifaceted relationships with China cannot be reduced to being only its competitor.[60] It was particularly noteworthy that in late July 2020 in the highly publicised sail through the South China Sea led by a US carrier group, Australia deployed five ships while Japan, with a much larger navy than Australia, contributed only one.

The Indo-Pacific

For some years, Australian and US security analysts have sought to shift and broaden the primary strategic focus from East Asia to the Indo-Pacific. East Asia has long been the central concern of Asia-Pacific security. With China's emergence as the dominant regional power, and its increasing military activity in the Indian Ocean, the concept of Indo-Pacific security has become widely adopted. The intention, again, is to draw India into regional security to balance China.

Australia has become a champion of the Indo-Pacific region as a strategic concept rather than the longstanding and more understandable Asia-Pacific region. The former has quickly become common parlance among politicians and strategic analysts, especially since President Trump began using it in 2017. Trump's former national security adviser, John Bolton, has described the phrase 'Free and Open Indo-Pacific' as being a 'bumper sticker, not a strategy'.[61]

India, however, stands apart from East Asia, as we shall discuss below. As such, the Indo-Pacific is a construct by defence and strategic policy analysts with little operational content. It makes about as much practical sense as would an Atlanto-Pacific concept, albeit it works for Australia as it uniquely has both extensive Pacific and Indian ocean coastlines. Nevertheless, it has achieved wide buy-in from the US, regional governments, and India itself. To underscore the strategic change in emphasis, the United States Pacific Command in May 2018 was renamed the United States Indo-Pacific Command— although its reach extends only to the west coast of India, whereas Australia views the region as extending to the east coast of Africa.

The Indo-Pacific accords well with the views of the self-proclaimed 'offensive realist' strategic analyst John Mearsheimer.[62] Mearsheimer has proposed the concept of 'buck-passing' in international relations theory. It holds that whenever a new power emerges, existing powers will try to encourage someone else to balance it. Mearsheimer argues that the balancing of a new power is inevitable; it's just a matter of who does it.[63] And with the Indo-Pacific concept, Australia and the US are trying to 'pass the buck' to India.

India is a most unpromising candidate to balance China because of its own security priorities, and its long history post-independence of pursuing a non-aligned foreign policy. India does have its own security interests to manage with China, but these do not involve competing for influence in East Asia. India has never been part of East Asian security concerns. Economic interests would be expected to drive security concerns and India has relatively few economic interests in East Asia apart from the Indian diaspora throughout South-East Asia. It is much less economically integrated with East Asia through trade and investment than is the Asia-Pacific itself.

The Middle East, Africa and Europe are of much greater economic interest to India.

India's trade with the major economies of East Asia has hardly changed over the past decade (see Figure 10). Having grown strongly during the 2000s along with its own economic reforms and rapid growth in the region, India's exports to East Asia peaked in 2011 and by 2018 had still not fully recovered. Meanwhile, its imports continued to grow strongly, with the bilateral trade deficit widening throughout the period. In East Asia, China is by far the biggest market and main source of imports for India (see Figure 11).

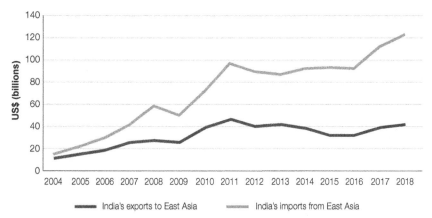

Figure 10. India's Trade with East Asia, 2004–18
Note: East Asia comprises China, Hong Kong, Taiwan, Japan and South Korea.
Source: India's Department for Promotion of Industry and Internal Trade, various years

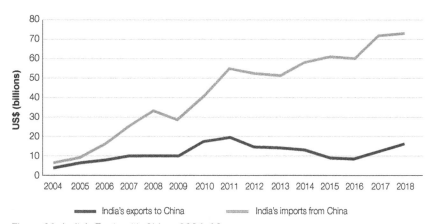

Figure 11. India's Trade with China, 2004–18
Source: India's Department for Promotion of Industry and Internal Trade, various years

In 2018, China and Hong Kong together accounted for 70 per cent of India's exports to the main economies of East Asia. India's total trade with Japan (see Figure 12) was 58 per cent of China and Hong Kong's combined, and with South Korea it was 30 per cent.

India's exports to Europe began to grow more strongly again from 2015, after having peaked in 2010 (see Figure 13). In 2018, India's exports to Europe were almost 50 per cent greater than to the main East Asian economies and 75 per cent greater than to China. Of the individual European markets, the UK, Germany and the

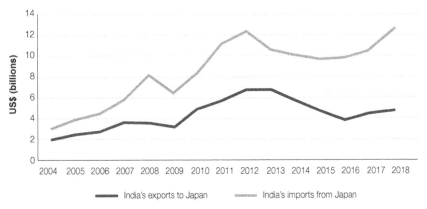

Figure 12. India's Trade with Japan, 2004–18
Source: India's Department for Promotion of Industry and Internal Trade, various years

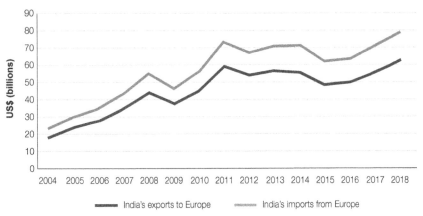

Figure 13. India's Trade with Europe, 2004–18
Source: India's Department for Promotion of Industry and Internal Trade, various years

Netherlands each accounted for about 15 per cent of India's exports in 2018.

Notwithstanding the relative smallness of export markets in the Middle East, in 2018, Indian exports there were almost the same size as to Europe, $62 billion compared with $61 billion, and significantly greater than to East Asia.

Underlying the relative lack of economic integration of India with East Asia, India's combined exports to Europe and the Middle East in 2018 were nearly three times as great as to East Asia. Acknowledging that India's imports from the Middle East are inflated by its heavy dependence on oil and refined petroleum products sourced from there, imports from Europe and the Middle East combined were some 40 per cent higher than from East Asia, where China accounted for about 50 per cent of India's total imports.

In terms of total trade flows, India overwhelmingly looks west to the Middle East (see Figure 14) and beyond that to Europe. In 2018, East Asia accounted for less than 50 per cent of total trade with Europe and the Middle East. The picture is the same for FDI, with Europe dominating FDI flow to India, accounting for more than East Asia and the Middle East combined. Japanese FDI in India peaked in 2016 around the time of high-level visits by the countries' respective leaders but has been declining since (see Figure 15).

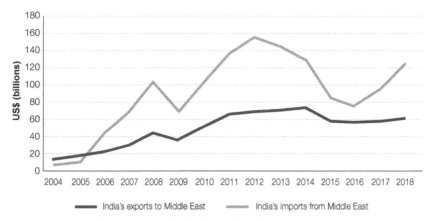

Figure 14. India's Trade with the Middle East, 2004–18
Source: India's Department for Promotion of Industry and Internal Trade, various years

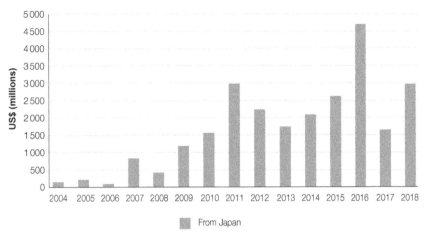

Figure 15. India's FDI Inflow from Japan, 2004–18
Source: India's Department for Promotion of Industry and Internal Trade, various years

In 2018, FDI from Japan, at around $3 billion, was less than FDI from the Netherlands alone, which invested $4 billion.[64]

For its security, India also looks mainly west, but to Pakistan where, since partition in 1947, it has faced its most severe security challenges. Kashmir remains contested territory between India and Pakistan, with no apparent path towards resolution. Both are nuclear armed states and support opposing sides in Afghanistan.

India's disputes with China in several places along its Himalayan border are not part of East Asian security. If anything, this dispute belongs to Central Asian security concerns. When military clashes occur between India and China at points on the disputed borders, they receive a lot of domestic and international attention but India and China have contained these episodes to minor skirmishes. They have not led to full military conflict since the Sino-Indian War in 1962. The June 2020 clash in the Galwan Valley may mark a departure from the previous management of border disputes, but international opinion regards China as the aggressor, and the incident has done substantial harm to China's standing, with little appreciable gain.[65]

India's other major security interest with China is ensuring its dominance in the Indian Ocean. It is here that proponents of the

Indo-Pacific believe that India can be brought in to play a checking role against China. China's port constructions in the Indian Ocean, notably Gwadar in Pakistan and Hambantota in Sri Lanka, have been colourfully described as China's 'string of pearls'. Gwadar and Hambantota predate the BRI, and whether they are to be used for military purposes remains to be seen.[66]

Gwadar and perhaps the other 'pearls' arise from local conditions creating opportunities. China's strategy for the Indian Ocean is not the unrealistic and unrealisable one of challenging Indian primacy but to ensure that it can protect and defend its vital shipping lanes, especially to keep supplies of crude oil flowing. Even if China's 'pearls' are of military value, they are unlikely to challenge India's dominance of the Indian Ocean by virtue of India's geographic presence. India, of course, does not welcome what China is doing, but it will most likely continue to pursue its security through its traditional approach of vigorous self-reliance and maintaining maximum flexibility to form temporary alliances as its interests dictate.

India and China could well reach a tacit understanding that, in view of their limited interests in each other's domains, they will avoid 'intruding strategically into the other's backyard'.[67] As Hugh White points out, rather than joining a grand coalition against China in the Indo-Pacific, India is more likely 'to cut a deal' with China to divide the Indo-Pacific region between them. If that were to occur, it would be a most difficult and challenging position for Australia to find itself in, akin to Mongolia's contemporary juggling of Russia and China.[68]

India and China may well reach a grand bargain, whereby they each allow the other to control their respective littorals. It has been noted that China has been respectful towards Indian interests in the Bay of Bengal and to India challenging China's activities in the South China Sea. This could have far-reaching implications for the Quad's cohesion and for the entire Indo-Pacific project.[69]

India has resisted formal alliance arrangements, although during the Cold War it did lean towards the Soviet Union, including for procuring military equipment—Russia is still an important supplier of advanced arms to India. India has long been an observer at the Chinese-initiated SCO, formally established in 2003; in 2017, together with Pakistan, it became a formal member. The organisation's stated purpose was to stymie the rise of violent fundamentalism in Central Asia, but from the beginning, the SCO was conceived of as, and continues to be, a grouping that consciously stands apart from arrangements created and led by the West.[70] It has been described as an 'alliance of non-western civilisations, comprising Chinese, Russian, Muslim, Hindu and Buddhist'.[71] In many ways, it marks the first institutional innovation of the bounded new order, one that was conceived of and created by China. It remains to be seen if India will participate in SCO's regular joint military exercises.

Significantly, India's membership of the SCO involves a much more formal, high-level and substantive commitment than either to the Quad or to the vague notion of the Indo-Pacific. If anything, this underscores the key point that India sees its security and its relations with China through very different lenses than Canberra or Washington. India's joining the SCO underlines both its foreign policy flexibility and its unwillingness to be enlisted in the cause of balancing China, as US and Australian strategic policy advisers hope. It is as if Australia has been sleepwalking into the new order. Far from resisting China's efforts at recasting the order, India has been an active participant in this. In addition to the SCO, with an explicit military dimension, India was a founding member of the BRICS Development Bank. When the AIIB was established, it joined immediately, and it became the second-biggest contributor of funds after China, despite at the time experiencing heightened border tensions with that country.

There are two major areas of strategic contest in the world today, and these are likely to remain so for any sensible planning horizon. One is East Asia, with the potential for conflict around the Korean Peninsula, Taiwan Strait, South China Sea and Sea of Japan, along with civil upheaval in Hong Kong which may draw in the international community. The second is Eurasia, especially Central Asia, where China and Russia are competing and where Russia is threatening Europe's eastern edges.

Compared with these areas of acute and persistent strategic competition, the Indian Ocean presents few challenges that the dominant power, India, will not be able to manage without involving the international community, and no issues over which the international community would become involved via security or other treaty-level alliances. India's relations and conflicts both with Pakistan and China have over seventy years not been internationalised.

For Australia and the US, bringing India into East Asian security was seen as 'bookending [their] Asian defense policy with two major powers with shared democratic values' in opposition to China.[72] Looking past India's deeply held non-aligned approach to security, which has in the past seen it draw close to the Soviet Union when it felt it needed options beyond the US, the wishful thinking has been that China's rise will so challenge India that it will seek security relations with the US and its allies. While at times such closeness would be of value to India, it will seek to manage its relations with China in its own way.

As Allan Gyngell argues, 'fear of abandonment' lies deep within Australia's foreign policy and public attitudes to its place in the world. Quoting Watkin Tench from the First Fleet, which arrived in Sydney Cove in 1788, Gyngell writes that 'every morning from daylight until the sun sunk did we sweep the horizon, in the hope of seeing a sail'.[73]

After the British Empire, then Pax Americana, Australia now finds itself again having to confront its existential fear of abandonment, and 'how this small group of people [can] protect an audacious claim to a vast continent'.[74] Gyngell is writing of the early colonists, but notwithstanding the tremendous achievements of Australians in generating great wealth and culture from the continent, the anxiety remains today. Australia is in search of a grand strategy for the new order. AUKUS created Sept. 2021

Containment by military alliance

CHAPTER 6

STRATEGIES FOR THE NEW WORLD ORDER

Australia's strategic objective should be a stable and prosperous region in which all countries' voices can be heard within a framework of agreed rules. It has long been a working assumption of Australian foreign policy that China's stability is central to that. Australian interests are best served by a successful China, engaging constructively in the region. Australia should seek friendly relations with China, not as an end in itself but as a means of protecting and advancing Australia's interests. For its part, China seeks regime survival, territorial integrity and recognition of the legitimacy of interests.

The time has come for Australia's foreign and strategic policy to be based on a contemporary understanding of how profoundly the world order has been changed by China's inexorable rise. Barring political implosion in China, which is always *possible* but still not highly *probable*, despite Xi Jinping's increasingly authoritarian control of domestic politics, it is likely that China's ascendency will continue for many more years. China is also now the dominant power in East Asia. But with substantial US presence in the region, an immensely powerful Japan, and few friends and no allies, it is unlikely to become a regional hegemon and pose any threat to Australia's security. Indeed, as China will remain Australia's most important market for as far as the eye can see, it will continue to make the biggest contribution to Australia's economic security, which of course is the cornerstone of national security. Australian policymakers will need to navigate the new bounded multipolar order with great skill.

Failure to appreciate the new reality in which Australia finds itself has led to several strategic miscalculations, each of which is based on the premise of a Chinese threat to Australia's national interests and hence the assumption that strategic competition with China is Australia's only sensible policy option. As discussed in the following section, several of these are likely to lead to strategic disappointment. An alternative policy agenda is then suggested in the rest of this chapter, including a ten-point framework of an Australian grand strategy for the new order.

Strategic Miscalculations

Australia's policy of the past four years, of joining the US in competition with China, has been a strategic miscalculation. It is dependent on the US' continued willingness and capacity to lead the old global order, which, in any event, has now been eclipsed by the return to a multipolar order. Australia and the US have sought to broaden strategic competition through the Quad and more recently the Indo-Pacific. As both concepts have balancing China as their strategic purpose, and China views them as seeking to contain it, they effectively require other countries in the region to take sides. Most, of course, will avoid doing this, or they will lean towards China because of its economic importance.

To the extent that the US is viewed by the region as being in relative decline, it will not be able to lead. Australia's move to align itself so closely with the US in strategic competition with China contributes to mistrust and suspicion, and it makes regional cooperation on issues of common security more difficult to achieve. It works against one of Australia's core strategic objectives, notably regional stability, and diminishes Australia's voice in the region.

It is not possible for Australia to provide regional leadership if it is unable to engage directly with China at the highest political levels. Moreover, it will be taken less seriously and be less respected by regional partners if it is not able to manage its relations with China. Strategic cooperation rather than US-led strategic competition with

China offers not only the most constructive means by which to protect and advance Australia's interests in the region, it is also the most realistic in view of China's regional weight and influence.

Pacific Pushback

In 2016, Canberra added the 'Pacific Step up', a stepping-up of engagement, to policies intended to counter Chinese influence in the western Pacific, traditionally regarded as an area of influence of Australia and New Zealand.[1] This was a knee-jerk reaction to perceived fears that China would establish some sort of naval facility in the area. China would probably like to do that, but what it would mean for Australian security is unclear. The Pacific Ocean is very large, and its smaller islands are a long way away from its mainland shores. These concerns about naval bases being established by potential adversaries seem to belong to outdated textbooks on warfare.

The increased attention paid by Australia to the Pacific is welcome, but doing it in this way invites Pacific island states to draw China and Australia into bidding contests for projects and influence.[2] If anything, it will feed the cynicism of Pacific islanders towards Australia over what they see as Australia's inaction on climate change—rightly or wrongly, climate change and rising sea levels, not China's presence in the region, are seen by Pacific island states as the existential threat. Shortly after the 2019 Pacific Islands Forum meeting in Tuvalu, at which Prime Minister Morrison was criticised over Australia's climate change policies, Kiribati and the Solomon Islands switched diplomatic recognition from Taipei to Beijing. As if to make a strong diplomatic point to Australia and the US, this occurred on the eve of the Australian prime minister's visit to Washington.[3] The Solomons also joined the BRI. Australia would be better served by working with, rather than against, China in the Pacific, but for that it would require cooperative relations between Canberra and Beijing.

Wishful Thinking on India

Similarly, Chinese naval expansion in the Indian Ocean is unlikely to threaten India's pre-eminence there, as it would involve a considerable stretching of resources and capacity. The Indian Ocean and land borders with Pakistan and China will continue to hold India's attention, but it has relatively minor economic and hence security interests in East Asia, just as Australia has relatively few interests in the Indian Ocean.

As Peter Varghese, one of Australia's foremost proponents of the Indo-Pacific concept, said in a report to the Australian Government, 'as a single strategic system it is very much a work in progress. It is both an act of imagination and a recognition of an emerging structural shift in [Australia's] strategic environment'.[4] Varghese makes the point that the Indo-Pacific as a 'coherent strategic system ... is a long way off'. This awaits a time when India's 'strategic and economic interests draw her into acting' as a strategic player in the Asia-Pacific. The Indo-Pacific as a coherent strategic reality as distinct from a concept is likely to be illusory, or wishful thinking. It is true, as Varghese argues, that Australia would be more comfortable in an order where India is an important player, notwithstanding its reluctance to pursue human rights agendas or advocate for democracy.[5]

East Asia the Main Game for Australia

Australia's strategy will need to remain, as in the past, focused on East Asia, where most threats are to be found. North Korea remains the most volatile problem, but territorial disputes between China and Japan, and Russia and Japan, also need careful management. The potential for China–Taiwan conflict, though still remote, has been elevated by the re-election as president in January 2020 of DPP leader Tsai Ing-wen. In an address to the NPC meeting in May 2020, Premier Li Keqiang did not use the longstanding formula of 'peaceful reunification', instead referring only to 'reunification'.[6] How neighbouring states can find a stable accommodation with China over the South China Sea is also a pressing matter.

US security doctrines typically come and go with each new administration. The Pivot was Obama's and was enthusiastically embraced by both sides of Australian politics. But as often is the case with such policy pronouncements, it underachieved. It was replaced by the Trump administration's Indo-Pacific concept. While a Joe Biden administration is likely to continue Trump's policy of strategic confrontation with China, it would be wise for Australian foreign policy to be alert to the prospect of a major shift in US strategic positioning.

Approaching a Bounded, Multipolar World Order

Strategy also requires an accurate appreciation of others' strengths and vulnerabilities. China's grand strategy derives from a position of weakness. As argued in previous chapters, China is a highly constrained superpower. It is Prometheus bound by limits of geography, history, global resource dependency, and its party-state system of political and social organisation, which, through the Party's narrative, constricts its deployment of soft power. China has no military alliances and, arguably, no reliable friends of strategic moment, except perhaps Pakistan, which has nuclear weapons.

Absolute size of population, economic weight and, perhaps, technological strength will sustain China's leading role. It has constructed a bounded order and has shown considerable entrepreneurship in institutional formation, with examples that include the SCO, New Development Bank, BRI Fund, AIIB and increasingly institutionalised elements of the BRI. At the same time, China has lifted its engagement with existing multilateral institutions such as the UN, WTO and the World Bank, where its interests can be advanced. In response to criticism and pushback on elements of the BRI and ODA funding, Beijing has begun to explore how to work with multilateral institutions to improve transparency, accountability and effectiveness.

The order has thus been changed, but it is not obvious what threats to Australia this new world order contains. Certainly it has a diminished role for the US, to which the US is having great difficulty adjusting. However, since neither the US nor China would risk war, with the ultimate threat of nuclear conflict, then the US over time will most likely accommodate China's leading role as Britain came to accommodate the US by the early twentieth century.

This was all inevitable, with China accounting for one-fifth of the world's population and having sustained historically unprecedented rates of economic growth for the past forty years. The emergence of such a great power so swiftly in East Asia, and the accompanying power shifts this has entailed, required all states in the region to change. They have done so and will continue to do so. Still, by attaching itself so closely to the US and joining it in strategic competition with China, for the time being, Australia has chosen to expose itself to some of the same geopolitical tensions that the US is experiencing.

All great powers on occasion behave badly when it is in their interests to do so. Some, at the same time, also provide valuable public goods, such as the US' idealism, which can inspire people to seek greater freedoms. Most, however, do not. It is natural for smaller states to seek to restrain the potential for big powers to do harm. The multilateral set of global rules and institutions was intended to achieve this. Whatever the value of these arrangements may be, great powers will prosecute their own interests outside of the agreed, multiple frameworks of rules—as, for example, the US did with its 2003 invasion of Iraq and China did in 2016 over The Hague decision on the South China Sea. It is also important for smaller powers to find creative ways to work together, to both engage the great powers and to raise the costs of bad behaviour.

Australia's strategy for managing the rise of China has been incremental, reactive to others' agendas, and as such, incoherent, other than the search to somehow retain vestiges of the old order. It clings to the US, and enthusiastically promotes the Quad grouping and the Indo-Pacific concept to contain China. It assumes that Australia's interests with respect to China are identical to those of the US, which potentially they are not. The US is the dominant power seeking to hold its position against the ascendant power. Australia has not sought to develop a strategy based on engagement and constructive cooperation, as proposed in its *2017 Foreign Policy White Paper*.

An Australian Grand Strategy

In the multipolar new world order, the US may still be our first call for security, but it can no longer be the only one. Australia will need to develop a grand strategy for itself as it seeks to find security and protect its interests. For a country that has throughout its history relied on great powers for its security—first the UK and then the US—this will require new thinking.

A grand strategy for Australia, to start with, would involve recognising that for the first time in our history, we are alone in the world. It would therefore be based on building coalitions of nations which themselves seek stability and order in East Asia, and who are also, like Australia, seeking to balance security and economic interests between the US and China.

The Foundations of Australia's Strategy

For Australia, a grand strategy would have at least ten foundations.

First, it should be based on a reasonable assumption of the US' continuing military pre-eminence, together with the realistic question of whether and under what circumstances the US would use its military power in direct conflict with China, possibly also Russia. Australian policymakers' comfortable assumption that the US is prepared to defend Australia, or other states in the region, can no longer be taken for granted.

Second, Australia needs to continue to work on its alliance relationship with the US, and to assist the US in recognising how its interests are directly aligned with Australia's own security. Over time, this may become less obvious to policymakers in Washington as they find accommodation with other powers in a multipolar order.

Third, the strategy must acknowledge that China will be the dominant power in the East Asian region, and that this power will continue to grow, based on the assumption of continuing domestic political stability and economic growth—albeit with this growth moderating over time, and converging with existing developed-country levels of economic growth in a range of 2–4 per cent.

Fourth, the best defence begins at home. Australia needs to ensure that, at all times, it keeps its own house in order. Essential elements of Australia's national security are economic performance based on rising productivity; increased defence expenditure made possible by higher economic growth; an expanded diplomatic effort, with a much greater investment in Australia's cultural diplomacy and soft power in the region; and a disciplined and consistent policy towards China.

Fifth, Australia, in protecting and advancing its interests, will need to return to activist middle-power diplomacy involving coalition building across a range of issues, from economics and trade, to the environment, and arms control in the East Asia region. This will require Australia to work with states that share its values, but also with those that do not. Australia's interests should drive its foreign and security policies. This does not mean disavowing values. Australia's values should define who we are when we sit at an international negotiating table, not which table we sit at.

Sixth, in practical terms, the biggest strategic challenge facing Australia, along with all its regional neighbours, is how to manage China's dominance while being highly dependent on it economically. In recent history, there has never been such a major economic power that has stood so far apart from international norms of political and social organisation. In view of its regional weight, China will seek to influence the behaviour of neighbouring states in ways which advance its own interests and security. So regional states need to find common purpose when dealing with China, to remind Beijing that a push against one is a push against all. Thoughts of Australia diversifying its economic relationship with China, other than at the margins, are nothing other than wishful thinking. The com-plementarities between the Chinese economy and Australia's are so profound that Australia's economic dependency on China will not change, not unless Australians choose to accept a major cut in their living standards.[7]

Seventh, Australia needs to strengthen its bilateral relations across the entire East Asian region, but especially in South-East Asia. Australia's relations are of uneven quality. It has worked hard with Japan, less so with South Korea, and a big effort has been made with Indonesia and Singapore. These relationships will need to be sustained and deepened, including, where this does not already occur, through bilateral military-to-military exchanges and exercises.

The recently concluded bilateral military arrangement with Vietnam is an excellent case in point. The Australian military also has assisted the Philippines army to deal with an insurgency threat in the south of the country. This should all lead to longer and more enduring forms of bilateral military cooperation. However, the depth of the relationships tails off fairly quickly from there. Australia is also often inconsistent in how it manages relationships. It embraced former Philippines president Benigno Aquino III, especially after his strong stance against China in the South China Sea, encouraged by the Obama administration, but it has allowed the relationship to cool in response to our distaste for President Duterte's human rights abuses during his anti-drug campaign, while supporting anti-insurgency efforts in Mindanao.

Balancing these complex elements—moral conviction and security in the case of the Philippines—is an unfamiliar challenge for Australian diplomacy. It wasn't always so. An earlier generation of Australian diplomats could set ideology and values to one side and adopt a pragmatic, realist approach to working with regional neighbours on issues of common interest.[8] It will be necessary to once again learn how to find carefully nuanced trade-offs if Australia is to build closer, more robust and enduring relationships across the region. Building trust will require deft statesmanship at the highest levels, and consistency in policies and discipline in public statements will be a key to this—something that Australian leaders have not been particularly good at in recent years.

Australia's grand strategy should involve working with those with common interests in maintaining regional balance and continued economic growth. Like-minded partners will be those that share these objectives, not necessarily Australia's values. Communist, authoritarian Vietnam, which has a poor human rights record, and against which Australia's local ethnic Vietnamese community is generally opposed, is in accord with our regional objectives just as much as democratic South Korea.

Indeed, Australia's relationship with Vietnam is something of a model of realist foreign policy. In most respects, it embodies the values that so upset Australian policymakers with China. The only material difference is that it is much smaller than China and less threatening as a result. Most importantly, it is an enemy of China and as such has been cultivated in recent years by the US. Accordingly, Australia has done the same.

Other front-line states facing China's immediate influence, such as Laos and Cambodia, similarly have been neglected. Australia was quick to support democratic renewal in Myanmar, but equally quick to cool its ardour in the face of human rights abuses of ethnic minorities, thereby creating opportunities for China's influence, which Myanmar's leaders had sought to resist.[9]

Eighth, looking beyond the region, Australia should engage with other states with liberal values and democratic traditions, wherever they may be in the world. As US leadership of the liberal international order fades away, other actors in the multipolar order will need to provide leadership in the face of provocations from authoritarian states.

Australia's grand strategy should aim to support and elevate liberal values in the new order. Here, Australia should seek common cause and build coalitions involving states from Europe, Latin America and the Indian subcontinent, as well as those in the East Asian region. Australia has done this successfully in the past with, for example, the Canberra Commission on the Elimination of Nuclear Weapons, initiated in 1995, and the Cairns Group of agricultural free-trading nations that was founded in the mid-1980s.[10] In these endeavours, Australia brought together states from across the world. Faced with China's weight and influence, promoting liberal values while pursuing interest-based foreign policy will be a major challenge, requiring deft diplomacy.

Ninth, and of the utmost importance, Australia's grand strategy should be to engage with China cooperatively and constructively across the entire spectrum of regional and also global concerns, especially those that impinge directly on China's security, such as the environment, water resources, energy, and asymmetrical threats such as terrorism, transnational crime, cyberwarfare and the militarisation of space. To do these things requires Australia to recognise the legitimacy of China's interests and its party-state.

Tenth, meanwhile, active engagement with China in cultural diplomacy should be another essential element of Australia's statecraft, accorded at least the same priority as other elements. Cultural diplomacy that promotes richer people-to-people interactions will break down stereotypical views. Australia should come to understand that China is not a monolithic society, with all its people mindlessly following the dictates of the party-state. And in China, people should know that Australia is a diverse, tolerant, multicultural society that can and does, mostly, think for itself. People in Australia have their own minds, and authority is challenged as part of Australia's culture.

Australia's Role in Middle-Power Diplomacy

From the 1980s, Australian foreign and trade policy concentrated increasingly on middle-power diplomacy. This involved putting less weight on great-power relationships, or supplementing them when they were found wanting, and working with coalitions of 'like-minded' countries on specific policy objectives. Middle-power diplomacy requires significant investment in diplomatic resources, and for the diplomacy, which is capable of taking a broader view of Australia's interests, to guide foreign policy, rather than the security and intelligence establishment which today leads on Australia's China policy.[11]

Multilateral Coalition Building

Australia has a strong tradition of building coalitions and alliances multilaterally on issues that bear on its security and interests, be it at the UN around issues of peace and disarmament, or the General Agreement on Tariffs and Trade (GATT) and its institutional replacement, the WTO, promoting free trade and strong rules and disciplines. In the UN in particular, Australia has contributed to global security by working with other states with similar interests to promote multilateral agreements; for example, on nuclear non-proliferation, chemical weapons, the control of small arms, and land mines. These are important elements in an international framework of norms, if not legally binding rules.

The Hawke government was unusually innovative by the standard of most Australian governments when it came to international coalition building and prosecuting a policy agenda around issues that the government believed had broad domestic support. For example, the Hawke government led an international effort against vested interests to impose financial sanctions on the apartheid regime. Similarly, with the Protocol on Environmental Protection to the Antarctic Treaty, which was ready to receive signatures in 1991, Australia found common cause with its arch trade rival France, with which it had sharp disputes over nuclear testing in the Pacific. In 1986, the Hawke government established the Cairns Group which, led by Australia, made a major contribution to including agriculture in the Uruguay Round of multilateral trade negotiations, despite opposition from European states and Japan.

This innovation continued in 1995 when prime minister Paul Keating established the Canberra Commission on the Elimination of Nuclear Weapons, which was chaired by then foreign minister Gareth Evans. The commission brought together former politicians, bureaucrats, Nobel laureates and other notables from both the developed and developing worlds to prepare a report on the eradication of nuclear weapons.

Regional Coalitions

It is in the Asia–Pacific region that Australia has made some of its most significant contributions to local initiatives, which have involved it working constructively and cooperatively with ASEAN states, individually and collectively. These have included the establishment of APEC and the associated summit, the Cambodian peace settlement, and the Bali Process on people smuggling and trafficking.

APEC was initially proposed by prime minister Hawke in a speech he made on his first visit to Seoul in 1985. Although, as intended, this was the big headline from the speech, the habits of consultation and cooperation had been well established for many years in the region under the Pacific Economic Cooperation Council (PECC), a joint Japanese–Australian initiative dating from 1980.[12] PECC was a one-and-a-half track process, bringing mainly academics and businesspeople together with government officials, as well as some interested public officials in their 'private' capacities, to discuss regional integration, trade and investment liberalisation, and cooperation with the Asia-Pacific region. APEC was to be an inter-governmental group at the foreign minister or trade minister level.

Problematically, then Malaysian prime minister Mahathir Mohamad had a visceral dislike of Australia and was determined to spike APEC. He was jealous that Australia had had the policy alacrity, imagination and capacity to launch a region-wide initia-tive.[13] Indeed, Australia was being described as 'white trash' in policy circles in Singapore and Malaysia, where arrogance was prevalent before the 1997 Asian financial crisis.[14] It is not that Australia did not deserve some of the opprobrium it received, but its policy activ-ism certainly was resented in some quarters.[15] It is testament to the achievements of Australian diplomacy that so much was achieved in the face of such hostility.

Bob Hawke had an intuitive sense of Australia having to make its own way in the world. When he first floated the APEC initiative, it did not include the US—China, of course, also was not part of it, as first it was necessary to settle how to deal with Taiwan, at that time a much bigger economic partner for most members of the region than was mainland China. The US saw not being included as a challenge, albeit an unintended one, to its dominance in East Asia. To Washington, it was the height of impertinence and betrayal that Australia could propose a regional initiative in its own right and not include the US as a foundation member.[16] Much scrambling and dissembling ensued and, as if it had never been omitted, US membership was eased into the Australian presentation of the APEC proposal.

At the time, it was audacious to believe that the US would not be a member of any and all East Asian arrangements. After all, it was the dominant regional power by far and the absolute guarantor of regional security, which was delivering ever-increasing prosperity, and this also took place during the Cold War. This obviously had not been an accidental omission but rather was a reflection of a region beginning to emerge with a powerful sense of identity, free of global power rivalry.

South-East Asian ambivalence, and Malaysia's hostility in particular, ensured that APEC had an awkward start. As Gareth Evans observed sardonically when reflecting on this, APEC was 'four adjectives in search of a noun'.[17] Another challenge was to find a formula by which China and Taiwan would be able to join, which was derived in 1991 after some more years of Australian diplomacy, despite US-led sanctions on China following the military assault on protesters in and around Tiananmen Square on 4 June 1989. The significance of this should not be underestimated. The APEC nomenclature for Taiwan, 'Chinese Taipei', has since become the standard fix for international organisations such as the WTO.

APEC's next major development was also led by Australia. Paul Keating, while challenging Hawke to become leader of the parliamentary Labor Party in December 1991, presented himself as someone who had close affinities with, and deep insights into, Asia. In fact, Keating's first visit to China was as the Australian treasurer in May 1989, to attend the first meeting of the ADB. He arrived in Guangzhou with little interest in the country, but witnessing the rapid growth of the economy and engaging with China's leaders on economic policy left an indelible impression on him. For Keating, China's re-emergence as a global power had a sense of inevitability about it.[18]

Keating went on to create the APEC leaders summit, a singular achievement which he personally conceived and led. Initially, the Canberra bureaucracy, which had been dealing with pushback from Malaysia and elsewhere in South-East Asia, was sceptical. It was timid, where Keating was bold. It wanted to protect the gains to date, whereas Keating had a vision of something grander. As Keating tells it, while sitting next to US president Bill Clinton at a dinner, he sketched on the back of a napkin what the proposed summit would look like and why the US should back it. But Allan Gyngell recalls that the proposal resulted from a long, congratulatory letter that Keating had written to the newly elected Clinton.[19] Either recollection could be correct. Clinton claims credit for the whole thing in his memoir.[20]

Keating believed that if APEC had a summit, then the US would have to be fully involved. The US president would have to participate each year and substantive agendas would be required to justify the meetings. For the first time, the Asia–Pacific region would have a summit that brought together its leaders on an annual basis.

Over the course of these summits, leaders have regularly departed from the bureaucrats' scripts and dealt with issues of immediate concern. The Shanghai summit in 2001 discussed the 9/11 attacks on the twin towers of Manhattan's World Trade Center and supported the worldwide effort to counter terrorism. For China to associate itself with an issue of primary concern to the US, one which was not part of APEC's economic agenda, was a significant development. The leaders, of course, also have supported further initiatives for trade liberalisation. The summits provide an opportunity for leaders to exchange positions in informal settings, which can often be much more direct and constructive than scripted formal meetings. They also provide a point of contact at times when relations are strained. In 2014, at the nadir of China–Japan relations over the Diaoyu/Senkaku Islands dispute, Prime Minister Abe visited China to attend the Beijing leaders' summit. An understanding was reached, if not agreed, that Japan would at least acknowledge that China had a claim, even if it rejected it.[21] The subsequent gradual improvement in China–Japan relations can be dated from that APEC meeting.

Australia has twice worked closely with Indonesia on developing responses to issues besetting the East Asian region. The first was the Cambodian peace settlement of 1991, led by Australian foreign minister Gareth Evans and Indonesian foreign minister Ali Alatas. It required years of careful and often frustrating diplomacy, the goal of which was to bring about a lasting peace settlement involving China and Vietnam to end the suffering of the Cambodians. Australia played a leading role in bringing sustained peace to the region.

The Bali Process on people smuggling and trafficking was another example of Australia working closely with Indonesia to try to deal with a problem that had become a major source of tension between the two countries. In August 2001, when the MV *Tampa* arrived at Christmas Island with 438 mainly Afghan people rescued from a stricken fishing boat in international waters, prime minister John Howard saw that the refugee inflow was about to become a flood. With Australia's onshore detention centres already at capacity, he declared that anyone arriving by boat in this manner could not step foot on Australian soil and thus be able to avail themselves of domestic legal privileges to determine their refugee status, and utilise the extended appeals process. The curtain had come down.[22] As the point of departure for most of the boat people was Indonesia, Howard and his foreign minister, Alexander Downer, publicly ramped up the rhetoric, pointing a finger at Indonesia for not doing enough to stem the outflow and demanding that it do more. In the politics of South-East Asia, this was toxic and it poisoned relations.

Howard won the 2001 election convincingly but still had to deal with the problem of boat arrivals, the big numbers of people waiting in makeshift camps in Indonesia, and the frosty relations with that country. However, it was Indonesia, not Australia, that broke the ice. Soon after the Australian election, Indonesian foreign minister Hassan Wirajuda proposed visiting Canberra to discuss the problem. He was accompanied by a senior official, Marty Natalegawa, who had a PhD from the Australian National University and whose children lived in Sydney; he was later to become Indonesia's ambassador to the United Nations and subsequently foreign minister. Over dinner in Parliament House, Wirajuda proposed to Downer that the way forward was to deal with people smuggling in a regional context, rather than simply treating it as a contentious issue in the bilateral relationship. Downer embraced the suggestion, and Australia and Indonesia set about organising the first regional conference on people smuggling, which became known as the Bali Process, in recognition of the meeting's location. The inaugural conference was held in April 2002, just four months after the initiative had been launched.[23]

The Bali Process focuses on policy coordination and practical measures to thwart the people smugglers. It has been an important example of functional diplomacy in the region and is a useful model of what can be achieved in terms of cooperation and coordination to tackle concrete security challenges.[24] It has been the last successful Australian-led regional foreign policy initiative utilising Australia's previous strengths in middle-power diplomacy.

In 2008, prime minister Kevin Rudd attempted to launch a major foreign policy effort in East Asia. Unfortunately, its execution was found wanting. Rudd floated the idea of an Asia Pacific Community that would bring together both traditional security and economic issues in the same forum, but he did so ahead of consultations with regional partners. ASEAN was immediately suspicious that—whether by design or inadvertently—it would be marginalised by the proposal. Undeterred, Rudd pressed a retired senior diplomat, Dick Woolcott, back into service. He was to be sent on the road again, as he had been when Hawke was creating APEC, nearly quarter of a century earlier.[25]

It may have been possible for Hawke to get away with a top-down public announcement in the mid-1980s to create APEC, which was to be a much more modest body dealing with economic and trade matters, and which built on years of consensus-building work inside PECC. But it was another thing entirely twenty-five years later when the region had changed so much, and the subject was to be the politically sensitive area of security between states. The initiative ran out of puff before it really got started, and this was to be the end of Australia's activist regional diplomacy.

Rudd did successfully broaden Australia's efforts on the global stage. His government, and those that succeeded his, campaigned successfully for Australia to become a member of the UN Security Council, which for decades Australia had not sought to do. The Howard government, for one, had held the UN in high disregard, preferring the comfort of its close relationship with the US, especially with the bonds that were believed to have been created with Bush and Cheney following 9/11, and Australia's commitment of troops to Afghanistan and Iraq.

Under Rudd, Australia also led international attempts to create the G20 in the wake of the GFC of late 2008. An intense diplomatic effort went into ensuring that a broader grouping than the G8—Russia had been brought into the G7 by that time—would be created that was more representative of the balance of economic power in the world.

———————

Within multilateral and regional bodies and groupings, Australia has a diplomatic tradition of activism in support of many initiatives, including in the WTO to secure the launch of the Doha Round of multilateral trade negotiations.[26] But over the past two decades, Australia has been seen to be regionally inactive. This is a concern and points to a failure of political leadership. Soon after I arrived in Beijing as ambassador to China in 2007, senior foreign ministry officials said to me in private that they lamented Australia's absence from regional diplomacy, noting that there had been a time when China looked to Australia to lead on local initiatives. They said Australia had been able to advance initiatives, such as APEC, when, if China attempted to do so, it would have been blocked by 'others' (read, the US).

Australia now needs to rediscover its traditions of diplomatic activism and innovation and take the initiative to shape the new world order through coalition building, with or without the active participation of the US. With the rise of China, the re-entry of Russia, and the emergence of other authoritarian states as influential actors in the new order, the task of multilateral coalition building has become very much harder, and it is likely to become even more so in the future. It was a different period in the 1980s and 1990s as the US-led order provided a stable international environment, with widely shared interests and values to engage countries in coalitions to serve common strategic objectives. Nonetheless, much needs attention in the global commons, and the interests of all states can still be advanced by global cooperation and collective action.

A Policy Agenda for a Grand Strategy
An ASEAN Hedging Strategy
In March 2018, the presence of ASEAN heads of government in Australia, meeting at prime minister Turnbull's initiative, was an

event of major significance. Ten years prior, even five, the idea of ASEAN's leaders meeting in Australia would have been laughable. Australia has long been seen by ASEAN as an outsider in the Asia-Pacific region, notwithstanding our massive economic integration and our valuable and welcomed cooperation across many areas, including defence, counterterrorism, people smuggling, organised crime and disaster relief. ASEAN members have always sought to protect the integrity of the group and to make it central to East Asian affairs.

Australia's liberal democracy, with its robust independent media that criticises regional governments for human rights abuses or ethnic discrimination, or highlights independence movements such as that for West Papua, or Indonesian military atrocities in East Timor, sits awkwardly with the more authoritarian political systems of our neighbours and their controlled or cowed media. Australia's adversarial parliamentary system and media also jar with consensus-based public discourse in the region.

Successive Australian governments sought to navigate a way through this, with varying degrees of success. Dick Woolcott famously described Australia as the 'odd-man-in' in Asia.[27] But we were never comfortable with being an insider, and neither was ASEAN comfortable with having us there. The recent change in ASEAN's attitude towards Australia is attributable to the rise of China. It thus points to the potential for new initiatives and coalition building with Australia's regional neighbours.

All countries in the region are trying to work out how to accommodate China's rise while not undermining their own sovereignty. They recognise that China is now, and will continue to be, the dominant power in the region through its economic and, increasingly, military weight. In an important respect, they are like Australia. They all seek China's markets and investment but are trying to work out how to manage China's overweening influence. Accordingly, this convergence of interest between ASEAN countries and Australia in the face of China's rise provides an opportunity for Australia to develop with its neighbours a hedging strategy for managing China, while providing strategic space for its continued ascendency.[28]

Australia should be clear and explicit about what it intends to do with such a strategy, namely encourage China to adhere to rules and norms that seek to minimise conflict while respecting the sovereignty of all states in East Asia. We should also explore ways to make new rules and create new architecture that reflect contemporary realities in the region, together with China.

A major challenge for Australia, however, is that many of the governments in the region have dubious democratic and human rights credentials. An effective hedging strategy will require us to work closely with governments that we do not like. Some of these states, such as Laos and Cambodia, have been, or are well advanced in being, groomed by China as client states, but none have as yet fully sublimated their national interests. Prime Minister Hun Sen's ruling Cambodian People's Party is establishing one-party, authoritarian rule, while members of Cambodia's exiled opposition party refer to the country as having become a colony of China.[29] Laos is probably the most closely aligned with China. The July 2018 election in Laos only underscored how far the country has moved in that direction. Some see Laos as the first domino to fall in a strategy by China to extend its control over South-East Asia.

Laos and Cambodia, however, are two of the smallest countries in South-East Asia in terms of population and economic size. They also have a history of local opposition to an ethnic Chinese presence in their economies. Meanwhile, several major countries in the region—Indonesia, Singapore and Malaysia—still lean heavily towards the US in foreign policy and strategic terms. The Philippines historically has been strongly pro US, but under Duterte it has become more balanced between the US and China, and at times leans towards the latter.[30]

Collectively, ASEAN is the most obvious body with which Australia should engage on a China-hedging strategy. Australia does not need formally to join the group for it to add substantial geopolitical weight to ASEAN, and vice versa. Already there are the ASEAN-plus processes and the ASEAN Regional Forum. A hedging strategy focused on our area of immediate strategic interest, namely East Asia, should seek to strengthen and broaden each of our bilateral relationships across South-East Asia, as well as with ASEAN collectively.

A key element of such a strategy would be realistic solidarity, though it will take a lot of diplomatic effort to achieve this. This means that, while allowing for the reality that each country's interests will prevail in its dealings with China, beneath this, China should know that if it pushes hard against one, it will be pushing hard against them all. The South China Sea is a case in point. A coordinated position from the region, including Australia, would have had much more impact in Beijing than various individual responses—even if Laos and Cambodia, and perhaps Thailand, would not have engaged actively.

If Australia's security is truly under challenge from China, which itself is not self-evident and thus needs to be argued by those who claim it to be, then Australia needs to work much harder, more creatively and more skilfully on its relations with South-East Asia.

Regional Security Architecture

In 2018, in a speech at the West Point Military Academy in New York state, Kevin Rudd urged his audience of future US military leaders to accept both the reality and inevitability of China's influence over East Asia, and to begin to develop strategies with which to manage China's behaviour in ways that better align with regional objectives of peace and stability.[31] Rudd's 2008 Asia Pacific Community was to be a step towards this idea of a regional security mechanism. In one of the most dangerous places on earth, it is remarkable that no such mechanism for states to engage multilaterally on security has been established, nor is there any momentum behind such an idea.

East Asia has lacked the kind of comprehensive security architecture that has proven so useful elsewhere, such as the Organization for Security and Co-operation in Europe (OSCE). In the mid-2000s, when the so-called six-party talks—involving the US, Japan, China, Russia, South Korea and North Korea—promised to make progress on removing North Korea's nuclear and missile programs, the idea of a new regional security mechanism based on this group was actively promoted, including by then US secretary of state Condoleezza Rice.[32] It was the first multilateral and regional security dialogue in East Asia. At the time, Chinese scholars were openly supportive of the notion that it could evolve into a broader dialogue.[33]

While Australia was not a party to the talks, it sent envoys from Canberra to lobby in Beijing, Seoul and Tokyo, as well as Washington, to ensure the participants understood Australia's concerns and interests. Being more economically dependent on the region than any other participant, Australia had vital national interests at stake in regional peace and stability. Australia also had a military alliance with the US which, depending on the circumstances under which conflict might occur, could involve us invoking the Australia, New Zealand, United States Security Treaty (ANZUS). Accordingly, participants in the six-party talks understood Australia's interests and at some stage may have recognised and accepted the legitimacy of its participation in any new security mechanism that might have emerged.

The six-party talks progressed to the point where an agreement with North Korea was about to be reached on denuclearisation and the ending of its missile program, in return for a peace treaty and recognition by the US. Typically, at the last minute, Pyongyang reneged, and the process was abandoned amid acrimony and frustration, especially on the part of the US.[34] Still, it is interesting to speculate on what regional security might look like now had such a mechanism been put in place. Chinese officials at the time were open to the idea, although internal policy discussions had not advanced to the point where Beijing had a formal position. The suggestion was attractive to China on a number of fronts. First, it would bring other countries into the process of managing the North Korean problem and so ease pressure on China to shape North Korea's behaviour. Second, it would have been the first formal recognition by the US of China as a great power in the region, to be treated as an equal alongside other powers. Third, Beijing probably hoped that, over time, such a mechanism would weaken the US' main alliances with Japan and South Korea.[35]

The fact that no arrangement for East Asian security has yet been established, despite the extent of regional economic integration, dense networks of bilateral free-trade agreements, and ASEAN and APEC summitry, points to immense obstacles.[36] But while it is a big challenge, so too were many of the other regional initiatives on which Australia took the lead. The degree of difficulty should not decide what policy challenges and initiatives are taken up, but rather the potential benefits that may be derived.

At a minimum, an East Asian security mechanism would adopt a wide definition of 'security', to cover, for example, traditional areas of armament and disarmament; non-state actors; energy; resources; transportation; food; the environment; and economic matters. It would, of course, require considerable diplomatic agility and consultation. It would be a bottoms-up process, proceeding on the basis of dialogue and confidence building. Whether China, the US and Japan—the great powers of the region—were involved from the outset would be a tactical question, but ultimately, to address the big risks in the region, all three need to take part. The mechanism's primary objective would be to build mutual trust in East Asia and, in doing so, reduce the prospect of armed conflict.

The absence of any such over-arching arrangement for the region can be expected to draw countries together to try to fill the gap. This occurred in March 2020, in the midst of COVID-19, when US Deputy Secretary of State Stephen Biegun convened a telephone meeting involving the Quad, plus Vietnam, South Korea and New Zealand, to discuss responses to the pandemic.[37] It is not clear why these three additional countries were invited to participate, and not Singapore and Indonesia, for example, but broadening out the Quad membership would certainly address one major criticism of it. As currently convened, it comprises three of China's strategic competitors and Australia—which, under the existing Australian policies, is a de-facto strategic competitor. Adding additional members to the Quad would help to dilute the sense that its primary purpose is to contain China and to introduce competing blocs into the Asia-Pacific region.

Membership could be expanded around functional issues, with different countries participating at different times, and these meetings could over time become building blocks for a broader security arrangement. For this to happen, it would be important that, as the Quad-plus group expanded and interacted more often, it would leave open the possibility of engaging with China on issues of common interest, such as pandemics. Also, if an expanded Quad became a more permanent feature in East Asia, its name should change to reflect more accurately its purpose as a nascent regional security organisation, and of course China should be invited to join.

Learning to Live in the New Order

Australia will need to increase its defence commitment in the new order from the current level of 2 per cent of GDP to something like 3 per cent. With the enormous economic impact of COVID-19, this will be challenging not just for Australia but for governments everywhere. Hugh White has argued that this figure needs to be raised to at least 3.5 per cent, and that Australia may need to consider a nuclear weapons capability launched from submarines if Australia's neighbours acquire nuclear capabilities.[38]

Australia also is under-represented diplomatically. It ranks eighth on diplomatic influence, just one level above its economic resources, but its diplomatic service is smaller than other comparable countries.[39]

In addition, Australia will need to learn to say 'No' to America and be able to disappoint China without offending it. Huawei is relevant in both cases. Many countries have come under enormous US pressure to impose blanket bans on Huawei participating in any aspect of 5G telecommunications systems, yet they have found ways to resist US pressure while maintaining traditionally close ties, including with some members of the Five Eyes intelligence-sharing arrangement. When blocking Huawei, Australia not only implemented a blanket ban, it also chose the most high-profile way of doing so, making China's leadership lose face and blissfully unaware of the domestic political implications for them in doing so.

Australian politicians need to learn that foreign policy is about getting the outcomes Australia wants, not what is said in public. Public commentary on foreign policy by prime ministers and foreign ministers carries a great deal of weight beyond Australia's shores. Certainly, China's leadership and its elites are highly sensitive to what other leaders say about their country. So it is gratuitous and against Australia's interests when our leaders make statements such as Julia Gillard did when she was prime minister that 'Japan is Australia's closest partner in Asia', or as Tony Abbott did as prime minister in saying that Australia was 'a strong ally of Japan'.[40] (The latter is technically wrong as Australia does not have a formal alliance with Japan.) Although each statement may have been accidental, most likely they were part of deliberate messaging to China. Both were unnecessarily provocative.

Similarly, in April 2020, Prime Minister Morrison's call for an independent investigation into the origins of COVID-19 was clearly directed at China. It was made in the midst of a slanging match between Beijing and Washington over where blame for the virus and its consequences should be attributed. It was also made following a telephone discussion between Morrison and Trump. While the request for an independent review of the causes of the virus and how governments responded was unexceptional, the timing, tone and context of Morrison's call were inevitably seen as provocative by Beijing.

Australia also was initially alone in this, not having done the basic diplomacy of a middle-level power and sought to build a coalition of countries to support its position and speak collectively. Eventually, the EU gathered a widely based group of supporters, including Australia, and a review process was established within the WHO. By then, however, further serious damage had been done to Australia–China relations, and China again reverted to economic coercion.[41]

Learning to trust our regional neighbours is a big step for Australia to take. It means bringing countries like Indonesia into Australia's confidence before making major policy announcements that affect regional security and national interests. When president Obama made his Pivot to Asia statement in Darwin in 2011, accompanied by an effusive Julia Gillard, an enterprising ABC journalist in Jakarta asked Indonesian foreign minister Marty Natalegawa what he thought of the joint US–Australia announcement that US marines would be based in Darwin for training. Natalegawa looked directly into the camera and said that 'he did not know that Australia saw

Indonesia as an imminent military threat', such was the annoyance of one of Australia's closest friends.[42]

A Forward-Looking Agenda of Strategic Cooperation with China

Of course, none of this is possible unless we improve our bilateral relations with China. A circuit-breaker for the current impasse is required. Australia did eventually choose to join China's initiative of the AIIB, despite US pressure not to, and it was able to keep its relationship with the US in top order. The AIIB has since continued to develop as a transparent, multilateral rules-based organisation, and Australia's participation has helped to shape it. Similarly, Australia should formally associate itself with the BRI, not as some sort of concession to Beijing, but because we recognise that this is a significant development in geopolitics, that we have something to contribute in shaping its evolution, and that it is in Australia's interests to have at least one foot in China's bounded order. Inside the BRI, Australia, together with like-minded countries in Europe and other liberally inclined states, can seek to exert influence and align the BRI more closely with multilateral principles and ideas.[43] Australia could also seek to work cooperatively with China on ODA in the Pacific. Beijing has already started to look at how its ODA can better align with the principles of transparency and accountability that apply in multilateral agencies.

To the extent that China threatens Australia through political interference, predatory investment, cyber-attacks, intellectual property theft, the pillaging of commercial secrets, and more, then Australia, as the EU proposes to do, needs to harden its internal defences. The Australian Government has already done this successfully with its anti-foreign interference legislation, greater investment in cybersecurity, intelligence sharing with its Five Eyes partners, and greater public awareness in the country's universities of the multiple roles of Confucius Institutes and inherent risks in science and technology collaborative work. Australia needs to recognise that it is a tough hard world full of risks and bad people and governments, but that should not be at the expense of engaging with China in our national interest.

A big agenda is beckoning for cooperation across a wide range of regional and multilateral issues, all of which go to China's security and, like environmental pressures and pandemics, can only be adequately addressed through international cooperation. Collaboration in these areas plays to Australia's considerable strengths. To do so, however, requires that Australian policy towards China return to its long-standing premise of strategic cooperation, based on recognising the legitimacy of China's interests, and not on strategic competition.

CONCLUSION

Imagine a world suddenly racked by a mysterious pandemic which, in a few months, carries over half-a-million people to their graves and continues to rage. A world where millions are infected and there is no vaccine, nor any certainty about immunity. Where already strained relations between the dominant power and an ascendant power boil over into acrimonious accusations, attributing responsibility to one another. Where cooperation breaks down seemingly irrevocably between those two powers, and the dominant power decides to walk away from the one global institution that has any chance of organising a coordinated and hence effective response.

Imagine a world in which the dominant power, with which Australia has firmly aligned itself, is displaying characteristics of a failed state, with the highest absolute number of deaths in the world, a collapsing health system and insufficient supplies of medical equipment. Where the poor are dying at faster rates than the rich. And where cities are being torched nightly as the black underclass protests extrajudicial murder by white police officers.

Imagine, too, that the ascendant power has been able to manage its way through the crisis, that its businesses are returning to work, that it is using the crisis to seek strategic advantage and further submit its peripheral areas to its central control. This ascendant power does not share the values of the dominant power and its allies. It views such things as human rights as second-order considerations on the road to a great national rejuvenation. And despite its lack of the rule of law and its technological prowess being directed in part to the surveillance of its citizens and censorship, its population, which accounts for one-fifth of humanity, by and large supports the system or acquiesces happily enough.

Imagine that the ascendant power now feels strong enough to be impervious to international criticism, certainly able to brush off challenges from the dominant power's allies. And that it knows it can cut deals with the dominant power regardless of these irritating allies. The ascendant power may also feel it is in its interests to keep propping up the dominant power for an indefinite time to benefit from the public goods, especially regional security, that are provided by that power at great expense. Imagine what Australia's policymakers might do in this dystopian world.

In this world of heightened risks and uncertainty, Australian foreign policy has become weaponised with respect to China. As Australia's intelligence, security and military establishment has taken control of Australia's foreign policy towards China, legitimate domestic policy discussion is cast increasingly in terms of being for or against the national interest and supporting or undermining Australia's security. Business proponents of improved bilateral relations with China are criticised as putting personal greed above national security. In this way, the huge economic interests Australia has in maintaining good relations with China are delegitimised. Politicians who argue for greater balance in Australia's policies towards China are attacked as somehow being unpatriotic. A senior government senator has said, 'We have Labor people willing to be basically apologists or ventriloquist dolls for the communist regime in China'.[1] The Opposition has become so wedged over China that it has been silenced.

China's bad behaviours, both within Australia and towards its regional neighbours, have reinforced each other to create a powerful narrative that China must be resisted at every turn. It was once a no-brainer that good relations with China were valuable for Australia—not as an end in itself, but as necessary to advance Australia's national interests, including but not limited to economic interests. This is no longer the case, and even hard-edged realist arguments for engagement with China are now dismissed as a new form of appeasement. It has never been explained why it is legitimate for major US arms manufacturers to fund the Australian Strategic Institute, which is a leading proponent of the China 'threat', but not for Australian resource companies to support China Matters, which seeks to promote informed discussion of China within Australia.[2]

Australia needs to find its way to a shared understanding of its long-term interests and from that maintain a disciplined and consistent foreign policy that is premised on Australia finding security _in_ its region—be it defined as East Asia or the Indo–Pacific—and not _from_ the region, as Paul Keating has said.

Australia has an abundance of soft power and needs to show its attractiveness to the world. It has some strategic weight with resources, but iron ore is one of the most plentiful minerals on earth and China will eventually diversify away from Australia for security reasons, if nothing else, while China's steel-intensive growth will fall over time. Australia's great attractiveness lies in a successful and open multicultural society that draws in students and tourists— people voting with their feet. Australia needs to project this to the world through ramped-up cultural diplomacy programs, at the same time avoiding divisive and racially tinged public discussion of security and foreign policy. It needs to emphasise individual rights and freedoms, and avoid identity politics that elevate sub-group interests above those of the individual and hence the community at large. Above all, Australians need to be confident in the strength of their institutions—the rule of law, independence of the judiciary, accountability of security agencies to parliament, and independence of the media. Australia faces threats from all major powers in the new order, perhaps none more so than China, but it also has the resilience to resist and overcome. Political leaders in Australia should be building confidence among the public in the country's institutional strengths, not spreading fear.

An activist, imaginative, smart and modest foreign policy needs to be well resourced. Diplomacy, after all, is the only instrument realistically available to ensure Australia's security. Australia itself can never fund the military defence of the continent, nor can Australia confidently rely on other states to protect us. In the new world order, the safest premise on which to build security policy is that we are on our own. Diplomacy therefore should not be seen as a cost but as an investment in Australia's future security.

The recent shift in Australia's policy towards China, from strategic cooperation to strategic competition, has seen relations deteriorate to their lowest point since December 1972, when official relations began. For three years now, China has frozen official bilateral contact. The Australian prime minister has been unable to speak to any of China's leaders concerning COVID-19. China has imposed trade measures against Australia, with a justification ranging from nil to questionable, and the Australian trade minister has not been able to speak to his counterpart in Beijing.

It may be fair to complain that China in this has behaved badly. But big powers do that, and smaller ones suffer what they must. Nevertheless, China's behaviour has lacked subtlety and has for many countries reached a point where it must be resisted. China needs to practise its foreign policy in a way that reflects and does credit to its great power status, not diminish it.[3]

Arguments about where moral responsibility lies for us having arrived at this nadir do not lead to a policy for dealing with the world as it is. While policy advisers may prick the moral indignation of their political bosses and feed a sense of grievance at being treated unfairly, this is not a strategy by which to advance a country's interests. Nor is it enough to say that it is all China's doing and Australia just needs to wait until China's behaviour changes. The asymmetry of power suggests that this is unlikely to be an effective strategy.

After four years of increasingly cooler bilateral relations, China may well have concluded that it does not matter much whether relations are restored to the level accorded to all of Australia's regional partners and other US allies. The view forming in Beijing may well be that, if Australia has chosen to be a strategic outlier, then 'so be it'.

From Beijing's perspective, why bother speaking with the monkey when you can talk to the organ grinder.

China has its major problems too: issues with its economy, which is the key to regime stability and survival; issues with its environment, which is existential and as much about water as air; an inherently brittle and therefore potentially unstable political system, without an institutional mechanism for the transfer of power; absence of the rule of law and an independent media, so few checks and balances apply; low levels of trust in government regulatory standards and public health issues, hence epidemics, and tardy responses from lack of transparency; and much more as well. All too often, policy towards China is discussed without reference to China's constraints and challenges, as if it were a protean actor that can exercise power at will.

China sits in the middle of its bounded order, which stretches to the west across Eurasia into parts of the Middle East and Africa, and south and east to parts of South-East Asia and the Pacific. It has powerful like-minded states like Russia at its side for the time being, and is recalibrating its relations with other powerful neighbours, especially Japan. It is secure among the autocracies, including Turkey, Iran and Saudi Arabia, and the authoritarian democracies, such as the Philippines, Thailand and Venezuela. It has cultivated neo-tributary states in South-East Asia, such as Laos and Cambodia. Remarkably, it has secured, at least publicly, quietude from Islamic states, including Turkey, Indonesia and Pakistan, over its treatment of the ethnic Turkic-speaking Uighurs and Kazakhs.

As China has been shaping its new order over the past two decades, with some exceptions, such as Indonesia and Singapore, this has been a world largely out of reach of Australian foreign policy. Where Australia has had the opportunity to connect, notably through the BRI, it has turned its back and instead sought to elevate its engagement with the Quad and the Indo-Pacific, together with the US, to contain China. At least, that is how Beijing views it.

Other actions which may have been perfectly reasonable in terms of Australia's national interest—the blanket ban on Huawei, anti-foreign interference measures, the call for an investigation into the origins of and early actions on COVID-19—were presented in ways that made the leadership in Beijing lose face. Australian policymakers may scoff at and reject notions of 'face', and argue, with much merit, that it is a one-way street in which China is the victim and the other party, Australia, must atone in some way. But this is the world in which we live, and better ways of advancing our interests need to be found. For Australia, East Asia is the primary area of our economic and security interests. A grand strategy begins with working out how to deal with China. It should recognise that we are caught in the greatest power shift in modern history.

The verities and assumptions that for so long have underlined Australian foreign and security policy, and given Australia so much comfort, no longer hold. Australia will need to develop a much more independent foreign policy, one where diplomacy has a far greater role than at any other time in our history, and which is based on a hard-headed, realist assessment of our national interests. This will require developing a grand strategy around being alone in the world and having to work creatively and hard at building alliances and groupings to advance our interests, often working with countries whose values we may not share, and even abhor.

Key participants in the multipolar order that now prevails are authoritarian states of great economic size or area, or strategic location. Australia will need to engage with such states as it would engage with like-minded states with competitive political systems. Differences in values will prevent cooperation in some areas, notably human rights, but many other possibilities will exist, such as for addressing asymmetrical security threats like terrorism, the environment and pandemics.

Australia's diplomacy in recent years can best be described as underwhelming. For the past decade, Australia has lacked the confidence and will to pursue an activist middle-power diplomatic agenda in the Asia-Pacific region. It has found no convincing answer to the rise of China and its dominance in the area. As unfashionable as it is at present to say so, Australia's interests are best served by a policy of engagement with China, not containment.

What does AUKUS represent for Australia's interests?

→ Australia remains a follower, not a activist

POSTSCRIPT: COVID-19

COVID-19 is both a global medical emergency and, in the responses to it, an economic shock of as yet unknown size. As the virus continues to rampage in the US and much of the developing world, and 'second waves' threaten in Beijing and Melbourne, where governments previously had been thought to have routed it by resolute action and public support, the shape of the post-COVID-19 world order cannot be discerned with confidence as no one yet knows when the pandemic will end. A return to 'normality' in people's lives will require a vaccine, but it is unknown when that might be found, if at all.

On the eve of the virus, the global order had already been fracturing along the lines discussed earlier in this book.[1] The inexorable rise of China and the US' retreat from leadership of the international system were well advanced to the point where analysts were writing about the 'New Global Disorder', or even as has been done here positing that a 'New Global Order' has already arrived.[2]

Towards the end of the Obama Administration, the US had begun to conclude that the post-1970s strategy of engagement with China had failed. China, from a Washington perspective, had not become a 'responsible stakeholder in the international system and was becoming more authoritarian and less amendable to US global leadership'. US policy towards China changed, based on China as a strategic threat. Henceforth, competition was to replace cooperation, containment to replace engagement.[3] This was supported on both sides of the aisles—Republican and Democrat—in the US.

Trump had set out an aggressive agenda towards China in his 2016 election campaign, blaming China for the US' perceived economic woes, despite the gathering strength of the US economy at the time. The centrepiece of his China pushback was the Trade War, which sought a return to managed trade between the great powers and a rejection of the global rules-based system for trade.[4] Many other issues had also become major points of dispute between the US and China, including Huawei, the state-sponsored and subsidised Made in China 2025 technology challenge, theft of intellectual property, and assertive foreign policy positions in East Asia. But trade was central to Trump's China policy. The trade agreement reached in December 2019 had promised a degree of calm in US–China relations, at least until the 2020 elections were out of the way. COVID-19 changed all of that.

By the time the virus struck at the end of 2019, other countries were well advanced in their reassessments of relations with China. During 2019, the EU followed with a fundamental reappraisal of its relations with China and concluded that China was also a 'systemic' rival to the EU, but it also remained committed to continued engagement with China on issues of mutual interest.[5] Australia as shown in this study had long followed the US in repositioning its policy towards China as one of containment in practice, if not in its pronouncements. With the onset of the pandemic, Australia's relations with China have become even more strained. The freeze imposed by China on high-level contact is said to be the 'new new normal'.[6] Australia has decided to tough it out and not seek to find a new accommodation with Beijing.

China's bad behaviour on multiple fronts, from the South China Sea, to cyberattacks on a massive scale, to running political interference as it boosted its sharp power as a major instrument of its statecraft, intellectual property theft and forced transfer of technology, subsidies to SOEs, predatory foreign investment practices abroad while keeping tight restrictions on foreigners in China, and so-called 'wolf warrior' diplomacy, predictably led to hostile and combative reactions by other powers. The EU is again reassessing its policies towards China in view of the pandemic and hardening its stance across a range of areas.[7]

Beijing's handling of the early stages of the pandemic characterised by the party-state's usual practice in such emergencies of denial and dissembling, before action and transparency, angered governments and citizens around the world.[8] Whatever mitigating arguments may be made about the lack of understanding in the early days about the viruses' infectiousness and mortality, and the clunkiness of China's internal information flows and decision-making, the speed of its global transmission and the ensuing economic damage on perhaps an unprecedented scale meant that international anger would be vented on China and directed towards the party-state. The Chinese public is also asking who knew what and when did they know.[9] The WHO inquiry initiated by the EU may help to answer these questions.

From Beijing's perspective, President Trump's blaming China and references alternatively to the Wuhan Flu, China Flu and the Kung Flu, and assertions that the virus had escaped from a military laboratory in Wuhan, were met with reciprocal hostile rhetoric from Beijing.[10] Publicly attributing responsibility to Beijing inevitably was seen as a direct attack on the authority and legitimacy of the CPC. A massive propaganda campaign within China was already underway, seeking to unite the country around the party and its leadership under Xi Jinping. Unprecedented lockdown measures were being imposed as the country was joined in a fight against the virus. More than ever, Beijing could not tolerate the slightest criticism. In this highly fraught domestic political context in China, the Australian prime minister's perfectly reasonable, but misjudged in terms of its execution, demand for an international inquiry became explosive.[11]

As with Australia being the first to impose a blanket ban on Huawei participating in 5G, its stridency over the South China Sea, and then leading without a coalition of like-minded countries a public call to investigate the origins of COVID-19, Australia has unnecessarily made itself a target for the CPC to attack. It looks as if Australia deliberately set about making the Chinese leadership lose face.

In foreign policy, COVID-19 became quickly weaponised and saw a deep deterioration in US-China relations, and even more so in Australia-China relations. In recent years, Australia has become something of the 'canary in the coal mine' for US-China relations: it adopts less nuanced and more confrontational positions thereby drawing to itself strong reaction from China. While all Australian official contact is frozen, the US and China, fortunately for the world, continue to engage officially at the highest levels. Following a meeting in Hawaii in June 2020 between Secretary of State Pompeo and China's State Councillor responsible for Foreign Affairs, Yang Jiechi, mutual public criticism was dialled back for a while, but China soon again became a focus of US electoral politics.[12]

Decoupling and the End of Globalisation?

The pandemic has heightened public awareness and concern globally over the world economy's deep interdependencies via global supply chains. Well before the pandemic struck, 'decoupling' was becoming an increasingly vogue subject on the foreign policy and business conference circuit. These concerns arose in the context of the US–China Trade War and heightened technological competition, especially in advanced technologies such as artificial intelligence, semi-conductors and biosciences.

As the World Economic Forum has argued:

> the trend today is not one in which these two countries are just competing across common domains but one in which each is looking to design its own systems—its own supply chains, 5G networks and global investment institutions. Already investment flows between the two have dropped, each has moved to restrict technology from the other, and some analysts predict China will look to reduce its dependence on the US dollar by holding more foreign currencies [non-US dollars].[13]

Decoupling was a threat that the Trump Administration made as a part of its changed strategy towards containment, especially denying

China access to advanced technology. Beijing, however, may now see little to fear from a decoupled world which may occur increasingly on its own terms.

Its capital markets are strong, stable and attracting more inflows, in turn strengthening the renminbi as an international currency. It is attracting gratitude from many countries for leadership and support in the international response to the virus. It is exerting much more influence in multilateral institutions than before—mainly because of its strong bilateral relationships around the world which will be bolstered substantially by its COVID-19 aid.

Meanwhile, Beijing is pushing on with its ambition to create a digital bounded order across Eurasia and into South-East Asia, parts of South Asia, Africa and the Pacific. At the 2nd Silk Road Forum in Beijing in 2019, Xi Jinping set out China's proposal for a 'digital Silk Road' encompassing not only infrastructure and physical equipment supplied by Chinese firms, notably Huawei and EZT, but also Chinese derived norms and regulatory arrangements, and digital border payments services supplied by firms such as Tencent and Alibaba.[14]

The BRI is, however, also under challenge from heavily indebted participant countries which have been hit badly by COVID-19. Beijing has had to renegotiate non-performing loans before, but it has never faced so many debtors at the same time. This is a significant risk to Beijing's own financial stability, at a time of lower domestic economic growth and efforts to deleverage its financial system. Widespread debt cancellation or rescheduling could increase domestic dissatisfaction and scepticism about the BRI.[15]

These Chinese vulnerabilities may push Beijing to work more cooperatively with multilateral creditor groups, such as the Paris Club. Beijing is not a member and continues to demonstrate a preference to manage debt-relief bilaterally, but this could change in the face of large-scale renegotiations. Although its messaging during the pandemic emergency has been to 'go it alone' and to portray itself as a generous provider of medical equipment and assistance, other creditors will resist and benefits from debt restructuring are unlikely to be allowed to be used to repay BRI loans, raising the likelihood of defaulting on BRI debt.[16] Without the cooperation of other creditors and permitting greater transparency around its BRI lending that would be required, 'debt distress along the Belt and Road will be a serious threat to China's own financial sustainability.'[17]

As can be seen from China's digital expansion along the BRI and the challenges of debt restructuring, COVID-19 is reinforcing powerful trends that push and pull in both directions of coupling and decoupling. It is too early to say which will prevail.

Governments and people around the world were shocked when they initially learned how dependent they had become on global supply chains for critical emergency equipment and supplies, and that all supply chains seemed to lead back to China. Although China suffered a big setback to its soft power in the early days of the pandemic over its lack of transparency and confusion, China has been able to reposition itself by supplying equipment and other material assistance on scale. China has supplemented this with intense diplomatic activity involving central and eastern European states through the '17+1' mechanism, the SCO, with a group of Pacific island states and other bodies, including the WHO. The US Administration has been passive in its diplomatic efforts.[18]

The revealed vulnerability and hence dependency on China, however, led to an immediate and intense reaction.[19] It drew a gathering backlash in the US, the EU and elsewhere against open markets and trade liberalisation. This united conservative and radical protectionists in calls for greater economic self-sufficiency. Trade-exposed industries quickly hopped on the bandwagon.

COVID-19 has given significant impetus to trade protection arguments and a retreat from globalisation. China is seen as a major beneficiary of the globalisation of the past thirty years and hence a major culprit in creating 'unfair' dependency by other states on it and thus eroding their sovereignty.[20] Governments which are all having to deal with shock increases in unemployment are susceptible to short-term protectionist arguments.

The reality, however, is that the world is coupled for good reason. A deeply integrated global economy has evolved because it is efficient to do so and delivers goods as cheaply as possible, thereby raising consumer welfare. While policies to promote domestic production on the grounds of national security are legitimate, they come at a cost and politicians need to explain to their publics what the cost may mean in terms of lower growth and welfare.

Australia as an open trading economy that has benefited so much from China's economic growth is itself not immune to arguments to decouple. In Australia's case, this argument usually takes the form of diversifying away from its heavy reliance on China as a market for both goods and services. But as the most recent detailed study of this has shown, the profound complementarities of the Chinese and Australian economies, the sheer size of the Chinese economy, and the absence of any viable alternative market of the size of China's mean that decoupling for Australia would come only at a heavy price. Economically, Australia is inextricably tied to China unless Australians are prepared to accept a big cut in their living standards.[21] Australian foreign and strategic policy needs to be reconfigured to reflect fully this reality.

A Post-COVID-19 Order

The impact of COVID-19 on the new order is still uncertain, but if the immediate developments are continued with China returning to business as usual ahead of most countries, and restarting its engines of economic growth before the rest of the world, then most likely the existing trends described elsewhere in this book will deepen and become more entrenched. The US' chaotic response could delay both recovery from the disease and even more so cause protracted economic recovery. Saddled with historically high debt and unemployment, it will be materially weakened in its contest with China.

China itself will also need to manage problems of debt and potential social instability from weaker growth and rising unemployment. BRI debt could be a further drag, not only on China's finances but importantly on the people's tolerance of Xi Jinping's global ambitions and the costs of BRI and an expanding military. These are dangerous times for China's leaders as they try to balance the projection of stability and a return to normalcy against an increasingly hostile Western-world opinion, and a virus that is scarcely under control.

Overall, the pandemic is likely to entrench further the new multi-polar, bounded world order. It is likely to highlight China's strengths and the US' weaknesses. The US has been here before, such as when it fell behind the Soviet Union in the Space Race and following the humiliation of its defeat in the long Vietnam War. On both occasions it recovered rapidly and convincingly. It has now been in Afghanistan longer than any other war in its history. Like all other invaders of Afghanistan, it will leave with its strategic objectives for entering the war unfulfilled. As former US secretary of defense, Robert Gates wrote recently, that US foreign policy has become over militarised.[22] He suggests the US needs to return to using the full range of its instruments of statecraft. But in the past it has not faced such a formidable opponent, and one which may emerge from COVID-19 relatively stronger. Short of an unthinkable military conflict with China, COVID-19 might hasten a reassessment in the next presidential term of its policies of confrontation.

Australia has firmly nailed its colours to the US mast and with or without its great ally, it is an unattractive future. Australia looks set to be locked into an unproductive relationship with China that will destroy value in trade and investment on both sides. Certainly, Australians will pay a price through lost economic opportunity and will be poorer than they otherwise would have been.

Australian policymakers who insist this is the 'new' normal and welcome it as Australia standing up to a bullying China, have not prepared the public for the economic consequences of these policies. Moreover, in foreign policy, positions which were once thought immutable can change overnight. In this, like all great powers, the US has form, and may do so again in its relations with China. The impact of COVID-19 is so severe that leaders in the US and China might once again decide that cooperation on the big risks of the day offers better prospects for advancing their interests. Australia could find itself outside of the conversation.

[handwritten: → AUKUS]

[handwritten: Does Australia Truly understand the total consequences of joining this "White Boys Alliance"?]

ACKNOWLEDGEMENTS

I am deeply grateful to the people who kindly read the text in full or part, and who contributed data, references and other material at a moment's notice on my requests for help. They were Jocelyn Chey, Xu Xitao, Linda Jackobson, Dirk van de Kley, Ross Garnaut, Stephen Fitzgerald, Stephen Wyatt, Zhaung BJ, Syd Hickman, Kevin Hopgood-Brown, James Laurenceson and Allan Gyngell. In over thirty years of working on Australia's foreign and trade policies, including living in China for nearly eighteen years in total, many people have guided my thinking and understanding about these matters and shaped my intellectual development. They are too many to list fully and it would be too invidious here to list a sample. They know who they are. Melbourne University Publishing's Publisher and CEO, Nathan Hollier, kept the faith despite many missed deadlines, and provided invaluable encouragement. Paul Smitz patiently, persistently and professionally edited the entire text. None are responsible for what is now being presented to the public, other than myself.

NOTES

Introduction

1 Literature on the subject has grown hugely since 2016. For an overview, see Peter Hartcher, 'Red Flag: Waking up to China's Challenge', *Quarterly Essay*, no. 76, 2019; Hartcher's arguments are rebutted in *Quarterly Essay*, no. 77.

2 Subsequently, the EU built an international coalition which China itself supported for the World Health Organization to conduct an independent inquiry without implying responsibility.

3 Jennifer Hewett, 'The Rupture with China Is Permanent', *AFR*, 23 June 2020.

4 Prime Minister Morrison's November 2019 meeting in Bangkok on the sidelines of the Association of Southeast Asian Nations summit did not mark a thaw. A meeting on the sidelines of a multilateral meeting is of a second order of diplomatic protocol and importance compared with a bilateral visit to one another's capitals.

5 Malcolm Turnbull, *A Bigger Picture*, Hardie Grant, Melbourne, 2020, pp. 422–6.

6 Department of Foreign Affairs and Trade, *Opportunity, Security, Strength: the 2017 Foreign Policy White Paper*, Australian Government, Canberra, 23 November 2017. At this time, the National Security Committee of Cabinet had, according to Turnbull, formed the view that 'China's goal was to supplant the United States as the leading power in the region, and that was plainly not in [Australia's] interests'— Malcolm Turnbull, *A Bigger Picture*, Hardie Grant, Melbourne, 2020, p. 422.

7 The White House, *New National Security Strategy for a New Era*, Washington, DC, 18 December 2017.

8 Ibid.

9 Brookings Institute, 'Brookings Experts on Trump's New National Security Strategy', *Brookings*, 21 December 2020, https://www.brookings.edu/research/brookings-experts-on-trumps-national-security-strategy (viewed May 2020).

10 The White House, *New National Security Strategy for a New Era*, Washington, DC, 18 December 2017. Of course, the claim that Australia has fought alongside the US in every war since World War I is historically wrong. Australia has not fought in the US' many wars in the Western Hemisphere.

11 Ben Smee and Christopher A Walsh, 'How the Sale of Darwin Port to the Chinese Sparked a Geopolitical Brawl', *The Guardian*, 18 December 2016. Turnbull recounts this as the only difficult moment in his relations with Obama—Malcolm Turnbull, *A Bigger Picture*, Hardie Grant, Melbourne, 2020, p. 298.

12 Michelle Grattan, 'Morrison Blocks Chinese Bids for NSW Power Grid', *The Conversation*, 11 August 2016, https://theconversation.com/morrison-blocks-chinese-bids-for-nsw-power-grid-63821 (viewed May 2020).

13 Department of Home Affairs, 'Critical Infrastructure Resilience', Australian Government, Canberra, 23 January 2017, https://www.homeaffairs.gov.au/about-us/our-portfolios/national-security/security-coordination/critical-infrastructure-resilience (viewed May 2020).

14 The Treasury, 'FIRB Chair Appointment', Australian Government, 8 April 2017, https://ministers.treasury.gov.au/ministers/scott-morrison-2015/media-releases/firb-chair-appointment (viewed May 2020).

15 *Global Times*, 19 April 2018.

16 Malcolm Turnbull, *A Bigger Picture*, Hardie Grant, Melbourne, 2020, p. 435.

17 Ibid.

18 *Financial Times*, 'Britain's Ties with China Are Set for a Change', 11 June 2020; *Financial Times*, 'Mike Pompeo Calls on UK to Choose Sides on China', 10 June 2020.

19 Shirley Yu, 'The Belt and Road Initiative: Modernity, Geopolitics and the Developing Global Order', *Asian Affairs*, vol. 50, no. 2, 2019, pp. 187–201.

20 Richard McGregor, *Xi Jinping: the Backlash*, Penguin, Sydney, 2019.

21 Kurt M Campbell, *The Pivot: the Future of American Statecraft in Asia*, Hachette, New York, 2016, pp. 230–50.

22 Michael Phillsbury, *The Hundred-Year Marathon: China's Secret Strategy to Replace America as the Global Superpower*, St Martin's Press, New York, 2015.

23 Geoff Raby, La Trobe University Oration, October 2019.

24 Michael Evans, 'Australian Strategy and the Gathering Storm in Asia', *Quadrant*, April 2020, p. 18.

25 John Pike, 'Worldwide Chokepoints', *GlobalSecurity.org*, 8 April 2018, https://www.globalsecurity.org/military/world/chokepoints.htm (viewed May 2020).

26 According to the 2020 Global Firepower index, which excludes nuclear weapons but uses fifty indices to normalise for absolute size to reveal effectiveness, Japan ranks fifth after India, while the US, Russia and China are the top three (in that order). Japan has about half of China's firepower, which, considering its much smaller numbers of active personnel, attests to its superior technological capabilities. Japan ranked nineteenth in manpower compared with China, which has the biggest military in terms of manpower—*Global Firepower*, 'Global Firepower 2020', 2020, https://www.globalfirepower.com (viewed May 2020); Jessica Dillinger, '29 Largest Armies in the World', *WorldAtlas*, 7 January 2020, https://www.worldatlas.com/articles/29-largest-armies-in-the-world.html (viewed May 2020).

27 In 2019, China substantially outweighed the US in diplomatic influence in Asia—Lowy Institute, 'Asia Power Index 2019', https://power.lowyinstitute.org (viewed May 2020).

28 Geoff Raby, 'Why the Bell Must Toll for WHO Chief Tedros', *AFR*, 18 April 2020.

29 Shashi Tharoor and Samir Saran, *The New World Order and the Indian Imperative*, Aleph Book Co., Delhi, 2020. To be fair, the authors challenge the notion of

'order', specifically the idea of a postwar liberal order as a myth, that it was a system of global governance based on coercive diplomacy 'which provided a means to amass and maintain power and wealth without the use of military force' (p. xiii).

30 Oliver Stuenkel, *Post Western World: How Emerging Powers Are Remaking Global Order*, Polity Press, Cambridge, UK, 2016.

31 Martin Jacques, *When China Rules the World*, 2nd edn, Penguin, London, 2014. Jacques was among the first to argue that China's political system will not be changed by economic growth and rising incomes but will revert to more traditional forms of Chinese political and social organisation and represent a 'new modernity' to challenge existing ones. He uses 'civilisation state' for China as distinct from 'nation state' (p. 244).

32 James Kynge, 'China Was the Real Victor of Asia's Financial Crisis', *Financial Times*, 3 July 2017.

33 Robert B Zoellick, 'Whither China: From Membership to Responsibility', speech to National Committee on US–China Relations, New York, 21 September 2005.

34 Graeme Dobell, 'Great Australian Foreign Policy Speeches: Rudd at Peking University', *The Interpreter*, The Lowy Institute, 18 August 2014, https://www.lowyinstitute.org/the-interpreter/great-australian-foreign-policy-speeches-rudd-peking-university (viewed May 2020).

35 Oliver Stuenkel, *Post Western World: How Emerging Powers Are Remaking Global Order*, Polity Press, Cambridge, UK, 2016, pp. 10–11. The Shanghai Cooperation Organisation was announced in 2001, its charter signed in 2002, and it came into force in 2003.

36 Vice President Pence referred positively to the US nineteenth-century missionary efforts in China in his Hudson Institute speech in which he endorsed the NSS position that China was a strategic competitor of the US. See, for example, Presbyterian Historical Society, 'The Last Years of a China Mission', The National Archives of the PC (USA), 31 March 1986.

37 Martin Jacques, *When China Rules the World*, 2nd edn, Penguin, London, 2014.

38 Richard McGregor, *The Party: the Secret World of China's Communist Rulers*, Penguin, London, 2011, ch. 2.

39 Yan Xuetong, *Leadership and the Rise of Great Powers*, Princeton University Press, Princeton, 2019, pp. 203–5.

40 www.reddit.com, 'Taiwan's Territorial Claims', 21 November 2019.

41 Julie Bishop, 'Change and Uncertainty in the Indo-Pacific: Strategy, Challenges and Opportunities', twenty-eighth IISS Fullerton Lecture, Singapore, 13 March 2017.

42 Nicholas Lardy, *The State Strikes Back: the End of Economic Reform in China?*, Peterson Institute, Washington, DC, 2019.

43 Xinhua, 'China Lifts Foreign Ownership Limits on Securities, Fund Management Firms,' www.xinhuanet.com, 1 April 2020.

44 Frank Tang, 'China's Economic Strategy Shift Shows Xi Jinping is Preparing for "Worst Case" Scenario', *South China Morning Post*, 25 May 2020.

45 Although there is much in this book with which Rory Medcalf would disagree, he would at least agree that we share the same policy objective of peace and stability through coexistence with China. Rory Medcalf, *Contest for the Indo-Pacific: Why China Won't Map the Future*, La Trobe University Press, Melbourne, 2020, p. 247.

46 David Shambaugh, *China Goes Global: the Partial Power*, Oxford University Press, Oxford, 2013, pp. 315–17.

Chapter 1   China's Grand Strategy and the New World Order

1 Peter Hopkirk, *Foreign Devils on the old Silk Road: the Search for the Lost Treasures of Central Asia*, John Murray, London, 2006.

2 Henry Kissinger, *World Order*, Penguin, London, 2014.

3 Oliver Stuenkel, *Post Western World: How Emerging Powers Are Remaking Global Order*, Polity Press, Cambridge, UK, 2016, p. 2.

4 Wang Jisi, 'China's Search for a Grand Strategy: a Rising Great Power Finds Its Way', *Foreign Affairs*, March/April 2011; John J Mearsheimer, 'Bound to Fail: the Rise and Fall of the Liberal International Order', *International Security*, vol. 43, no. 4, 2019, pp. 7–9; Angela Stanzel, Nadege Rolland, Jabin Jacob and Melanie Hart, 'Grand Designs: Does China Have a Grand Strategy?', European Council on Foreign Relations, 18 October 2017, http://www.ecfr.eu/publications/summary/grands.designs_does_china_have_a_grand_strategy (viewed May 2020).

5 Sulman Wasif Khan, *Haunted by Chaos: China's Grand Strategy from Mao Zedong to Xi Jinping*, Harvard University Press, Cambridge, 2018, p. 236.

6 Ibid., p. 237.

7 Wang Jisi, 'China's Search for a Grand Strategy: a Rising Great Power Finds Its Way', *Foreign Affairs*, March/April 2011.

8 John S Van Oudenaren, 'The Chinese Communist Party's Obsession with the Threat of a Colour Revolution Is Revealing', *The Diplomat*, 1 September 2015. The Party has viewed the West's promotion of human rights and democracy as intended to overthrow the Party.

9 Ibid.

10 Wang Jisi, 'China's Search for a Grand Strategy: a Rising Great Power Finds Its Way', *Foreign Affairs*, March/April 2011.

11 Sulman Wasif Khan, *Haunted by Chaos: China's Grand Strategy from Mao Zedong to Xi Jinping*, Harvard University Press, Cambridge, 2018, p. 44.

12 Ibid., p. 243.

13 Ibid.

14 Shirley Z Yu, Belt and Road Initiative: Defining China's Grand Strategy and the Future World Order, a thesis in the field of government for the degree of Master of Liberal Arts, Harvard University, March 2018, p. 83.

15 Xi Jinping, 'Davos World Economic Forum', *China Daily*, 17 January 2017.

16 Shirley Z Yu, Belt and Road Initiative: Defining China's Grand Strategy and the Future World Order, a thesis in the field of government for the degree of Master of Liberal Arts, Harvard University, March 2018, pp. 8–9.

17 Yu argues that not only is 'Pax Sinica' the real meaning of 'Common Destiny', but that it is likely to happen. Ikenberry is much more hopeful about the future of liberal order—G John Ikenberry, 'The Future of the Liberal World Order: Internationalism after America', *Foreign Affairs*, vol. 90, no. 3, 2011. The quote is from Sarwar A Kashmeri, *China's Grand Strategy: Weaving a New Silk Road to Global Primacy*, Praeger, Santa Barbara, CA, 2020, p. 7.

18 Hal Brands and Charles Edel, *The Lessons of Tragedy, Statecraft and World Order*, Yale University Press, New Haven, CT, 2019, pp. 134–6.

19 The pushback against the BRI and China's interference under the United Front Work Department are discussed more fully in Chapter 5; see also Richard McGregor, *Xi Jinping: the Backlash*, Penguin, Sydney, 2019. Russia's 'near abroad' as a major strategic policy priority for China was discussed by Singapore's Prime

Minister Lee Hsien Loong, 'The Endangered Asian Century: America, China and the Perils of Confrontation', *Foreign Policy*, July/August 2020.

20 Malcolm Turnbull, *A Bigger Picture*, Hardie Grant, Melbourne, 2020, p. 419.

21 John J Mearsheimer, in 'Bound to Fail: the Rise and Fall of the Liberal International Order', *International Security*, vol. 43, no. 4, 2019, postulates an emerging 'bound' order to replace the liberal, international order, in which great powers both engage in an international order of rules, such as the WTO, and within their own—bound—orders that include at least one great power and exclude another great power. The BRI has these characteristics, although notionally it is open to the US to join. The US won't, of course, because that would hand leadership to China.

22 Pooja Bhatt, 'What China's Defence Paper Tells Us about Beijing's Regional Ambitions', *The Interpreter*, The Lowy Institute, 2 August 2019.

23 Kathy Gilsinan, 'How the US Could Lose a War with China', *The Atlantic*, 25 July 2019; David Lague, 'Special Report: US Rearms to Nullify China's Missile Supremacy', *Reuters*, 6 May 2020.

24 Graham Allison, 'The Thucydides Trap: Are the US and China Headed for War?', *The Atlantic*, 24 September 2015; Margret MacMillan, *The War that Ended Peace: the Road to 1914*, Random House, New York, 2013.

25 Graham Allison, *Destined for War: China, America, and the Thucydides Trap*, Harcourt, Boston, 2017, p. xvi.

26 Arthur Waldron, 'There Is no Thucydides Trap', *SupChina*, 17 June 2017.

27 Crispin Rovere, 'Book Review: Graham Allison's *Destined for War*', *The Interpreter*, The Lowy Institute, 4 July 2017.

28 Oliver Stuenkel, *Post Western World: How Emerging Powers Are Remaking Global Order*, Polity Press, Cambridge, UK, 2016, p. 8.

29 Joshua R Itzkowitz Shifrinson, *Falling Giants, Rising Titans: How Great Powers Exploit Power Shifts*, Cornell University Press, Ithaca, NY and London, 2018, pp. 160–74.

30 Quoted in Graham Allison, *Destined for War: China, America, and the Thucydides Trap*, Harcourt, Boston, 2017, p. 151.

31 Yan Xuetong, *Leadership and the Rise of Great Powers*, Princeton University Press, Princeton, 2019, pp. 88–90; Shirley Yu, 'The Belt and Road Initiative: Modernity, Geopolitics and the Developing Global Order', *Asian Affairs*, vol. 50, no. 2, 2019.

32 Rory Medcalf, *Contest for the Indo-Pacific: Why China Won't Map the Future*, La Trobe University Press, Melbourne, 2020, p. 15.

33 Shirley Yu, 'The Belt and Road Initiative: Modernity, Geopolitics and the Developing Global Order', *Asian Affairs*, vol. 50, no. 2, 2019, pp. 182–9.

34 Halford John Mackinder, 'The Geographical Pivot of History', *Geographical Journal*, vol. 23, no. 4, 1904, p. 436.

35 Shirley Yu, 'The Belt and Road Initiative: Modernity, Geopolitics and the Developing Global Order', *Asian Affairs*, vol. 50, no. 2, 2019, p. 47.

36 Richard Feinsberg, 'Review of Eric Rutkow: *The Longest Line on the Map: the United States, the Pan-American Highway and the Quest to Link the Americas*', *Foreign Affairs*, May/June 2019, p. 207.

37 The pushback against BRI investment and loans from a number of countries is discussed at length in Chapter 5.

38 World Bank, 'Belt and Road Economics: Opportunities and Risks of Transport Corridors', Washington, DC, June 2019, pp. 4–5, 37.

39 These are popular headline numbers. A recent World Bank report puts the total value of investment commitments by China at \$575 billion and identifies seventy-one countries along the main 'corridors' (these are the countries of East and South-East Asia, the Pacific, Eurasia, the Middle East, and Sub-Saharan Africa—ibid., pp. 4–5, 37.

40 Ibid., pp. 39–40.

41 Ibid., p. 40.

42 U.S. Energy Information Administration, 'World Oil Transit Chokepoints', 25 July 2017, p. 6.

43 Sarwar A Kashmeri, *China's Grand Strategy: Weaving a New Silk Road to Global Primacy*, Praeger, Santa Barbara, CA, 2020, p. 151.

44 Daniel S Markey, *China's Western Horizon: Beijing and the New Geopolitics of Eurasia*, Oxford University Press, Oxford, 2020, preface.

45 From personal visits and conversations in 2010 as ambassador and in 2015 while leading a business delegation.

46 Robert D Kaplan, *The Return of Marco Polo's World: War, Strategy and American Interests in the Twenty-First Century*, Random House, NY, 2018, p. 260.

47 Private conversation, 2014.

48 Fang Jin, 'The Belt and Road Initiative: Progress, Problems, and Prospects', in Daniel Remler and Ye Yu (eds), *Parallel Perspectives on the Global Order: a US–China Essay Collection*, CSIS, Washington, DC, September 2017, pp. 90–3.

49 World Bank, 'Belt and Road Economics: Opportunities and Risks of Transport Corridors', Washington, DC, June 2019, pp. 4–5.

50 Oliver Stuenkel, *Post Western World: How Emerging Powers Are Remaking Global Order*, Polity Press, Cambridge, UK, 2016, p. 11; John J Mearsheimer, 'Bound to Fail: the Rise and Fall of the Liberal International Order', *International Security*, vol. 43, no. 4, 2019.

51 G John Ikenberry, 'The Illusion of Geopolitics and the Enduring Power of the Liberal Order', *Foreign Affairs*, May/June 2014; G John Ikenberry and Darren J Lim, 'China's Emerging Institutional Statecraft: the Asian Infrastructure Bank and the Prospects for Counter-Hegemony', Project on International Order and Strategy at Brookings, April 2017, p. 2.

52 Alicja Bachulska and Richard Q Turcsanyi, 'Behind the Huawei Backlash in Poland and the Czech Republic', *The Diplomat*, 6 February 2019.

53 Mearsheimer provides a typology of order, with both international and bounded orders coexisting and overlapping. The international approximates to US-led unipolar moment, and the bounded where one superpower leads an order with one superpower outside it, as exists now with the US and its allies refusing to participate in the BRI and/or AIIB, and China outside the TPP, while the US and its allies are outside the SCO. Coverage of orders range from what he calls 'thick', where rules have a substantial effect on the behaviour of states (for example the WTO), or 'thin', such as APEC, which has little or no direct effect on members' behaviour. Types of orders range from realist through to agnostic and ideological (liberal)—John J Mearsheimer, 'Bound to Fail: the Rise and Fall of the Liberal International Order', *International Security*, vol. 43, no. 4, 2019, pp. 11–16.

54 Ibid., pp. 9–10.

55 Elena Collinson, 'Australia's Tilt on China', *ACRI Facts*, University of Technology Sydney, 4 July 2017.

56 Andrew Clarke, 'Julie Bishop and the Australia–China relationship', *AFR*, 17 May 2018.

57 David Hurst, 'We Will Simply Disconnect', *The Guardian*, 25 May 2020.

58 Michael Evans, 'Australian Strategy and the Gathering Storm in Asia', *Quadrant*, April 2020, p. 26.

59 Shirley Z Yu, Belt and Road Initiative: Defining China's Grand Strategy and the Future World Order, a thesis in the field of government for the degree of Master of Liberal Arts, Harvard University, March 2018, pp. 41–3. Regression analysis shows no correlation between BRI membership and 'democratic' forms of social and political organisation.

60 The Victorian Government has taken the position that BRI membership poses little or no downside risk, while not participating denies Victoria potential opportunities that may follow signing the MOUs.

61 Shirley Z Yu, Belt and Road Initiative: Defining China's Grand Strategy and the Future World Order, a thesis in the field of government for the degree of Master of Liberal Arts, Harvard University, March 2018, p. 4–7.

62 Richard McGregor, *Asia's Reckoning: China, Japan and the Fate of U.S. Power in the Pacific Century*, Penguin, New York, 2018, p. 351.

63 Kishore Mahbubani, in conversation with John Mearsheimer and Tom Switzer, Centre for Independent Studies, webcast, 7 May 2020.

64 Robert D Blackwell and Jennifer M Harris, *War by Other Means: Geo-economics and Statecraft*, Harvard University Press, Harvard, 2016; Graham Allison, *Destined for War: China, America, and the Thucydides Trap*, Harcourt, Boston, 2017, p. 21.

65 Richard Maude, 'Looking Ahead: Australia and China after the Pandemic', Asia Society Policy Research Centre, Melbourne, May 2020.

Chapter 2 The Ties that Bind China

1 Peter C Perdue, *China Marches West: the Qing Conquest of Central Asia*, Harvard University Press, Harvard, 2010.

2 Ross Terrill, *The New Chinese Empire and What It Means for the United States*, Basic Books, New York, 2004, p. 230.

3 Mark B Smith, *The Russian Anxiety: and How History Can Resolve It*, Allen Lane, London, 2019, p. 19.

4 *Global Firepower*, 'Global Firepower 2020', 2020, https://www.globalfirepower.com (viewed May 2020).

5 Mod.gov.cn, 2020, http:/www.mod.gov.cn/topnews/2019-03/05/content_4837244.htm (viewed May 2020); *ChinaPower*, 'What Does China Really Spend on Its Military?', 2020, http://chinapower.csis.org/military-spending (viewed May 2020).

6 *ChinaPower*, 'What Does China Really Spend on Its Military?', 2020, http://chinapower.csis.org/military-spending (viewed May 2020).

7 Adrian Zenz, 'China's Domestic Security Spending', *China Brief*, https://Jamestown.org/program/chinas-domestic-security-spending-analysis-available-data (viewed May 2020).

8 Michael Smith, 'Inside China's Re-education Camps', *AFR*, 26 July 2019.

9 Halford John Mackinder, 'The Geographical Pivot of History', *Geographical Journal*, vol. 23, no. 4, 1904, p. 436.

10 He argues that a geopolitical centre is determined not by physical geography but the capabilities of the countries that reside there—Yan Xuetong, *Leadership and the Rise of Great Powers*, Princeton University Press, Princeton, 2019, pp. 93–4.

11 Quoted in Margaret Scott and Westenley Alcent, 'Revisiting the Pivot: the Influence of Heartland Theory in Great Power Politics', discussion paper, Macalester College, Washington, DC, May 2008, p. 1.

12 Ibid., p. 2

13 Henry Kissinger, *World Order*, Penguin, London, 2014.

14 Robert D Kaplan, *The Revenge of Geography*, Random House, New York, 2012, pp. 212–13.

15 Ibid.

16 Ben Doherty, 'Explainer: What Is the Deadly India–China Border Dispute About?', *The Diplomat*, 17 June 2020.

17 Nguyen Minh Quang, 'The Bitter Legacy of the 1979 China–Vietnam War', *The Diplomat*, 23 February 2017.

18 Ibid.

19 Ibid.

20 Ibid.

21 Ibid.

22 Quoted in Margaret Scott and Westenley Alcent, 'Revisiting the Pivot: the Influence of Heartland Theory in Great Power Politics', discussion paper, Macalester College, Washington, DC, May 2008, p. 1.

23 Mark B Smith, *The Russian Anxiety: and How History Can Resolve It*, Allen Lane, London, 2019, p. 380.

24 Ibid.

25 Ibid., p. 20.

26 Halford John Mackinder, 'The Geographical Pivot of History', *Geographical Journal*, vol. 23, no. 4, 1904; Mark B Smith, *The Russian Anxiety: and How History Can Resolve It*, Allen Lane, London, 2019, p. 246.

27 Ibid.

28 Yu Lei, 'China–Russia Military Cooperation in the Context of Sino–Russian Strategic Partnership', *Asia Europe Journal*, 8 July 2019.

29 Vasily Kashin, 'Russia and China Take Military Partnership to New Level', *The Moscow Times*, 23 October 2019.

30 Ibid.

31 Peter C Perdue, *China Marches West: the Qing Conquest of Central Asia*, Harvard University Press, Harvard, 2010.

32 Robert D Kaplan, *The Revenge of Geography*, Random House, New York, 2012, p. 203.

33 Darren Byler, 'The Disappearance of Perhat Tursun', *SupChina*, 5 February 2020.

34 Geoff Raby, 'Why the Bell Must Toll for WHO Chief Tedros', *AFR*, 18 April 2020.

35 Linda Jackobson, private conversation.

36 *China Daily*, 'Speech Delivered by Xi Jinping at the First Session of the 13th NPC', 21 March 2018.

37 Chris Buckley and Chris Horten, 'Xi Jinping Warns Taiwan', *New York Times*, 1 January 2019.

38 Linda Jackobson, private conversation.
39 *RTHK News*, 'Liaison Office not Subject to Article 22', 18 April 2020.

Chapter 3   Rich Country, Poor Country

1 Dwight Perkins, 'Completing China's Move to the Market', in Ross Garnaut and Yiping Huang (eds), *Growth without Miracles*, Oxford University Press, New York, pp. 37–40. Zhao Ziyang was premier and then party general secretary and Wan Li was vice premier.

2 R Ash, 'The Evolution of Agricultural Policy', *China Quarterly*, December 1988.

3 C Watson, 'The Second Phase of Economic Reform in China', *Current History*, September 1985.

4 *Beijing Review*, no. 44, October 1984.

5 Geoff Raby, 'The Neither This nor That Economy', in Ross Garnaut and Yiping Huang (eds), *Growth without Miracles*, Oxford University Press, New York, pp. 19–35.

6 Ronald Coase and Ning Wang, *How China Became Capitalist*, Palgrave McMillan, London, pp. 68–103.

7 Zhao Ziyang, *Prisoner of the State: the Secret Journal of Zhao Ziyang*, Simon and Schuster, New York, 2009.

8 Janos Kornai, *The Economics of Shortage*, North Holland Press, Amsterdam, 1980.

9 Madeline O'Dea, *The Phoenix Years: Art, Resistance and the Making of Modern China*, Allen and Unwin, Sydney, 2016.

10 The data for this section is drawn from standard statistical sources commonly used, such as China's National Bureau of Statistics (NBS), the General Administration of Customs of China (GACC), the World Coal Association (WCA), and for crude oil, LNG BP Ltd, Worldsteel, IEA and *Reuters*. These sources are indicated in the relevant tables and graphs.

11 Stephen Wyatt, 'Iron Ore Price Wars', *AFR*, 23 July 2007.

12 James F Carlin, 'Tin: Statistics and Information', United States Geological Survey, 2008–12.

13 David E Hamilton, 'Herbert Hoover: Life Before the Presidency', Miller Center, University of Virginia, 2019.

14 Armand Hammer, 'On a Vast Market', *Journal of International Affairs*, vol. 39, no. 2, winter 1986.

15 Ibid., p. 21.

16 NBS, various years.

17 International Trade Administration, 'China Commercial Guide', U.S. Department of Commerce, 2020, http://www.export.gov/article?id=China-Oil-and-Gas (viewed May 2020).

18 Rystad Energy, 'North America Becomes Self-Sufficient in Oil', press release, 7 March 2019.

19 Nicolas Loris, 'Does the US Still Need Middle East Oil?', *The Heritage Foundation*, 17 January 2020.

20 Douglas Ritchie, 'Chinese Outward Foreign Direct Investment', *China Go Abroad*, n.d., http://www.chinagoabroad.com/en/commentary/Chinese-outward-foreign-direct-investment (viewed May 2020).

21 Blanche D'Alpuget, *Hawke: the Prime Minister*, Melbourne University Press, Melbourne, 2010, pp. 126–9.

22 Personal communication with Professor Garnaut.

23 Private conversation with author.

24 Stephen Wyatt, 'Iron Ore Price Wars', *AFR*, 23 July 2007.

25 Conversation with minister Downer. I was the official who made the observation about Mme Fu.

26 On the current episode of 'wolf-warrior diplomacy', see Zhiqun Zhu, 'Interpreting China's "Wolf-Warrior" Diplomacy', *The Diplomat*, 15 May 2020.

27 Stephen Wyatt, 'China Warns Miners in Iron-ore Standoff', *AFR*, 21 September 2007.

28 Stephen Wyatt, 'Snub Bodes Ill for Iron Ore Negotiations', *AFR*, 7 October 2008.

29 Stephen Wyatt, 'Iron Ore Contract Price Posturing Begins', *AFR*, 21 September 2007.

30 Angus Grigg and Lisa Murray, 'BHP, Rio and the Doomed $40 billion Chinalco Deal: Who Knew What When?', *AFR*, 3 August 2018.

31 Regular representations objecting to this were made to the Australian embassy in Beijing.

32 Michael Allan McCrae, 'The Worst Mining Deal Ever', *Mining.com*, 15 February 2013.

33 Stephen Wyatt, 'Rio Coup by Chinalco's Xiao Cements Place in Corridors of Power', *AFR*, 14 February 2009.

34 Angus Grigg and Lisa Murray, 'BHP, Rio and the Doomed $40 billion Chinalco Deal: Who Knew What When?', *AFR*, 3 August 2018.

35 Stephen Wyatt, 'Jilted Suitor Laments Broken Iron Ore Dream', *AFR*, 6 June 2009.

36 Official discussion with Vice Chairman Zhang.

37 Stephen Wyatt, 'Rio Caught between Old and New China', *AFR*, 13 July 2009.

38 Yue Qu, Cai Fang and Zhang Xiaobo, 'Flying Geese in China', *East Asia Forum*, 22 November 2012.

39 David Shambaugh, *China Goes Global: the Partial Power*, Oxford University Publishing, Oxford, 2013, pp. 176–7.

40 Leonard K Cheng and Zihui Ma, 'China's Outward Foreign Direct Investment', in Robert C Feenstra and Shang-Jin Wei (eds), *China's Growing Role in World Trade*, Chicago University Publishing, Chicago, 2010, p. 547.

41 Ibid., p. 548.

42 Ibid., p. 549.

43 David Zweig and Jianhai Bi, 'China's Global Hunt for Energy', *Foreign Affairs*, September 2005, pp. 14–15.

44 Douglas Ritchie, 'Chinese Outward Foreign Direct Investment', *China Go Abroad*, n.d., http://www.chinagoabroad.com/en/commentary/Chinese-outward-foreign-direct-investment (viewed May 2020), p. 2.

45 Ibid.

46 Ibid.

47 Brad Thompson, 'Billion-dollar Write Down for China's Flagship Sino Iron Project', *AFR*, 12 March 2018.

48 Douglas Ritchie, 'Chinese Outward Foreign Direct Investment', *China Go Abroad*, n.d., http://www.chinagoabroad.com/en/commentary/Chinese-outward-foreign-direct-investment (viewed May 2020), p. 3.

49 Ibid.

50 The source has not been found so it could well be apocryphal, but it captures well the dilemma and security vulnerability. Shambaugh refers to the 'Malacca Dilemma' but without citing a source as well—David Shambaugh, *China Goes Global: the Partial Power*, Oxford University Publishing, Oxford, 2013, p. 163.

51 David Zweig and Jianhai Bi, 'China's Global Hunt for Energy', *Foreign Affairs*, September 2005, p. 11.

52 Stephen Kuper, 'The Indo-Pacific's Maritime Choke Points: Straits of Malacca', *Defence Connect*, 14 June 2019.

53 U.S. Energy Information Administration, 'World Oil Transit Chokepoints', 25 July 2017, p. 2.

54 Ibid., p. 6.

55 Douglas Ritchie, 'Chinese Outward Foreign Direct Investment', *China Go Abroad*, n.d., http://www.chinagoabroad.com/en/commentary/Chinese-outward-foreign-direct-investment (viewed May 2020), p. 2.

56 Australian Government, *Foreign Investment Review Board Annual Report, 2019*, Canberra, 2019.

57 Betty Huang, Avaro Ortiz and Tomasa Rodrigo, 'China: Five Facts about Outward Direct Investment and Their Implication for Future Trend' [sic], *China Economic Watch*, March 2019, p. 1.

58 Ibid., p. 2.

59 Ibid.

60 Ibid.

61 One of the most common misunderstandings by non-economists, and not too few economists, is confusing comparative advantage with absolute advantage. An economy might be lower cost at producing all goods and services than another economy. An optimal allocation of resources will occur, however, if some products are not produced where an economy is comparatively less efficient. That is, more resources would be saved for producing other goods in each economy, and the two countries enter into trade to satisfy demand.

62 NBS, various years.

Chapter 4 Soft Power, Sharp Power

1 Bo Yibo Memoirs, Wilson Center Digital Archive, 1991, http://digitalarchive. wilsoncenter.org/document/117029 (viewed May 2020).

2 Richard McGregor, *The Party: the Secret World of China's Communist Rulers*, Penguin, London, 2012, p. 1.

3 Wang Jisi, 'China's Search for a Grand Strategy', *Foreign Affairs*, March/April 2011.

4 Tom Mitchell, 'Xi Distracts from Own Failings with Hong Kong Security Law', *The Financial Times*, 21 May 2020.

5 Kat Devlin, Laura Silver and Christine Huang, 'U.S. Views of China Increasingly Negative amid Coronavirus Outbreak', *Pew Research Center*, 21 April 2020.

6 Eleanor Albert, 'China's Big Bet on Soft Power', Council on Foreign Relations, 9 February 2018; Joseph S Nye, Jr, 'Why China Is Weak on Soft Power', *New York Times*, 17 January 2012.

7 Bruno Macaes, *The Dawn of Eurasia: on the Trail of the New World Order*, Penguin, London, 2018, pp. 125–6.

8 Maria Repnikova and Kecheng Fang, 'Behind the Fall of China's Greatest Newspaper', *Foreign Policy*, 29 January 2015.

9 Xinhua, 'Xi Stresses Stronger Cultural Confidence', www.xinhuanet.com, 4 March 2019.

10 Tanner Greer, 'Xi Jinping Knows Who His Enemies Are: a Review of *Inside the Mind of Xi Jinping*' (by François Bougon, 2018), *Foreign Policy*, 21 November 2019.

11 Damien Ma, 'Beijing's "Culture War" Isn't about the US—It's about China's Future', *The Atlantic*, 5 January 2012.

12 Joseph S Nye, Jr, 'Why China Is Weak on Soft Power', *New York Times*, 17 January 2012.

13 Joseph S Nye, Jr., 'The Decline of America's Soft Power', *Foreign Affairs*, May/June 2004.

14 G John Ikenberry, 'Review of Joseph S Nye Jr, *Soft Power: the Means to Success in World Politics*', *Foreign Affairs*, May/June 2004.

15 Joseph S Nye, Jr., 'How Sharp Power Threatens Soft Power: the Right and Wrong Ways to Respond to Authoritarian Influence', *Foreign Affairs*, 24 January 2018.

16 Frances Stonor Saunders, *Who Paid the Piper? The CIA and the Cultural War*, Granta, London, 1999/2000.

17 Joseph S Nye, Jr., 'How Sharp Power Threatens Soft Power: the Right and Wrong Ways to Respond to Authoritarian Influence', *Foreign Affairs*, 24 January 2018, p. 5.

18 Malcolm Turnbull, *A Bigger Picture*, Hardie Grant, Melbourne, 2020, pp. 429–31.

19 Oddly, Turnbull is still in denial over the damage this caused to relations, dismissing those who said it harmed relations as 'unhinged'—ibid., p. 430.

20 Staff reporter, 'The Famous Mao Slogan, that He Never Even Used', *South China Morning Post*, 25 September 2009, https://scmp.com//article//693526/famous-mao-slogan-he-never-even-used (viewed May 2020). Jocelyn Chey brought this to my attention.

21 Jocelyn Chey, 'The Gentle Dragon', *Yale Global,* 29 November 2007; Jocelyn Chey, 'Confucius Redux: Chinese "Soft Power", Cultural Diplomacy and the Confucius Institutes', *Sydney Institute Papers,* January 2008; Jocelyn Chey, 'Cultural Diplomacy and Australia–China Cultural Relations', *Willow Catkins: Festschrift for Dr Lily Xiao Hong Lee,* The Oriental Society of Australia, 2014, pp. 343–75.

22 *The Economist* reported that, in 2009, the website of Edinburgh University's Confucius Institute promoted a talk on campus by a 'prominent' dissident whose works had been banned in China—*Economist*, 24 October 2009.

23 Quoted in ibid.

24 Bethany Alle-Ebrahimian, 'America's Oldest Confucius Institute to Close', AXIOS, www.axios.com, 18 January 2020.

25 Human Rights Watch, 'China: Government Threatens Academic Freedom Abroad: New 12-Point Code of Conduct to Help Education Institutions Respond', 21 March 2019.

26 Ibid.; Elaine Pearson, 'More Must be Done to Protect Academic Freedom under Threat from China', *The Age*, 7 April 2019.

27 Eleanor Albert, 'China's Big Bet on Soft Power', Council on Foreign Relations, 9 February 2018.

28 David Shambaugh, 'China's Soft Power Push', *Foreign Affairs*, July/August 2015.

29 Ibid.

30 Merridan Varrall, 'Behind the News: Inside China Global Television Network', Lowy Institute, 16 January 2020.

31 Ibid.

32 Ibid.

33 *Pew Research Center*, 'U.S. Views of China', 21 April 2020.

34 Laura Rosenberger, 'China's Coronavirus Information Offensive', *Foreign Affairs*, 22 April 2020.

35 Wolfgang Munchau, 'China Is Pitting EU Countries against Each Other', *Financial Times*, 25 May 2020.

36 *Pew Research Center*, 'U.S. Views of China', 21 April 2020.

37 Ibid., p. 7.

38 Ibid., p. 9.

39 Ibid., p. 11.

40 Ibid., p. 17.

41 *Pew Research Center*, 'People Around the Globe Are Divided in Their Opinions of China', 5 December 2019.

42 Jeremiah Cha, 'People in Asia-Pacific Regard the US More Favourably than China, but Trump Gets Negative Marks', *Pew Research Center*, 25 February 2020.

43 Ibid.

44 *Reporters without Frontiers, 2020 World Press Freedom Index.*

45 Xi Jinping, speaking during an inspection tour of Beijing, 25 February 2014.

46 McGregor, *The Party*, op.cit., p. 228.

47 Xi Jinping, closing meeting of the First Session of the National People's Congress, 20 March 2018.

48 Madeleine O'Dea, *Phoenix Years: Art, Resistance and the Remaking of Modern China*, Allen and Unwin, London, 2016.

49 Panos Kotzathanasis, 'All Zhang Yimou's Movies Rated from Worst to Best', *Taste of Cinema*, 11 June 2017.

50 Dan Levin, 'Film Festival in the Cross Hairs', *New York Times*, 9 August 2009.

51 Chris Uhlmann, 'We Can't Return to Business as Usual with China', *Sydney Morning Herald*, 29 April 2020.

52 Geoff Raby, 'China Needs a Grown-up Foreign Policy for a Changed Era', *Australia Financial Review*, 21 January 2019.

53 Evan Osnos, 'China's Culture Wars', *The New Yorker*, 5 January 2012.

54 Amy King and Shiro Armstrong, quoted in Shannon Tiezzi, 'Is China Ready to Take Its Economic Coercion into the Open', *The Diplomat*, May 2019.

55 Shannon Tiezzi, 'Is China Ready to Take Its Economic Coercion into the Open', *The Diplomat*, May 2019.

56 J James Kim, 'South Korean Caution and Concern about China', The Asian Institute for Policy Studies, 16 October 2019.

57 Ibid.

58 Ibid.

59 Peter Hartcher, 'Red Flag: Waking up to China's Challenge', *Quarterly Essay*, no. 76, 2019; Nathan Hondros, 'He's Hijacking China Debate', *WAtoday*, 29 April 2020.

60 Phillip Coorey, 'Opinion', *AFR*, 1 May 2010.

61 Han Han, quoted in Joseph S Nye, Jr, 'Why China Is Weak on Soft Power', *New York Times*, 17 January 2012.

62 Ibid.

63 Yun Sun, 'One Year on, the Role of the China International Development Cooperation Administration Remains Cloudy', *Brookings*, 30 April 2019,

https://www.brookings.edu/blog/africa-in-focus/2019/04/30/one-year-on-the-role-of-the-china-international-development-cooperation-administration-remains-cloudy (viewed May 2020).

64 Charles Wolf, Jr, Xiao Wang and Eric Warner, *China's Foreign Aid and Government Sponsored Investment Activities: Summary Report*, RAND Corporation, Santa Monica, CA, 2013, p. xiii.

65 David Dollar, 'Where Is China's Development Finance Really Going?', *Brookings*, 12 October 2017.

66 Sulagna Basu and Alexandre Dayant, 'China's Aid: Lend Your Money, (Don't) Lose Your Friend', *Lowy Interpreter*, 1 April 2019.

67 Cheng Cheng, 'The Logic Behind China's Foreign Aid Agency', *Carnegie Endowment for International Peace*, 21 May 2019.

68 Jamie Smyth, 'China Aid Wins Influence in the Pacific Despite Rising Concerns', *Financial Times*, 14 November 2019.

69 Ibid.

70 Denghua Zhang and Hongbo Ji, 'The New Chinese Aid Agency after Its First Two Years', ANU Canberra/Crawford School of Public Policy/Development Policy Centre, 22 April 2020.

71 Ibid.

72 Cornelia Tremann, 'China's Aid: the Image Boost', *Lowy Interpreter*, 21 September 2018.

73 Ibid.

74 Haibin Zhang, 'The Development and Transformation of China's Foreign Aid', in Daniel Remier and Ye Yu (eds), *Parallel Perspectives on the Global Economic Order*, CSIS, September 2017, p. 80.

75 Ministry of Foreign Affairs, 'New Starting Point for Cooperation and New Driving Force for Development: Opening Statement at the Leaders' Roundtable of Belt and Road Forum for International Cooperation', People's Republic of China, May 2017.

76 Michael Evans, 'Australian Strategy and the Gathering Storm in Asia', *Quadrant*, vol. 64, no. 565, April 2020, p. 26.

77 Ibid.

78 Reid Standish, 'China's Path Forward Is Getting Bumpy', *The Atlantic*, 1 October 2019.

79 Yong Deng, 'The Sustainability Challenge of China's BRI', 13 December 2019, East Asia Forum, https://www.eastasiaforum.org.

80 Yu Ye, 'China's Response to Belt and Road Backlash', *East Asia Forum*, 15 December 2018.

81 Xinsong Wang, 'One Belt, One Road's Governance Deficit Problem', *Foreign Affairs*, 17 November 2017.

82 James Crabtree, 'China Needs to Make the Belt and Road Initiative More Transparent and Predictable', *Chatham House*, 26 April 2019.

Chapter 5   Australia's Dystopian Future

1 The White House, *New National Security Strategy for a New Era*, Washington, DC, 18 December 2017; Jan Perlez, 'Pence's China Speech Seen as Portent of "New Cold War"', *New York Times*, 5 October 2018; The White House, *United States Strategic Approach to the People's Republic of China*, Washington, DC, 20 May 2020.

2 Max de Haldevang, 'Trump's Doctrine of "Principled Realism" Baffles the Foreign Policy World', *Quartz*, 26 September 2018.

3 Salvatore Babones, 'Trump's Foreign Policy Success Shows Principled Realism in Action', *The National Interest*, 26 September 2018.

4 Ibid.

5 'I think Australia is broadly comfortable with the Pence approach'—quoted in Jan Perlez, 'Pence's China Speech Seen as Portent of "New Cold War"', *New York Times*, 5 October 2018.

6 Richard Maude, 'Looking Ahead: Australia and China after the Pandemic', *Asia Society*, 13 May 2020, https://asiasociety.org/australia/looking-ahead-australia-and-china-after-pandemic (viewed May 2020).

7 The White House, *United States Strategic Approach to the People's Republic of China*, Washington, DC, 20 May 2020, p. 12.

8 Zha Daojiong, 'US Defence Strategy Is Not News to China', *East Asia Forum*, 11 February 2018.

9 Gary Sampson, 'Bypassing Trump's Fake Complaints Paves the Way for WTO Renewal', *AFR*, 6 May 2020.

10 European Commission, *EU–China: a Strategic Outlook*, joint communication to the European Parliament and the European Council, Strasbourg, 12 March 2019.

11 Ibid.

12 John J Mearsheimer, 'Bound to Fail: the Rise and Fall of the Liberal International Order', *International Security*, vol. 43, no. 4, 2019, pp. 8–9.

13 *ACRIFacts*, 'South China Sea: What Australia Might Do', Australia–China relations institute, March 2018.

14 Bob Carr, 'South China Sea Would Be a Lonely Patrol for Australia', *AFR*, 11 November 2015.

15 Phillip Coorey, 'Australia Misses Deputy Role in China's Asia Infrastructure Investment Bank', *AFR,* 29 January 2016; Michael Smith, 'Australia Has "Special Role" to Play in Asia Infrastructure Bank', *AFR*, 4 April 2017.

16 Kurt Campbell, *The Pivot: the Future of American Statecraft in Asia*, Hachette, New York, 2016, p. 276.

17 Geoff Raby, 'Northern Australia Takes Its Place on Xi Jinping's New Silk Road Map', *AFR*, 11 May 2016.

18 Phillip Coorey, 'Australia Misses Deputy Role in China's Asia Infrastructure Investment Bank', *AFR,* 29 January 2016; Michael Smith, 'Australia Has "Special Role" to Play in Asia Infrastructure Bank', *AFR*, 4 April 2017.

19 James Laurenson and Elena Collinson, 'Belt and Road Will Go Ahead With or Without Australia', *The Lowy Interpreter*, 22 May 2017.

20 Evelyn Goh, 'Rising China's Influence in Developing Asia', Yale NUS College Public Lecture, 10 April 2017; Evelyn Goh, *The Struggle for Order: Hegemony, Hierarchy, and Transition in Post-Cold War East Asia*, Oxford University Press, Oxford, 2013.

21 Rory Medcalf, *Contest for the Indo-Pacific: Why China Won't Map the Future*, La Trobe University Press, Melbourne, 2020, p. 194.

22 DFAT press release, 7 June 2018 and 4 November 2019.

23 Ankit Panda, 'Shinzo Abe's "Quadrilateral Initiative": Gone and Forgotten?', *The Diplomat*, 7 May 2014.

24 *The Hindustan Times*, 'PM Says India Not Part of "So Called Contain China" Effort', 11 January 2008.

25 Uttara Choudhury, 'India Can Thank Uncle Sam for Julia Gillard's Uranium Backflip', *Firstpost*, 16 November 2011.

26 Confirmed in private conversations at the time.

27 Nicholas Brendan, 'China Warns Canberra on Security Pact', *The Age*, 15 June 2007.

28 *The Hindustan Times*, 'PM Says India Not Part of "So Called Contain China" Effort', 11 January 2008.

29 Ibid.

30 Kevin Rudd, 'The Convenient Rewriting of the History of the Quad', *Nikkei Asian Review*, 26 March 2019.

31 Shinzo Abe, 'Asia's Diamond of Democracy', *Project Syndicate*, 27 December 2012.

32 Huong Le Thu, 'Southeast Asian Perceptions of the Quadrilateral Security Dialogue: Survey Findings', *ASPI*, October 2018, p. 7. Huong Le Thu also used the label 'Quad 2.0' for its second coming.

33 Angus Grigg, 'Interview with Prime Minister Abe', *AFR*, 20 January 2018.

34 A key finding of a 2018 report into attitudes in ASEAN towards Quad 2.0 is that it lacked clarity in purpose and objectives and was poorly explained—Huong Le Thu, 'Southeast Asian Perceptions of the Quadrilateral Security Dialogue: Survey Findings', *ASPI*, October 2018, p. 4.

35 The quote is from James Curran, 'Trump Exhumes the Diplomatic Carcass of the Security Quad', *AFR*, 17 November 2017.

36 Rory Medcalf, 'An Indo-Pacific Quad Is the Right Response to Beijing', *AFR*, 9 November 2017.

37 Tanvi Madan, 'The Rise, Fall, and Rebirth of the "Quad"', *War on the Rocks*, 16 November 2017, https://warontherocks.com/2017/11/rise-fall-rebirth-quad (viewed May 2020).

38 Shashi Tharoor and Samir Saran, *The New World Disorder and the Indian Imperative*, Aleph, New Delhi, 2020, p. 291.

39 Rageswari Pillai Rajagopalan, 'Will India Now Finally Invite Australia to the Malabar Exercise?', *The Diplomat*, 31 January 2020.

40 *The Hindustan Times*, 'India is Rather Too Cautious on the Quad', 24 January 2019.

41 *Economic Times*, 'Malabar Exercise with Australian Participation is not Quadrilateral Military Alliance', 3 February 2020.

42 Rageswari Pillai Rajagopalan, 'Will India Now Finally Invite Australia to the Malabar Exercise?', *The Diplomat*, 31 January 2020.

43 Ai Jun, 'NATO Naming China the Enemy Will Lead to Consequences', *Global Times*, 12 November 2019.

44 Ankit Panda, 'US, India, Australia, Japan "Quad" Holds Senior Officials Meeting in Bangkok', *The Diplomat*, 5 November 2019.

45 Iain Marlow, 'U.S. Security Bloc to Keep China in "Proper Place"', *Bloomberg*, 23 October 2019.

46 Iain Henry, 'Finally, Some Plain Talk on the Quad', *Lowry Interpreter*, 25 October 2019.

47 Patrick M Cronin, 'US Asia Strategy: Beyond the Quad', *The Diplomat*, March 2019; Annabelle Liang, 'Is the Quad Dead (Again)?', *The Diplomat*, March 2019.

48 Ibid.

49 Ibid.; Bo Seo, 'Beware China's Growing Offensive Capability', *AFR*, 13 February 2020; Andrew Tillett, '"Unbreakable": US Wants Missiles in Darwin', *AFR*, 4 August 2019.

50 Roland Rajah, 'Mobilising the Indo-Pacific Infrastructure Response to China's Belt and Road Initiative in Southeast Asia', *Foreign Policy at Brookings*, April 2020, pp. 3–4.

51 Sandy Milne, 'Connecting the Blue Dots after Covid-19', *Defence Connect*, 7 April 2020; Zach Montague, 'Can the "Blue Dot Network" Really Compete With China's Belt and Road?', *World Politics Review*, 4 December 2019; Mercy A Kuo, 'Blue Dot Network: the Belt and Road Alternative', *The Diplomat*, 7 April 2020.

52 Nayanima Basu, 'Blue Dot Network—US Answer to China Initiative that India Is "Interested" in', *The Print*, 10 March 2020; Sandy Milne, 'Connecting the Blue Dots after Covid-19', *Defence Connect*, 7 April 2020.

53 'Blue Dot Network is just Washington's Delusion', *Global Times*, 24 December 2019.

54 Shisheng Hu, Director of South and Southwest Asia and Oceania Studies, China Institute of Contemporary International Relations, *Global Times*, 1 January 2020.

55 'Explained: What is the Blue Dot Network, on the Table during Trump Visit to India', *Indian Express*, 26 February 2020.

56 Hugh White, 'Why India Is Not Going to Save Us from China's Power', *AFR*, 10 March 2020.

57 Chengxin Pan, 'Qualms About the Quad: Getting China Wrong', *Debating the Quad*, The Centre of Gravity Series, ANU, March 2018, p. 9.

58 Ibid.; Rory Medcalf, 'An Indo-Pacific Quad Is the Right Response to Beijing', *AFR*, 9 November 2017.

59 Rory Medcalf, 'An Indo-Pacific Quad Is the Right Response to Beijing', *AFR*, 9 November 2017.

60 Chengxin Pan, 'Qualms About the Quad: Getting China Wrong', *Debating the Quad*, The Centre of Gravity Series, ANU, March 2018, p. 11.

61 John Bolton, 'The Scandal of Trump's China Policy', *The Wall Street Journal*, 17 June 2020.

62 'Offensive realism' views the international system as being in a perpetual state of anarchy. Peace and war are determined by structural forces, not the will of individual leaders. In Mearsheimer's view, Kissinger would be a romantic for his belief that individual statesmen (like Kissinger himself) can shape history in the way that he believed his heroes Metternich and Castlereagh did—Robert D Kaplan, *The Return of Marco Polo's World*, Random House, New York, 2018, pp. 196–8.

63 Ibid., pp. 200–1.

64 Compiled from the Government of India, Department of Industry and Internal Trade of India, various reports from various years.

65 Russell Goldman, 'India–China Border Dispute: a Conflict Explained', *New York Times*, 18 June 2020.

66 Daniel S Markey, *China's Western Horizon: Beijing and the New Geopolitics of Eurasia*, Oxford University Press, Oxford, 2020, p. 9.

67 Hugh White, 'Why India Is Not Going to Save Us from China's Power', *AFR*, 10 March 2020.

68 Ibid.

69 Abhijit Singh, 'Is Beijing Seeking a "Grand Bargain" with New Delhi in the Indian Ocean?', *South China Morning Post*, 13 February 2020.

70 Rick Rozoff, *The Shanghai Cooperation Organisation: Prospects for a Multipolar World*, Centre for Global Research, Canada, 22 May 2009.

71 Ibid.

72 Humphrey Hawksley, *Asian Waters: the Struggle Over the South China Sea and the Strategy of Chinese Expansion,* The Overlook Press, New York, 2018, p. 148.

73 Quoted in Allan Gyngell, *Fear of Abandonment: Australia in the World since 1942*, La Trobe University Press, Melbourne, 2017, p. 5.

74 Ibid.

Chapter 6   Strategies for the New World Order

1 Christina Zhou and Michael Walsh, 'Australia Pledged to "Step up" in the Pacific Amid Growing Chinese Influence, but Are We on Track?', *ABC News*, 18 January 2020.

2 Ibid.

3 Alan C Tidwell, 'With Pacific Step up, a Chance to Step in', *The Lowy Interpreter*, 30 September 2019.

4 Peter Varghese, *An Indian Economic Strategy to 2035: Navigating from Potential to Delivery*, Department of Foreign Affairs and Trade, Canberra, April 2018, p. 378.

5 Ibid., pp. 377–9.

6 Minxin Pei, 'China Must Avoid Provoking the US with Threats to Taiwan', *Asia Nikkei Review*, 7 June 2020.

7 James Laurenson and Michael Zhou, 'Covid-19 and the Australia–China Relationship's Zombie Economic Idea', Australia-China Relations Institute, Sydney, May 2020.

8 Robert Zoellick, 'A Tribute to Richard Woolcott', *Asia Society*, 14 July 2010; Richard Woolcott, *The Hot Seat: Reflections on Diplomacy from Stalin's Death to the Bali Bombings*, Harper Collins, Sydney, 2003.

9 Hunter Marston, 'Has the US Lost Myanmar to China?', *The Diplomat*, 20 January 2020; Crisis Group, *Commerce and Conflict: Navigating the Myanmar–China Relationship*, report no. 305/Asia, 30 March 2020.

10 Gideon Rachman, 'Mid-Sized Powers Must Unite to Preserve the World Order', *Financial Times*, 28 May 2018.

11 Paul Kelly, 'National Security Cowboys Put Nation's Interests at Unnecessary Risk', *The Australian*, 9 May 2020.

12 Allan Gyngell, *Fear of Abandonment: Australia in the World since 1942*, La Trobe University Press, Melbourne, 2017, p. 174.

13 Ibid., pp. 174–5.

14 *AFR*, 'The Poor White Trash of Asia: a Phrase that Changed an Economy', 24 May 2015.

15 Allan Gyngell, *Fear of Abandonment: Australia in the World since 1942*, La Trobe University Press, Melbourne, 2017, p. 209.

16 Gyngell quotes foreign minister Gareth Evans saying that US secretary of state James Baker 'laid the real mark of Zorro on me, slash, slash, slash'—Ibid., p. 176; Robert Zoellick, 'A Tribute to Richard Woolcott', *Asia Society*, 14 July 2010.

17 Allan Gyngell, *Fear of Abandonment: Australia in the World since 1942*, La Trobe University Press, Melbourne, 2017, p. 175

18 Personal recollection. As counsellor (economic), I met Keating and his small party in Hong Kong and travelled by train to Guangzhou. His visit to Beijing coincided with the visit of general secretary Gorbachev to normalise Soviet–China ties and the Tiananmen Square demonstrations.

19 Allan Gyngell, *Fear of Abandonment: Australia in the World since 1942*, La Trobe University Press, Melbourne, 2017, pp. 198–200, and personal communications with Paul Keating.

20 Bill Clinton, *My Life*, Random House, New York, 2004.

21 Jonathan Kaiman, 'Japan's Abe and China's Xi Hold Ice-Breaking Meeting as APEC Starts', *The Guardian*, 10 November 2014.

22 Allan Gyngell, *Fear of Abandonment: Australia in the World since 1942*, La Trobe University Press, Melbourne, 2017, pp. 276–7.

23 Based on personal recollections. At the time, the author was First Assistant Secretary in DFAT.

24 DFAT, 'Bali Process on People Smuggling', press release, April 2002.

25 Paul Maley, 'Old Warhorse Richard Woolcott Back in Harness to Smooth Regional Ties', *The Australian*, 5 June 2008.

26 Craig VanGrasstek, 'The Launch: from Singapore to Doha, with a Detour in Seattle', in *The History and Future of the World Trade Organization*, World Trade Organization, Geneva, 2013, http://www.wto.org/english/res-e/ersd201109-e.pdf (viewed May 2020).

27 Allan Gyngell, *Fear of Abandonment: Australia in the World since 1942*, La Trobe University Press, Melbourne, 2017.

28 Gareth Evans doubts if ASEAN is up to the task—Gareth Evans, 'Four Ways to Improve Australia's Foreign Policy in the Age of Trump', *AFR*, 2 August 2018.

29 David Hutt, 'Does China Really Dominate Southeast Asia?', *Asia Times*, 23 August 2018.

30 Ibid.

31 Kevin Rudd, 'Understanding China's Rise under Xi Jinping', speech at the US Military Academy, West Point, 5 March 2018.

32 Hyug Baeg Im, 'Constructing Regional Security Community in East Asia from Difficult Conditions: from Community of Commerce to Community of Nations', *East Asia Community Review*, vol. 1, no. 75, 2018, p. 84.

33 Robert Ayson, 'The Six-Party Process: towards an Asian Concert?', in Ronald Huisken (ed.), *The Architecture of Security in the Asia-Pacific*, ANU E Press, Canberra, 2009, pp. 57–63.

34 Condoleezza Rice, remarks at the JP Morgan International Council Meeting, Shanghai, 26 October 2017.

35 Private discussions with officials, 2008–9.

36 Org Friedrichs, 'East Asian Regional Security: What the ASEAN Family Can (Not) Do', *Asian Survey*, vol. 52, no. 4, 2012, pp. 754–76.

37 Rajeswari Pillai Rajagopalan, 'Towards a Quad-Plus Arrangement?', *Indo-Pacific Analysis Briefs*, vol. 1, 2020.

38 Hugh White, *How to Defend Australia*, La Trobe University Press, Melbourne, 2019.

39 Lowy Institute, *2019 Power Index*, Sydney, 2019.

40 Allan Gyngell, *Fear of Abandonment: Australia in the World since 1942*, La Trobe University Press, Melbourne, 2017, p. 324.

41 Geoff Raby, 'PM's Virus Inquiry Was a Lose-Lose Call', *AFR*, 1 May 2020; Angus Grigg and Michael Smith, 'China's Big Chill Sets in as "Fear and Greed" return', *AFR*, 16 May 2020.

42 Geoff Raby, 'Australia and China at 40: Pivot, Divot and the US', the 2012 Richard Larkins Oration, Monash University, Melbourne, 8 August 2012; recollection from *ABC TV* broadcast.

43 Stephen Fitzgerald, 'Managing Australian Foreign Policy in a Chinese World', 2017 Whitlam Oration, Whitlam Institute, Western Sydney University, 16 March 2017.

Conclusion

1 Matt Coughlan, 'Sack Labor MP for China Spray: Nats Deputy', *Lakes Mail*, 22 May 2020; 'Former ASIO Boss "Exasperated" over China Apologists', *Sky News Australia*, 21 November 2019.

2 Bernard Keane, 'China Matters, Especially for Big Business', *Crikey*, 19 November 2019.

3 Geoff Raby, 'Beijing Kicks Own Goal by Booting Hastie and Paterson', *AFR*, 21 November 2019.

Postscript: COVID-19

1 Richard Haass, 'The Pandemic Will Accelerate History Rather Than Reshape It', *Foreign Affairs*, 7 April 2020.

2 Shashi Tharoor and Samir Saran, *The New Global Disorder and the Indian Imperative*, Aleph books, New Delhi, 2020.

3 *Foreign Affairs*, 'Did America Get China Wrong?', The Engagement Debate, July/August 2018.

4 Jacob Greber, 'Donald Trump's Trade War with China Has Only Just Started, Says Kevin Rudd', *AFR*, 20 September 2018.

5 EU Commission, 'EU-China – a Strategic Outlook', EU, Brussels, 12 March 2019; Dingding Chen and Junyang Hu, 'Are the European Union and China Systemic Rivals', *The Diplomat*, 8 April 2019.

6 Richard Maude, 'Looking Ahead: Australia and China After the Pandemic', Asia Society Australia, 13 May 2020.

7 Andrew Small, 'The Meaning of Systemic Rivalry: Europe and China Beyond the Pandemic', *European Council on Foreign Relations*, ecfr.eu, 13 May 2020.

8 Geoff Raby, 'Why the Bell Must Toll for WHO Chief', *AFR*, 17 April, 2020.

9 Christopher R Hill, 'What Does Washington Want From China?: Pique Is Not a Policy', *Foreign Affairs*, 11 May 2020.

10 David Nakamura, 'With "Kung Flu", Trump Sparks Backlash Over Racist Language', *The Washington Post*, 25 June 2020.

11 Geoff Raby, 'PM's Virus Inquiry Was a Lose-Lose Call,' *AFR*, 1 May 2020.

12 Wendy Wu, Teddy Ng and Robert Delany, 'Hong Kong and Other Disagreements Dominate US-China Hawaii Meeting', *South China Morning Post*, 18 June 2020.

13 World Economic Forum, 'Global Risks 2020: an Unsettled World', *WEF*, Geneva, January 2020,

14 'The Digital Side of the Belt and Road Initiative', *The Economist* 6 February 2020.

15 Minxin Pei, 'China's Expensive Bet on Africa Has Failed', *Nikkei Asian Review*, 1 May 2020.
16 Nick Crawford and David Gordon, 'China Confronts Major Risk of Debt Crisis on the Belt and Road Due to Pandemic', *The Diplomat*, 10 April 2020.
17 Ibid.
18 Kurt M Campbell and Rush Doshi, 'The Coronavirus Could Reshape Global Order', *Foreign Affairs*, 6 April 2020.
19 Andrew Foxall, 'Ending the Dangerous US Dependence on China', *National Review*, 26 May 2020.
20 Ibid.
21 James Laurenceson and Michael Zhou, *COVID-19 and the Australia-China Relationship's Zombie Idea*, ACRI, University of Technology, Sydney, May 2020.
22 Robert M Gates, 'The Overmilitarization of American Foreign Policy', *Foreign Affairs*, July/August 2020.

INDEX